The Traditional Ways & The NEW Alternatives

- **Money** Exactly How Much You Need
- **The Financing Plans** The Newest
- **Where to Find Mortgage Money**
- **The Real Costs** Taxes, Payments, Savings
- **The Middle Men** Who To Believe & Trust
- **The Housing Jargon** Real Estate Terms
- **Shelter** All Your Possibilities

A Home of Your Own For The LEAST Cash

The Home Buyer's Guide for TODAY!

Alan Hughes

ACROPOLIS BOOKS LTD.
Washington, D.C.

ACROPOLIS BOOKS LTD.
Colortone Building, 2400 17th St., N.W.,
Washington, D.C. 20009

Printed in the United States of America by
COLORTONE PRESS Creative Graphics, Inc.
Washington, D.C. 20009

Library of Congress Cataloging in Publication Data

Hughes, Alan, 1933-
    A home of your own for the least cash.

    1. House buying.   2. Housing–Finance.   3. Dwellings.
I. Title.
HD1379.H84   643'.12   81-19142
ISBN 0-87491-462-0   AACR2

Acknowledgments

While I take full responsibility for the accuracy of *A Home of your Own,* the suggestions, additions, red-penciling and counsel of the following people and organizations, on relevant sections submitted to them for review, are gratefully acknowledged:

Jenny Billig, realtor, Coldwell Bankers

Kenneth Hall, Federal Home Loan Bank Board

John R. Kupferer, Home Manufacturers Council, National Association of Home Builders

Albert B. Moore, Albert B. Moore Associates

Veronica Pickman, The Venture Group, Washington, D.C.

Morton Press, real estate lawyer

Steven T. Rehm, Federal Home Loan Mortgage Corporation

Beth Van Houten, Federal National Mortgage Association

Manufactured Housing Institute

Mortgage Insurance Companies of America

And a special note of thanks to my brother, Neil, who took the time from a busy overseas development banking schedule, to show how ARM's might be presented to consumers.

Alan Hughes

2189S01

Contents

Foreword

I f you are trying to buy a house despite the highest interest rates in U.S. history—and have found that available fixed-rate mortgages closely reflect the going market interest—don't give up hope! You CAN own a home that will fit both your needs and your family's for many years to come.

This book was designed as a guide both to affordable types of housing and to the complex process of selecting and financing your home. Since residential mortgage money at below-market interest is either very scarce, or involves complicated adjustable mortgage rates and indexes, *A Home of Your Own* begins with a general review of the more affordable types of housing available. Where some kinds of homes are described in greater detail it is because, in the author's opinion, they have not yet been widely covered on a nationwide basis.

If you see a lower-cost housing option that you like, you would borrow less money to finance it, which in turn would lower the monthly payments and the income level needed to qualify for the loan. It's assumed that readers of this book will be holding full-time jobs and can invest only a limited amount of "sweat equity" in their shelter—for this reason, no attempt has been made to describe "do-it-yourself" housing kits.

Most of the more affordable options described are traditional frame houses or dome houses built all or in part at a
factory, although some super-efficient site-built "foam
domes" employing innovative design and erection techniques
closely match their erected costs. The word "innovative" is
important to home buyers, and it does not mean "far out."
Instead, it refers to putting up a house with the best current
techniques available, which is not always the case in our
tradition-bound residential housing industry.

The housing "crunch" you face today is largely due to both
rapid increases in building costs (which drive up the prices of
traditionally built homes) and soaring interest rates (which
make it expensive to borrow the money necessary to pay for
them). Nationwide, the building industry has generally
reacted slowly to this situation, as far as adopting new
methods to cut costs is concerned. *A Home of Your Own* tries
to indicate the exceptions: those builders and manufacturers
who use modern technology to provide high quality housing
at a lower cost. Also outlined in Part I are the other affordable options of group living and urban/suburban rehabilitation of existing houses.

The second part of the book is a guide to locating a house
and financing the purchase. It begins with the search for a
good real estate agent, then describes the institutional
lenders and "shopping" for a mortgage, follows this with an
explanation of alternative financing techniques, and ends
with the closing process. For most U.S. buyers these proceedings are the most traumatic part of acquiring a home—a
purchase which, ideally, should not be much more complicated than buying a car or camper. However, the most
technologically advanced society in the world makes it no
simple matter for its citizens to acquire personal shelter.
Many other countries are far ahead of us in this respect.

The book also includes a comprehensive glossary of
building terminology, and a glossary of real estate and home
financing terms which should be adequate. Very few people
read glossaries for fun, but if you get to the point of drawing
up contracts for rehabilitation work—or simply have to clar-
ify the jargon in financial documents—these definitions
should come in handy.

As with all home buyers' guides, you'll want to know how much of A HOME OF YOUR OWN directly relates to your personal needs. The usefulness of each chapter will depend on your housing preferences and financial situation, but you will probably find that each section covers its topic in enough detail with little excess wordage. Many knowledgeable people have contributed information to the book. If A HOME OF YOUR OWN can help you acquire good shelter at an affordable price, the work of the author and everyone else will have been worthwhile.

Alan Hughes

PART I

Shelter in the Eighties

CHAPTER 1

The home
as an
Investment

Like many seeking affordable shelter in to-
day's housing market, the Maxwells were in their early 30's,
commuting to their separate jobs and fairly secure about
their future prospects.

John worked as an accountant. Anne had just returned to
teaching junior high school after a five-year layoff (she'd had
her second child two years ago). Their combined income of
$39,800 was enough to allow a few luxuries: they liked to take
a resort vacation each year and did a fair amount of entertaining and dining out.

But with the children getting older, their non-controlled
rental apartment was rapidly becoming too small for their
needs. And the rent kept going up. Faced with the third increase in four years, the couple took a careful look at what
they were getting for their $560 monthly payment to the
landlord.

Renting vs. Owning

After comparing the pros and cons of renting and owning,
John and Anne concluded that renting simply did not fit their
future plans—in spite of their not having to worry about long
term carrying costs and the (usually expensive) irritants of

home maintenance. As had so many before them, they found that renters have no real stake in the place called "home." They:

- Must include the landlord's profit as part of their monthly living expenses;
- May be evicted at the termination of the lease;
- Cannot deduct rent payments at income tax time;
- Build up no home equity and must count on assets *other* than the best one of all—a house in a good neighborhood—to hedge against inflation;
- Ditto, when establishing a credit rating;
- Can—where other renters are few—find it harder to be accepted into the community.

As with many other young couples in their income range, the Maxwell's assets had now diversified well beyond a savings account. For several years, they had been itemizing their deductions on form 1040A. They began to study the housing situation and realized that, as investments, most homes appreciate in value better than other types of property. A well-chosen house—unlike, for example, tax-free bonds—is almost unbeatable in keeping ahead of high inflation rates.

This value appreciation, *plus* the chance of getting a tax shelter with deferred capital gains, were the two things that finally convinced John and Anne to go shopping for the best house they could afford.

The Home as a Tax Shelter

You could define a tax shelter as an investment that allows the owner to deduct certain taxes, maintenance costs, carrying and other charges from his or her annual income tax. For instance, homeowners pay a relatively small lawyer's fee at closing. Investors purchasing a large office building would pay lawyer's fees in excess of the purchase price of any house the Maxwell's could have afforded.

Investors who can use tax shelters have this advantage over other investors: they can deduct very substantial cash outlays (for items specifically allowed by law) from the income on which they must pay taxes. They are able to retain a greater share of their money instead of handing it over to Uncle Sam.

A house, however, can give every homeowner a similar break at income tax time. The Maxwells found that, as owners, they could deduct:

- The amount of interest paid on the mortgage (most of the monthly payment goes towards interest in the early years);
- Local property taxes;
- Interest paid on second mortgages or home improvement loans;
- Any penalty charges for early payment of a mortgage (these are treated as interest by the I.R.S.);
- Credits, up to 15 percent of the first $2,000, for certain energy conserving home modifications specified in the Tax Bill passed by Congress in 1978.

New Rules for Home Financing

In their preliminary talks with real estate agents and homeowning friends, John and Anne learned that the ground rules in house financing had changed drastically. Back in the depression days and early post-war period, people took pride in paying off their mortgages as soon as possible—and celebrated the day when they finally owned their house "free and clear."

Then, as inflation rates started to soar in the mid-1970's, "leverage" became the byword in homebuying. Smart buyers carefully chose neighborhoods where housing prices were most likely to appreciate. They then bought with the lowest possible down payment and counted on the rapidly rising value of the house to outstrip inflation. Such a rise would also help offset the unpaid loan balance, on which the owner would continue to make payments in ever-cheaper dollars.

The Maxwells noted that the steep interest rates of the last two years had brought new practices, common in commercial real estate, into the home real estate market. Known as "creative" or alternative financing, most of the arrangements struck Anne and John as potentially dangerous to either buyer, seller, or both. They *did* like the "buy down," where a builder pays the lender an amount equal to about three percent of the interest rate for a period of years. They noticed that most of the developments in the area were offering some version of this plan, and mortgages at thirteen percent or fourteen percent were almost certainly "buy downs."

The couple decided that they would not care to get involved in most of the other forms of alternative financing without budgeting for the services of a top real estate lawyer.

Another effect of very high interest rates was that they tended to shut off available mortgage money from the traditional sources of these loans. Since the mid-1970's, inflation had made things very difficult for the lenders who originated home mortgages. These banks and savings and loan institutions could acquire mortgage loan money in three ways:

- From deposits by customers;
- By selling the mortgages they originated to large buyers in the "secondary mortgage market," and writing new mortgage loans with this money;
- By competing for funds in the capital market with other investors.

Even if you had regularly deposited part of your take-home pay in a savings account over the years, the sharply rising inflation rates of the middle and late 1970's would probably have forced you to look around for a better return on your savings. For example, mutual funds—some with excellent payment records—and treasury bills, backed by the full faith and credit of the U.S. Government, paid much higher rates than did savings institutions. Subject to legal limits on the interest they could pay, the savings banks saw a sharp dropoff in their deposit money.

Home mortgages were not faring very well in the nation's capital markets either. The restrictions imposed by the regulating agencies and federal and state laws, on the interest a lending institution could charge, made short-term financing and commercial loans much more profitable for large investors.

This left the secondary mortgage market as the main source of funds for your home loan—but here again, the laws of economics applied and no one wanted to acquire a portfolio of loans which were yielding less than the going market rate.

The first steps to make home mortgages more attractive to lenders were taken in the late 1970's. In 1979 Variable Rate Mortgages (VRM's) were offered by any federally chartered savings and loan institution (California banks started to offer these in 1976). This new loan had its interest rate keyed to the Savings & Loan Cost of Funds index, published twice a year in the Federal Home Loan Bank Board's *Journal.* The bank could change your interest rate once a year in accordance with the index, either raising it (lender's option) or lowering it (mandatory)—but within very tightly constrained limits of ± ½ percent a year. And by law, the total rate increases over the entire life of the loan could not exceed 2½ percent.

In 1980 the same federally-chartered savings institutions offered a Renegotiable Rate Mortgage (RRM), which gave the borrower stable payment rates over a 3, 4 or 5 year term (your choice) but then allowed the bank slightly more leeway in adjusting interest rates at each renewal period. These loans were keyed to the National Index of Mortgage Rates published monthly in the FHLBB *Journal.* The bank was required to lower its interest rate if the index rate moved downward. With a rising index, the bank could not increase your interest rate by more than ½ percent for each year of the renewal term (1½ percent for 3 years, 2 percent for 4 years, 2½ percent for 5 years). By law, the total increase in payment over the life of an RRM was limited to 5 percent.

Today, home mortgage money not only costs more, but many loans are tied to indexes which rise or fall with inflation and the prime rate.

The Maxwells learned that they might have to shop around quite a bit before finding VRMs and RRMs with tightly capped interest rate variations. They knew that, while the prime rate hovered around 20 percent, their chances of getting a traditional standard fixed-payment 30 year mortgage from any federally chartered institution were slim.

There were reasons for this scarcity of tightly constrained VRMs and RRMs: an April 1981 announcement by the Federal Home Loan Bank Board gave the savings and loans institutions it regulated much more latitude in adjusting interest rates. In June 1981, the largest buyer of mortgages in the secondary market—"Fannie Mae," the Federal National Mortgage Association (FNMA)—announced that it was prepared to buy eight different types of adjustable rate mortgages. This package of loan plans included five different indexes to which the loans were tied.

Four of the FNMA plans have no limitations on interest rates (caps), one has an 18¾ percent cap on interest payment increases and two have 7½ percent limits. Therefore, it's not hard to figure out why the capped VRM (2½ percent) and RRM (5 percent) have been phased out of federally chartered lending institutions' programs.

Anne and John still felt that a well-chosen home would be their best bet if high inflation persisted. But as owners, they would now also have to worry about the same inflation's effect on things like negative amortization (where increases in interest charges not covered by an agreed monthly payment are added back into the loan balance.) They made a mental note to be *very* careful in estimating their net worth and future income prospects. They also decided to try for a loan first at *state* chartered banks, which might still be limited by law to offering fixed payment mortgages, or the "Old" VRM or RRM.

Where You Live—It Can Double the Cost of Your House

The Maxwells liked the area where they lived and planned to buy their house there. They knew the key factor which most affects housing prices: location. (The $61,295 *average* acquisition cost for existing homes in their metropolitan area, estimated by the FHA for home mortgages they insure, came as no surprise.) Wide differences in house prices *can* come as a jolt to people who've been transferred to new areas. California real estate agents, in particular, have learned to live with reactions of shocked disbelief from clients used to other parts of the country.

Before making a move, it'a always a good idea to check housing prices in the area you're moving to and at least *try* to get an adequate allowance for the probable price difference between your old and new home. You can get information on average housing costs in each area through Department of Housing and Urban Development publications, the Federal Home Loan Bank Board and the savings and loan trade associations.

If you have travelled around the country to any extent, you've probably seen that the *overall* cost of consumer goods doesn't vary significantly from place to place. True, a large city will have discount stores for clothes and big-ticket appliances, but these savings will be offset in time by higher prices for items like fresh vegetables and fruit. The things that *do* vary considerably are housing prices and municipal taxes. And, if no mass transit system is available, the cost of commuting by car can be the third major variable in your budget.

As for the specific *features* to look for in a neighborhood, the Maxwells again had an advantage: they knew their area well. Two communities met their requirements (see Table I, Neighborhood Checklist):

- Most homes well maintained and appreciating in value;
- Streets and parks clean and attractive, with pleasant shade trees and minimal litter;
- Good police, fire, sanitation and other municipal services;
- Vandalism and public disturbance (noise) were about as low as could be expected;
- The school systems and public libraries were excellent;
- Hospitals were within a 30-minute drive;
- Public transportation routes were close, allowing the couple to get to their respective jobs without using their car.

The high taxes that the Maxwells would have to pay both municipalities for these services were a tradeoff. But since the tax situation was similar in all the other towns where they wanted to live, they decided to budget for these payments. And their chosen state gave home buyers a better deal than either of the bordering ones: its closing costs were quite a bit lower.

A Wide Range of Shelter Options Now Available

Either community allowed the couple three approaches toward acquiring a home: (a) purchase a new house from a builder or developer; (b) buy an existing house; (c) buy a lot and have a home of their choice—either manufactured or custom-built—erected on it.

Although Anne and John liked the idea of having a new frame house built to their specifications, they realized that such a home would probably be beyond their reach. Most houses of this type require much more labor to build, since they normally use more non-standardized wood sections for framing and finishing—which must be cut, drilled and nailed together at the site.

Even if they could have qualified for the six figure mortgage they would have needed for a custom-built home in the metropolitan area, the Maxwells were wary of taking out such a large loan. "Leverage" was a good option for first-time buyers in the fixed-payment era, but with the adjustable interest rates common in the 1980's a cheaper house meant less risk.

They did plan to look at the older used homes, and expected real estate agents to show them a number of these. But they also anticipated very few bargains.

An exception might be a house in poor condition, but this could cost them plenty later on, since neither John nor Anne had the free time or skills to handle major home repairs. They would have to hire contractors to do the work, which would mean high expenses for major improvements.

The next option they explored was manufactured housing. Two approaches, "modular" and "panelized," use the same materials as houses constructed piece-by-piece at the site, but are cheaper due to a factory's use of high volume standardized components. By combining these components in different ways, the manufacturers can offer a surprising range of styles and models: split-level or one to three stories high (see chapter 7).

A third type of manufacturer furnishes "pre-cut" house parts which are cut, numbered and pre-drilled or otherwise prepared for quick assembly. Home builders are large users of these components, although pre-cut kits are also advertised for the owner-builder. These kits are a good bet if you have the skills and spare time to put "sweat equity" into the job. But first make sure that a bank will finance your efforts, should a loan be needed for the project. For the same reasons that excluded the option of buying a used home needing major fixing-up—lack of time and the necessary skills—the Maxwells decided that pre-cut kits were not for them.

John and Anne were also considering many other types of homes, but gave them a lower priority. The reasons for this included the couple's life style preferences, reluctance in some cases by local lenders to finance a particular type of house, and community zoning restrictions.

However, these options are very popular with other buyers. The choices include condominiums and cooperative housing, single and double width "manufactured" (formerly "mobile") homes, Zero lot line houses, duplexes, pre-cut log houses, houseboats, geodesic dome houses and earth-sheltered homes. (See chapters 3, 7 and 8 for further details on these.)

One criterion applied to *any* house on the Maxwell's list: it would have to be energy-efficient! They were entering the housing market at a time when costs for all types of energy save one—solar—showed long-term upward trends. This meant that the cheapest home to operate—and the one most likely to sell for top price later—must be well insulated and designed, and sited for maximum passive solar heating and shading effectiveness.

Building Codes and Zoning Restrictions

The purpose of building codes is to ensure that the construction of new homes, and modifications to existing homes, conform to safe standards. Zoning restrictions affect the use to which the land will be put.

Together, these regulations can be used to prevent any one house from adversely affecting the value of other homes in the community. As a rule, the more desirable a town as a place to live, the more strictly it is apt to inspect for building code violations and enforce its zoning restrictions. Before getting too deeply involved in comparing different types of housing, it would be a good idea to check on what the area's residents consider "tacky" or too nonconformist in design.

If you decide on a new home, or major modifications to an existing one, you may still have problems with the building code—even if your home is acceptable to the town authorities. The reason is that many of these codes are outdated: they were written many years ago when cheaper materials and labor allowed more space in home design.

In the Maxwell's case, Anne had already begun to order catalogs from makers of manufactured homes serving their area. Many of the models listed in these brochures had fixed interior dimensions and offered only certain options for exterior finish and trim. So she and John decided to check the building codes in both their chosen communities for the following restrictions:

- Minimum lot size;
- Minimum or maximim house area (usually given in square feet);
- Restrictions on building height;
- "Setback" restrictions (distance of house from street);
- Minimum room sizes;
- Minimum door and window sizes;
- Fire retarding enclosure for the entrance/exits;
- Limitations on stair design, such as specified riser and tread sizes.

Since the couple were determined to have a basement, they didn't worry about restrictions on alternatives to a concrete or masonry foundation. And since both had full-time jobs and a family to look after, they didn't plan to do much of the work on the house themselves.

If you are a do-it-yourselfer, however, or just want to limit the initial cash outlay on the house, you should check the code for any restrictions on:

- Your right to complete a shell built by a contractor;
- The type of lumber that you can use for framing (can you shop around for used material or must it all be grade-stamped kiln-dried new wood);
- More than one family per home, if you are thinking of joint purchase or a duplex.

Table I: Neighborhood Inspection Checklist

Neighborhood Quality	Yes	No	Not Important
1. Are the homes well taken care of?	☐	☐	☐
2. Are there good public services (police, fire)?	☐	☐	☐
3. Are there paved roads?	☐	☐	☐
4. Are there sidewalks?	☐	☐	☐
5. Is there adequate street lighting?	☐	☐	☐
6. Is there a city sewer system?	☐	☐	☐
7. Is there a safe public water supply?	☐	☐	☐
8. Are the public schools good?	☐	☐	☐

Neighborhood Convenience			
1. Will you be near your work?	☐	☐	☐
2. Are there schools nearby?	☐	☐	☐
3. Are there shopping centers nearby?	☐	☐	☐
4. Is there public transportation available?	☐	☐	☐
5. Will you be near child care services?	☐	☐	☐
6. Are hospitals, clinics, or doctors close by?	☐	☐	☐
7. Is there a park or playground nearby?	☐	☐	☐

Neighbors			
1. Will you be near friends or relatives?	☐	☐	☐
2. Will you be near other children of your kids' age?	☐	☐	☐
3. Will you feel comfortable with the neighbors?	☐	☐	☐
4. Is there an active community group?	☐	☐	☐

Does The Neighborhood Have Any Problems			
1. Increasing Real Estate taxes?	☐	☐	☐
2. Decreasing sales prices of homes?	☐	☐	☐
3. Lots of families moving away?	☐	☐	☐
4. Heavy traffic or noise?	☐	☐	☐
5. Litter or pollution?	☐	☐	☐
6. Factories or heavy industry?	☐	☐	☐
7. Businesses closing down?	☐	☐	☐
8. Vacant houses or buildings?	☐	☐	☐
9. Increasing crime or vandalism?	☐	☐	☐

	Good	Fair	Poor
What is your overall rating of the neighborhood?	☐	☐	☐

Source: Homebuyer's Guidebook, U.S. Department of Housing & Urban Development

Table II: An Approximate Comparison of Housing Options

(Estimated cost per square foot of living space, erected single-story or split level structure of approximately 1600 square feet. Costs for land and excavated basement are *not* included).

	Range per ft²	Total for 1,600 sq. ft. home
(1) *Site-built finished house, wood frame construction*	$35–$45	$56,000–$72,000
(2) *Factory-built homes: finished* (within 100 miles of factory)		
(3) Modular/Sectional	$21–$26	$33,600–$41,600
Closed Wall Panelized Package	$22–$28	$35,200–$44,800
(3) Manufactured/Mobile Home	$18–$23	$28,800–$36,800
(4) *Factory-built homes: Weathertight Shells* (within 100 miles)		
Open Wall Panelized Package	$18–$23	$28,800–$36,800
Post and Beam framing	$17–$22	$27,200–$35,200
Log house	$18–$23	$28,800–$36,800
Modified-Geodesic Dome	$21–$26	$33,600–$41,600
(4) *Foam Dome Shell*	$20–$25	$32,000–$40,000

(1) Cost varies widely, depending on region and neighborhood. Mechanical equipment, appliances, fixtures and furnishings not included.

(2) Mechanical equipment, appliances, fixtures and furnishings not included.

(3) Delivery charges from factory can run as high as $10 per loaded mile.

(4) Includes finished exterior, windows and doors. Does *not* include plumbing, wiring, drywall and taping, or finished floors.

NOTE: These figures are based on conversations with several manufacturers. Since the policies of individual firms vary considerably, the figures shown are only given as a starting point for estimating purposes.

CHAPTER 2

How Much Can You Afford To Pay?

When Anne's parents decided to buy a house in the early 1950's they, like their daughter, were planning the biggest personal investment of their lives. Unlike Anne, however, they were able to make their decision on the basis of relatively clear and simple guidelines.

To begin with, they waited until their total net spendable income after taxes was four times the estimated annual expense for the house they wanted. They knew that careful budgeting would be necessary during the early years but, barring financial disaster, were sure that by following this "25 percent" rule they would be on time with their mortgage payments.

The loan itself cost less. Anne's father, a Navy petty officer in World War II, qualified for a Veterans Administration loan guarantee which eliminated the risk of default to the lender. Sure of getting its money back, the savings and loan institution which originated the mortgage was able to lower the down payment.

The interest charged was ridiculously low by today's standards. The bank still made a nice profit, however, since the cost of its incoming funds was even lower. These funds came from the deposits of many small savers who appreciated above all the *security* of the Federal insurance permitted on their savings accounts. Many people, in this early postwar period, had painful memories of savings wiped out in the wave of bank failures which followed the 1929 stock market crash.

With both the monthly payment and the term of the mortgage fixed, Anne's parents could sit down and figure out the unpaid balance at any point along the life of the loan. And the value of their house, in the 1950's, was expected to at least keep up with other types of investment.

Traditional Rules for Home Finance No Longer Apply

None of the rules her parents used apply to Anne and her husband today. On the contrary:

- House prices have soared to the point where many owners have to spend 30, 35 or even 40 percent of their net income to own their shelter. When they add their expenses for food, clothing and transportation, not much is left over for anything else;

- With house prices at this level, buyers must have substantial savings to make a 20 percent down payment. If they are buying their first house and haven't had the time to accumulate savings or other equity, they can lower the down payment through mortgage insurance—provided their income is high enough to qualify. At today's interest rates financing a greater portion of the selling price means monthly payments much higher than those of established owners lucky enough to be repaying single-digit interest.

- In order to get interest below the prevailing high mortgage rates in the market, it's not only possible, but probable that buyers will have to settle for an adjustable rate mortgage (ARM) tied to unpredictable economic indexes. In the Maxwell's case, their employers were unlikely to transfer them elsewhere. They had to at least consider keeping a house for a mortgage's 30-year term—and how their interest might fluctuate over that entire period.

- Should federal and state regulations allow it, terms on adjustable rate mortgages could even be extended to 35 or 40 years. A longer term would limit "negative amortization" on the outstanding balance—this occurs when the amount still owed to the lender gets larger in spite of your regular monthly payments. If the payment is fixed, it may not cover all the interest due, in which case the unpaid portion is simply added to the unamortized principal. Lenders can minimize this effect by extending the number of payments over a longer period.

Hard Times For Home Builders and Lenders

The housing industry, and the financial institutions which provide the money to keep it going, have had a particularly tough time during the last several years. Builders have been hit by the skyrocketing cost of almost everything, while "disintermediation" (the transfer of savings into short term investments which pay higher interest) plus the high cost of funds borrowed on the market have meant oceans of red ink for financial institutions.

The cost of land, labor and lumber—three items which home builders use in huge quantities—have climbed about 75 percent since 1975. Almost as high have been the cost increases for masonry, plumbing, fixtures and other products which go into a house. It is an increasing challenge for a builder to put up a solid, affordable house in the 1980's: many are solving it by using more and more pre-cut or pre-assembled components from assembly line manufacturers.

How Big a Mortgage?

If Anne had applied her parents' 25 percent guideline to her own case, she and her husband could have set aside about $506 each month for mortgage payments. This amount, if applied to a traditional (and now hard to find) fixed-rate mortgarage, would have met the payments for a $39,000 loan at 17 percent interest.

Adding the amount lent to a 20 percent down payment would have yielded a maximum amount of $48,750 to buy a house—not nearly enough where they lived to buy the types of homes they were considering!

The Maxwells used the following calculations to arrive at the $506 monthly figure:

- Their $40,000 gross income and four deductions put them in the 21 percent tax bracket (they used the standard deduction here because itemizing had so far given them only a slightly better deal);
- $40,000 × .79 = $31,600 after taxes;
- $31,600 × .25 = $7,900 per year for house expenses;
- $7,900 ÷ 12 = $658 (approx) each month.

Then, estimating that the price of their house might fall within $80–$90,000, they checked their county real estate guide and saw that municipal taxes might run around $110 a month for homes in this price range.

Comprehensive fire and theft insurance would cost them an additional $30 per month. In case they should buy a new home, they also decided to figure in the cost of a house warranty against possible defects in construction.

These two charges added $42 to their estimated monthly housing expense. Since both amounts are based on the value of the house, they are not affected by any changes in the estimated size of the monthly mortgage payment.

By subtracting $152 ($110 + $42) from the $658 figure the couple got the monthly $506 amount they could apply toward the mortgage under the 25 percent guideline.

The Maxwells then selected a price of $65,000 as being typical of what they might expect to pay for a house in their neighborhood. Assuming a 20 percent down payment, the 80 percent financed portion of the price would be about $50,000. Payments on a mortgage at 17 percent would run $712 each month and would mean allocating about 33 percent of net income for housing ($31,600 × .33 = $10,423 ÷ 12 = $870 − $152 = $718).

Since they hadn't recently bought any expensive items on credit and were making no time payments, Anne and John reluctantly decided that they could—just barely—buy a house in the $65,000 range and still make ends meet.

The 33 percent rule. If John had not firmly suppressed last year's sudden impulse to sell their old car and buy an expensive imported sedan on credit, their situation would have been worse.

In the case of home loan applicants already in debt, the limit traditionally used by lenders was 33⅓ percent of net income. This applies to *all* payments: those for housing plus payments for other items bought on credit. In recent years these limits have been increased to as much as 40 percent for applicants whose incomes are expected to stay ahead of inflation.

Since most expensive consumer goods are financed by short or medium term loans at the market rate—and the high performance car that John liked cost well over $15,000—the bank would have had to stretch the 33 percent rule considerably to lend the Maxwells the amount needed for such a home.

How Much Down Payment?

Anne and John had already weighed the pros and cons of borrowing enough money over the actual cost of the house to cover closing costs.

They would also have moving and settling-in expenses. Since neither had relatives to lend them such large amounts, they thought the mortgage might be the next best source of funds, if their liquid assets were not enough to cover the costs of moving in.

Assuming the bank agreed, one way to get enough money to cover these expenses from the mortgage was to lower the down payment. On an $85,000 house a 10 percent down payment compared to a 20 percent down payment would mean this much more cash:

Down payment	Loan amount
10% = $ 8,500	$76,500
20% = $17,000	$68,000
	$ 8,500 additional cash

By lowering the down payment they would, in effect, be borrowing $8,500 at a lower rate than market interest for short term consumer loans. The reduced down payment seemed to have a number of things in its favor:

- Leverage: they would be using less of their own money and borrowing a greater amount. Then, *if* the value of the house continued to rise, their equity would grow in relation to the debt. The Maxwells would benefit from increased net worth with less of their own money invested.
- They could invest the extra cash from a low down payment and get a rate of return higher than the increased mortgage payments.

Lower Down Payments and Mortgage Insurance

However, banks often waive mortgage insurance on loans if down payments are 20 percent or more, since the resale price of the house will usually cover the unpaid principal if they have to foreclose.

The principal reason for using mortgage insurance is to make up for the borrower's reduced equity in a house financed with a low down payment. Such mortgages are considered "high loan-to-value" and they are often the only way that first time buyers can afford a house.

Without some form of loan insurance or guarantee, mortgage loan officers tend to become distinctly uneasy at the thought of borrowers having ten percent or less equity in homes financed by their institutions. The lending industry has statistical evidence that borrowers are more likely to default when they have little to lose besides their credit ratings.

If the loan's risk portion (that part of it which sale of the house might not cover) or all of it is insured or guaranteed by a third party, however, the lender is protected against loss. This risk is assumed by the underwriter and the lender can then issue such mortgages on the basis of the borrower's ability to meet the monthly payments.

Being a veteran, Anne's father had qualified for a VA-guaranteed mortgage at no extra cost. Originally set up as a federal assistance program for returning servicemen, the expenses of running the VA home loan guaranty program were and are paid from public funds—qualified borrowers pay no insurance premiums.

For non-veterans there was the Federal Housing Administration home mortgage insurance program (the FHA is now part of the Department of Housing and Urban Development). Approved by Congress in 1934, the purpose of FHA insurance was to be a stabilizing force in the residential mortgage market, promote better housing standards and establish sound financing practices. By committing the full faith and credit of the U.S. government to paying claims resulting from default, the FHA radically transformed the home financing industry and brought order out of post-Depression chaos.

One result of the FHA's operations is a healthy and growing private mortgage insurance industry. Since the first mortgage insurance company, Wisconsin-based MGIC, began underwriting home mortgages in 1957, fourteen other companies have been formed. Together, they now insure more single-family homes than the government.

FHA insurance is still available and they currently insure up to $67,500 of a home loan ($90,000 in designated high cost areas). FHA insures 100 percent of the loan, not just the risk portion, and under their rules the house must first be appraised, both to determine a fair market value and to certify that it complies with FHA building and structural requirements.

Very Low Down Payments and "Leverage"

Back in the 1970's many people bought houses with 10 percent down payments and in a number of cases as much as 95 percent of the house was financed. Where the buyers had selected their houses and neighborhoods carefully, the market value of their dwellings soared. After a few years their equity in the house equaled or exceeded the unpaid mortgage principal.

Low down payments also benefited (and still benefit) buyers in high tax brackets. Since the large monthly interest payment can be deducted from their pre-tax income, the house is put to maximum use as a tax shelter.

But the Maxwells had misgivings about applying for the lowest possible down payment to finance, in today's market, the very best house they could get. For one thing, they read that housing prices had peaked in many parts of the country—and actually dropped when selling prices were adjusted for inflation.

The couple had, of course, seen other reports explaining how the pent-up demand for housing would explode again as soon as interest rates came down to reasonable levels. But, if such a buying surge occurred, would the Administration in power continue all the tax advantages of home ownership? Also featured in newspapers and magazines were articles by some well known economists who blamed the housing industry for soaking up a disproportionate share of the available investment capital.

These economists argue that America's competitive position in the world has declined because of inadequate investment in new factories, industrial long-term research and advanced product development. Much of this is financed by corporate bond issues, which exponents of the "too much money for housing" theory say sometimes have few takers while money has flowed into unproductive residential homes. John and Anne didn't fully understand the underlying reasons behind this argument, but they did notice that some of its proponents had names that lawmakers and administrators listen to respectfully.

So not only were the Maxwells unsure whether their home would appreciate like so many in the 1970's, but there was also the probability that to qualify they would have to settle for an adjustable rate mortgage. This might mean sharp rises in monthly interest payments or, if these payments were fixed, substantial negative amortization. The indexes to which adjustable rate mortgage plans are tied are all affected in different degrees by inflation and price increases, such as might result from a stoppage of oil imports from the Middle East or other political/economic crises overseas.

Had their income been higher, the Maxwells would probably have opted to pay down as little of their own money as possible, using the cash still on hand to pay for improvements, fixtures and furnishings. But their actual earnings meant very tight budgeting to repay even a 90 percent mortgage on the better types of houses in their area. Sleepless nights and frayed nerves would be the likely result of trying to keep up the even higher payments on a 95 percent loan. Rather than try for this much leverage, Anne and John decided that a lower priced house would put less strain on both them and their marriage.

Several of their friends, on the other hand, could have afforded to gamble on prices and indexes rising. John's cousin, a recent law school graduate now practicing in their city, was one. The young surgeon who had operated on Anne the previous year was another. Both these people could easily have qualified for a high loan-to-value mortgage in the expensive suburbs surrounding their city, including private insurance on the mortgages' 25 percent risk portion.

In both cases these young professionals were beginning careers where their incomes were certain to increase rapidly. The Maxwells earned comfortable salaries, but their paychecks were not in *that* class.

The Mortgage Insurance Companies of America, whose members' reason for being is to make low down payment loans possible—and who are in the business of writing *insurance,* not holding portfolios of deeds on defaulted homes—has this to say about adjustable rate mortgages:

- (Negative amortization): "loans where the initial monthly payment may not be sufficient to fully amortize the loan over (its) term" are an example of a design element with "serious risk features." (The borrower could in time possibly owe more than the property value.) "If not properly understood and used appropriately, this design feature can generate unmanageable default risk."

In other words, both the lender and the underwriter who make a low down payment possible will be especially careful with an ARM. If, in their opinion, an applicant qualifies, the risk is likely to be acceptable by the standards of prudent home loan management.

When Two or More Parties Jointly Buy a House

One approach which appeals to some buyers will halve the cost of housing expenses and municipal taxes. If they purchase their home jointly with another couple—or single person—the down payment, monthly loan payment, taxes and utility bills are all shared. In suburbs which allow joint ownership of a house, some builders are even offering new homes with two person or multi-family layouts.

Since both owners will not only share expenses but also will live quite close together, it's important that both be responsible people and *compatible*—for example, if one party likes listening to Indian music at high decibels, the other owner should also be partial to this sound!

Ideally, both should have comparable incomes and ages. They should already know each other well enough to avoid the rise of unexpected conflicts as they share the common areas of the house: living room, kitchen, garage, garden, cellar and attic. In fact, if you opt for joint ownership, or a "mingles" house, take a tip from similar urban town house arrangements and do *everything* possible before moving in to avoid squabbles about who is using how much of what and who is going to pay for it.

Many of the larger existing houses are especially attractive to joint owners, since their greater living space allows ample separate areas for each. You can prevent clashes down the line if you and your co-owners spend the extra money to install separate water heaters, electricity meters, kitchens and an equal number of bathrooms in each area. If you can afford it, and the layout of the house permits, separate heating/cooling systems will promote harmony in an era of high energy costs. Make sure that solid, sound-absorbing partitions divide the separate living areas. If the house has only a small garage, and both owners drive cars, make a 2-car garage a high-priority modification.

One of the newest options available to potential homeowners is "equity sharing" or "joint venture." This method of "teaming up" a buyer and an investor has been used very successfully in the commercial real estate field, but only now in home real estate. Here the real estate agent "matches" the buyer with an investor. They apply for financing together and take title to the property as "tenants in common," splitting the down payment, closing costs, taxes, monthly mortgage payments, insurance and condominium fees, if applicable. When the property is sold, both partners share the accumulated equity. However, only one partner, the original home buyer, actually lives in the home. He or she pays the co-owner/investor rent, fixed at a proportion of the fair market value rent, for the privilege of living in the home. Read more about this "creative financing" in Chapter 14.

In both joint occupancy ownership and equity sharing, it is important to have a good lawyer (preferably of a similar age and outlook) draw up an agreement which clearly sets forth the responsibilities of both owners—and how each will be protected if one should move out or fail to comply with the conditions to which both have agreed.

In the Maxwell's case, they did know one couple with whom they might have jointly and compatibly bought a bigger and better house than either could otherwise have afforded. But Anne felt that this would be too much like apartment living. Her active children were the deciding factor. She and John agreed that sole ownership or equity sharing would best fit their preferences, and that if necessary they would buy a cheaper house. But what sort of house should it be?

Singles and the Single-Family Home

One of their friends was surprised at what turned out to be the house of her dreams. Elaine Novak, a divorced and childless older woman who rented an apartment, was also shopping for a home—but for different reasons. Elaine liked privacy and didn't enjoy living so close to a lot of other people in a large building.

Her salary, as a mid-level manager in an insurance company, was $38,500—higher than John's, although less than the Maxwell's combined earnings.

When her marriage broke up in the early 1970's, the suburban home which she and her husband had owned was sold. Elaine moved into her apartment and since then had never seriously considered returning to the suburbs. She remembered that the lives of most of her neighbors had revolved around the raising and educating of children, activities which she hadn't been able to share.

Real estate agents, among others, now informed her that things were different and that she stood a very good chance of having neighbors in situations similar to her own. Before she started house-hunting, Elaine had believed that an urban town house was the only really viable homeowning option for single people—but learned that recent statistics didn't bear this out.

FHA figures, for example, showed that in 1980 42 percent of one-family houses were sold to single, separated, widowed, or divorced buyers* (the "SSWD's" in housing industry parlance). Elaine also learned that, since the enactment of the Equal Credit Opportunity Law in 1976, the same loan qualifying standards applied to her as to anyone else. Being female was no longer relevant when applying for a home mortgage. What now counted most were her solid net worth and good future earnings prospects.

Most of the manufactured homes and other types of alternative housing were of little interest to Elaine. Unlike the Maxwells, she had only looked at new and used traditional houses like the one she had known during her marriage. She was appalled at the way prices had climbed since her homeowning days!

It was a social get-together that rather ironically put Elaine in one of the more unusual kinds of alternative home. The invitation had come from people she had met during her sum-

---

*Characteristics of FHA Single-Family Mortgages, Section 203b, 1980 (Married Mortgagors: 79,079; Unwed Mortgagors: 33,212)

mer vacation at a nearby bay. It was for a "housewarming" on a floating shelter, a houseboat! Although she loved the shoreline, it had never occurred to her that she could both work at her job and still live in her preferred environment.

After talking to her hostess and then shopping for models and prices (learning that quite a nice houseboat costs around $40,000—much less than even a small house in her area) she made her decision and bought the one she liked with a $15,000 chattel mortgage. This medium-term loan carried a higher interest rate than a 30-year mortgage. But it was for a smaller amount and she could easily handle the payments to get what she wanted: her own home by the Bay with an unbeatable view!

So Elaine Novak discovered her dream house was a houseboat. What will yours be? The next chapters discuss the many options open to you—even on a very limited budget. From condominiums to geodesic domes, review your options. There are many more than you expect.

Table III

WORKSHEET FOR ESTIMATING WHAT YOU CAN AFFORD TO PAY FOR A HOUSE

STEP 1   FIGURE OUT YOUR REGULAR MONTHLY TAKE-HOME (NET) PAY AFTER DEDUCTIONS FOR TAXES, SOCIAL SECURITY, PENSION, UNION DUES, ETC. INCLUDE ONLY WHAT YOU CAN DEFINITELY COUNT ON.

	AN EXAMPLE	YOUR ESTIMATE
• Employment (after deductions)	$ 850	$
• Social Security, Disability/Pension Benefits Benefits, Welfare Payments, etc.	$ 0	$
• Alimony, Child Support	$ 0	$
• Interest on Savings Accounts	$ 15	$
• Stock Dividends, Bond Income, etc.	$ 0	$
• Other Income (such as, second job)	$ 135	$
TOTAL (NET) INCOME	$ 1,000	$

STEP 2 FIGURE OUT YOUR REGULAR MONTHLY EXPENSES (EXCLUDING RENT AND UTILITIES).

	AN EXAMPLE	YOUR ESTIMATE
• Food (groceries, eating out, etc.)	$ 250	$ 190
• Clothes (new clothes, laundry, etc.)	$ 60	$ 25
• Personal Care (cosmetics, hair care, personal hygiene	$ 25	$ 25
• Medical/Dental Bills (plus prescriptions)	$ 35	$ 20
• Home Furnishings and Expenses	$ 20	$ 20
• Recreation (movies, vacation)	$ 30	$ 50
• Gifts (birthdays, holidays)	$ 25	$ 13
• Car expenses (auto loan, insurance, gas, oil, maintenance, etc.)	$ 110	$ 100
• Life and Health Insurance	$ 50	$ 17
• Child Care Expenses	$ 15	$ 0
• Installment Loans (charge accounts, credit cards)	$ 30	$ 0
• Regular Savings	$ 30	$ 30
• All Other Miscellaneous Expenses	$ 20	$ 20
TOTAL (NON-HOUSING) EXPENSES	$ 700	$ 600

STEP 3   SUBTRACT THE TOTAL IN STEP 1 FROM THE TOTAL IN STEP 2 TO GET THE AMOUNT AVAILABLE FOR HOUSING EXPENSES.

	AN EXAMPLE	YOUR ESTIMATE
TOTAL AVAILABLE FOR HOUSING	$ 300	$

Source: U.S. Department of Housing & Urban Development

Table IV: Qualifying Guidelines Used For Home Mortgages

1. Monthly housing expenses may not exceed:
   - For FHA/VA: 35% of monthly income after deducting federal income tax.
   - For Conventional: 25%–28% of gross monthly income.
2. Total long term debt service may not exceed:
   - For FHA/VA: 50% of monthly income after deducting federal income tax, social security payments, state and local income tax.
   - For Conventional: 33%–36% of gross monthly income

---

*Note: These limits have been extended on conventional mortgages.

CHAPTER 3

Options for the Group-Oriented

Condominiums and Homeowners' Associations

Condominiums are the fastest growing and most popular type of group housing in the country. Their owners can get the tax and ownership advantages of a single-family home, usually at a lower price for a comparable area of square feet, and need only clean and maintain their interior living space.

If you live in a condominium, you do none of the messy jobs that the exterior of a detached single-family house and its grounds usually require. Instead, you pay your share of the maintenance contract, which is supposed to ensure that this work is done for you and the other residents.

Many condominium developments sound like the home of your dreams with the good life and resort facilities added—a theme that developers' ads seldom overlook. The tradeoff is loss of privacy, since your neighbors are close around you and, in a highrise, above and below you as well. Most of your fellow residents—and their children and pets, where permitted—will be equally anxious to enjoy the common facilities. You will get to know them well, whether you like them or not.

Generally speaking, only buyers wealthy enough to afford large, soundproof and expensive apartments—or detached units with entrances and grounds carefully laid out to provide the illusion of seclusion—get any real privacy in a condominium. Since the individual owners bear the operating expense on a pro-rated basis, it follows that this cost goes down as the number of homeowners increases. In the case of detached-unit suburban developments, the optimum density/ individual payment ratio is about ten units per acre—one for every 4,356 square feet. Any closer than this and maintenance charge reductions are outweighed by an irritating view consisting mostly of neighbors' windows, porches and garage doors. If 8 to 10 units per acre still doesn't give you enough elbow room, there's the option of a low density development—but these hardly qualify as housing for average incomes.

Group living can give people earning average salaries a shelter comparable to a single-family home—not only at lower cost but often with a variety of recreational facilities included. But you can expect to be *involved:* in resident's committees and general meetings dealing with everything from clubhouse privileges, children in "adults only" playing courts and the swimming pool, to maintenance standards and bids for major repairs.

By design, most condominiums are more culturally diverse than a neighborhood of single family homes. The exceptions are the very expensive developments and those aimed specifically at older retired people. When a community offers a selection of differently sized and priced dwellings, residential planners consider it to have an "optimum socio-economic mix."

Adequate rules—and their strict enforcement—are important in maintaining the community's intended quality of life when residents come from all types of backgrounds. All owners must abide by these rules. Before buying-in the list of regulations should be read carefully. If you do buy into a condominium, but don't choose to get personally involved in helping to run it, you must then abide by regulations decided entirely by others.

One federal agency which views communal living with particular approval is the Environmental Protection Agency (EPA). A 1974 EPA-sponsored study on land-use revealed that in today's society, clustered dwellings are the most environmentally sound and economical way to build residential communities. Unlike single-family homes on quarter-acre subdevelopments, clustering uses substantially less real estate to house the same number of people. And it does not encroach as much on productive farmland, destroy wildlife habitats, degenerate into urban sprawl, or make it impossible for residents to enjoy a "natural and pleasant" environment.

The study found that it is cheaper for builders to house a given number of families in clustered housing, which means the dwellings cost less. It is also more economical for the municipality to provide services, when dwellings are clustered together. Each family needs less power for heating and cooling when dwellings are enclosed within common walls, which conserves energy and lowers the monthly utility bill. And of special interest to the EPA: automobiles are used much less in properly planned clustered housing and the reduced exhaust pollution makes for cleaner air.

Homeowners' Associations. The purpose of a condominium's homeowners' association (HOA) is to own and operate on a non-profit basis the service and recreational facilities which serve the whole community. You automatically become a member when you buy-in. And, if membership fees are charged, the association can, if necessary, collect these dues by placing a lien on your unit.

The HOA's responsibilities include keeping up all the common property areas. This covers such items as snow removal, lawn mowing, electric utility lines, sewage pipes, underground TV cables and a long list of other jobs. If parts of the common property are damaged for any reason, it is up to the homeowners' association to ensure that proper repairs are made.

Homeowners' associations get the money to pay for all these services by levying a monthly maintenance assessment on individual owners which, like membership dues, *must* be paid. If the developer has stayed on to provide all or part of the community's services, the HOA must still exercise overall supervision over the way the work is done. Should the developer have departed, the HOA will have to hire outside contractors to do the work—which involves preparing, issuing, reviewing and awarding bids. However, in cases where the departed developer has retained a long term lease on recreational facilities, the HOA is powerless to control any subsequent rent increases for these unless state law says otherwise.

A homeowners association elects a board of governors or trustees to carry out all these functions. This board is also responsible for enforcing the regulations, which often leads to friction with offending homeowners. Typically, the elected governors have little training in handling their enormous responsibilities and, since the HOA is supposed to operate on a non-profit basis, their remuneration is often minimal or nil. Many elected officials will have "had it" after one term; and the resulting lack of qualified, willing candidates has forced a number of HOA's to hire professional managers from outside. This often leads to a smoother operation.

What you get. The availability of condominiums in your area depends on the enactment of a "Horizontal Property Act" or similar state legislation that allows individual dwelling unit estates to be established within a larger total property estate.

The vertical boundaries of each individual estate are its exterior walls. In a highrise, the horizontal boundaries are the floor and ceiling of the dwelling. You own everything inside these boundaries: the living space itself and any interior partition walls, kitchen equipment, bathroom and lighting fixtures, carpeting, curtains and so on—just as with a single-family home.

The common areas, in which you would own a share, include: hallways, lobby, elevators, mailroom, basement and the central heating/cooling/air purifying equipment, storage rooms and indoor parking areas. Outside the building you own part of the roof, exterior walls, outdoor parking areas, gardens, lawn, driveways and all recreational facilities retained by the community. Your share in the common property depends on the "unit value ratio" of your dwelling. This ratio is determined by dividing the appraised value of your unit by the total number of dwellings in the condominium. The higher your unit's price, the higher will be your ratio.

Condominium layouts. These communities can be designed to fit virtually any life style or architectural preference. Apart from some very innovative and expensive resort condominiums, however, the ones available in your area will probably fall into these categories: highrise, town house, planned unit development (PUD), garden apartment and villas.

Highrises. These are similar to rental apartment buildings, although more expensive condominiums will have a much fancier lobby, hallways and other public areas. Owners living in a highrise usually feel more secure against break-ins than those living in small detached units. If the highrise is well located, most of the apartments will have a very good view.

On the other hand, there's the problem of carrying a full load of groceries up the elevator, or running the gauntlet through the hallways and lobby in casual wear or curlers in order to pick up some urgent item at the store.

Exceptions to such luxurious standards, however, would be many of the converted rental buildings that are now offering condominium apartments. A large number of these were converted after they had outlived the depreciation period allowed by law, thereby becoming useless to their owners for tax writeoffs. By evicting the tenants, doing a minimal amount of remodelling and offering the old rental apartments for sale as condominiums, the owners could make a much greater profit. If you buy into one of these, it is you and your fellow owners who will have to maintain everything in working order (the former owner rid himself of that responsibility when he converted the building). The useful life of a rental apartment building can range from fifteen to thirty years, depending on IRS rulings and local tax officials—viewed in terms of the building's original mechanical equipment, this is a very long time indeed.

Before committing yourself to a condominium in a converted older building it's a good idea to have a building inspector go over the entire plant: elevators, heating and cooling systems, plumbing and wiring. If any of this equipment is old, it will be giving trouble much sooner than would new equipment in a new building. The replacement costs could force a homeowners' association with an inadequate contingency reserve into receivership. There is small chance of your unit appreciating in value while a court-appointed receiver is running the operation until debts are paid. Depending on the building's condition the reserve should be from 15 to 30 percent of the total annual maintenance assessment—make sure you are given this figure and discuss it with the building inspector, if possible.

Townhouses. These are usually built as two-to-four story narrow buildings in which each owner occupies one or two floors. They are typically row houses sharing common walls and are a space-efficient alternative for people who dislike high rise buildings but still prefer to live on expensive city residential real estate.

PUDs. Planned Unit Developments are the most sophisticated form of the clustering concept. The idea is to have a common architectural theme running through the development and either leave as much of the land as possible in its natural state, or else turn it into recreational areas that benefit the whole community.

The nature of planned unit developments is much influenced by standards the Federal Housing Administration established for the mortgages it insures on the individual dwellings. State and local planning boards in all parts of the country have adapted these FHA guidelines for their own areas. For example, FHA has laid down strict standards governing the intensity of land use in a PUD. The agency requires that a specified percentage of the open space must be reserved for the use of all the residents and that this may *not* include parking lots.

If developers want the units in their PUD to qualify for FHA-insured mortgages, the development will have to comply with FHA environmental impact standards. It will have to provide enough recreational facilities for the intended number of residents to satisfy FHA. And it may not use construction that FHA considers inadequate.

Provided the esthetic and environmental standards are met, the developers of a PUD have considerable freedom in the design of dwellings. These can include detached houses, highrise buildings, row houses or cluster housing. They may either use only one type of unit or else combine two or all of them together.

Developers may also include commercial areas or light industry in a PUD, provided that their architecture is in line with that of the residential dwellings and that they meet the environmental impact standards. In some cases the developers of a PUD will be creating a small, planned city from scratch.

If there are also isolated condominium housing clusters within the large condominium of the PUD, the owners living in them share in the common property of the PUD. PUD residents outside these smaller condominiums, however, do not share in their common areas—for which the cluster owners pay a separate maintenance fee.

Garden Apartments. These may or may not be surrounded by gardens, although some have an open balcony or one glassed-over as a greenhouse for plants. The term is usually used to describe a succession of buildings from two to several stories high, divided into condominium apartments sharing common exterior walls as vertical boundaries.

Villas. Here, your developer has borrowed from the promotional "hype" which has characterized the selling of single-family homes. Most of these "villas" will be rows of connected buildings two or three stories high. The term could just as easily be applied to a row of Quonset huts.

Financing a Condominium

From your point of view as a buyer, getting a mortgage for a condominium is the same as for a single-family home. The lender may have already checked out the development as a sound investment, and will apply the same standards to your qualifying for a loan as he would in the case of a single house. The closing costs, however, are often higher with condominiums, since these purchases involve more work for the real estate lawyer.

State laws are slowly evolving to prevent some of the abuses that have occurred in the past on condominium sales. Many buyers experienced in buying and selling condominium dwellings feel that the lawmakers should move faster. Here is where you can use the FHA Section 234 condominium insurance program as a guide in what can otherwise be a dangerous situation, depending on where you live. The FHA maximum loan amount of $67,500 ($90,000 in designated high cost areas) is high enough to buy a respectable unit in most condominium developments. Ask the developers if their units qualify for FHA mortgages. If they do, the development will have met FHA regulations on:

- Retention of a lease on land or recreational facilities. The FHA does not allow such leases and *all* of the condominium must be owned by its residents to qualify for FHA insurance. One of FHA's reasons for this rule is that otherwise your mortgage is affected by your assessment obligations to the homeowners' association. If the developer raises the rent on the leased facilities, the HOA is obliged to pay the increases by assessing its individual members. Inability to pay the additional amounts means that a lien can be placed on the individual property in spite of regular mortgage payments to the bank.

- Your down payment cannot be used for construction purposes. The money must be placed in an escrow account and kept there until all the units are completed and the developer has sold 80 percent of them to buyers. At this point he can transfer title to the new owners and collect his deposit money. (Otherwise, if the developer had gone bankrupt after using your money to pay construction expenses, you would be very far down the list of creditors in getting it back. When 80 percent of a condominium's units have been sold, the community is almost sure to be a success.)

- The FHA 80 percent requirement also protects you in case the units are not selling well. In a slow market many developers will rent unsold units and use the rental income to pay part of the development's fixed charges—which are quite high. While renting may benefit the developer, it's likely to have the opposite effect on residents who own their units. Suddenly they are a minority surrounded by renters who have no equity in the development. These will tend to be more casual about littering, obeying the rules and generally keeping up the common property. As a result, the value of your dwelling is likely to drop instead of appreciate.

Other Pitfalls for Condominium Buyers

Since relatively few condominiums qualify for FHA-insured mortgages, most buyers may have to finance the purchase with a non-insured mortgage requiring a 20 percent down payment. If they find a private insuror willing to underwrite a "conventional" mortgage this firm will have checked out the development as carefully as FHA. A good lawyer can be your most important ally when you buy into such a condominium and you should use one even with condominiums that meet FHA standards. From your personal viewpoint it's an advantage if your state law requires the legal documents to be in English instead of legalese.

The lawyer should carefully scrutinize the Enabling Declaration or Master Deed. This document states what you own, what the rules are, what your financial responsibilities are, how members are expected to conduct themselves and what they can and cannot do with their dwellings. It is the condominium's constitution and your dwelling stands as security that these regulations and assessments will be met.

Other than the practices specifically prohibited in qualifying for FHA mortgage insurance, the following additions or omissions in a condominium's voluminous Master Deed have often made the "good life" an expensive misery for many homeowners' associations:

Restrictions on common property. You may indeed be part owner of all common property, but a restriction on certain portions of it will prevent you from using them. Make sure that common areas which are easily accessible to all owners are not restricted for the use of particular dwelling units only.

Fixed share appraisal value. Your share in the common property is based on the appraised value of your unit and is added onto the purchase price. If prices in the development go up and some of your co-owners subsequently sell out, the unit value ratio and common property share of the new owners should still be based on the original appraisal value—unless all dwellings are to be reappraised together. Otherwise, new owners of appreciating units will own bigger shares, while yours becomes smaller and smaller. Remember that projects favored by a majority can be defeated by a smaller group of residents if their total investment is larger.

Management training. If you and your co-owners are typical of most condo communities you will be running a large and expensive complex without prior experience. Before they shoulder this burden alone, the developer should make sure that they get on-the-job training. If he has built other condominiums check with their residents. Has the developer ever departed as soon as his interest ended and left the new homeowners' association to fend for itself?

Prior debts. Has the developer's maintenance company presented the HOA with a large bill, as yet unpaid? If so, you and the other owners will have to pay it.

Adequate reserve funds. Does the homeowners' association have enough cash in reserve to cover major overhaul and repairs, based on a professional analysis of its plant? If the cost of repairs should exceed the cash on hand, you will be assessed your share of the additional money needed.

Unrealistic, low maintenance costs. These will usually be quoted you for new units, by salesmen anxious to make a sale. When you finally move in, the rate may have risen to several times the figure quoted. When buying used units you can always ask other residents what they pay for maintenance, and the seller should have records of recent payments.

Adequate property maintenance. The firm maintaining the common property should have condominium experience, since the value of all units in a run-down condominium will decline. Signing a *long-term* contract with a company belonging to the developer, however, is one way to risk poor maintenance.

Short term building warranties. If your state law requires 3-year warranties on condominium dwellings, you are likely to get better construction than with a 1-year warranty.

Cooperative Housing

The co-op is the oldest form of group home ownership in this country. While condominiums are much more common today nationwide, cooperatives still prevail in many areas—particularly the major cities of the Northeast. In a cooperative you are a shareholder with a stock certificate, whereas in a condominium you own your living unit in much the same way as you would own a single family house. Owning a share in a cooperative is very much like owning shares in any corporation, except that the shareholders are fewer and the laws affecting a housing co-op are different.

The Articles of Incorporation and By-laws for a housing corporation are specifically designed so that its stockholding residents can both own the property and jointly operate it. The legal rights and responsibilities of the corporate entity are very similar to those that apply to you as an individual. A housing cooperative must by law be a non-profit organization.

As a resident in a housing cooperative, your stock certificate gives you the exclusive right to occupy the unit you live in and the right to take part in running the corporation. Your participation can either be indirect (as a voter) or direct (as an elected member of the Board of Directors). Unlike the owner of a condominium unit, the resident in a cooperative does not receive a title to his or her dwelling unit.

The law permits only the elected Board as a whole to act for a housing cooperative. The reason for this is to eliminate one-person decisions, such as a chief executive officer might make in an industrial corporation. A housing cooperative's board is also kept small in number (usually between five and seven) so that there will be enough qualified candidates among the membership to be elected.

What makes a cooperative different from any other form of home ownership is the *corporation's* holding title to the individual dwelling units. It is the corporate entity that carries the mortgage, pays the taxes and fulfills the other obligations necessary to finance and operate the building or development. Through the corporation all members share responsibility for all the units, including yours. For this reason, you'll find that most cooperatives have strict controls over apartment remodeling.

When their corporation is a borrower or mortgagor, the members support it through their occupancy agreements, which usually run for three years. This eliminates individual payments on individual mortgages—it also means that financing a co-op dwelling is usually limited to a medium-term high interest loan. You cannot take out a long term self-amortizing mortgage to buy your stock certificate, and the holder of the corporation's mortgage will be directly concerned about the credit standing of prospective buyers.

A cooperative's Board has the right to veto any applicant's request to buy a stock certificate. The By-laws and local regulations usually prohibit turning away applicants from personal prejudice. However, the Board is sure to thoroughly investigate a prospective resident's credit standing and past payment record. Not only is the ability to make the down payment reviewed but the assurance of receiving regular monthly payments is of particular concern to the Board. If these go unpaid the other stockholders must make up the difference.

The monthly charges you pay are your share (based on the value of the dwelling unit you occupy) of the budget, as estimated by the Board of Directors. If the annual budget is overestimated you will receive your share of the unused amount in what's known as a "patronage refund." If not enough was budgeted to meet expenses, you will be assessed your share of the additional money needed. You are entitled to deduct on your income tax that portion of your payments which actually goes towards the mortgage interest and real estate taxes.

Should you decide to move out at any time, your membership certificate can be sold, subject to the Board's and mortgagee's approval. The By-laws will govern the certificate's transfer value, and both you and your lawyer should go over these carefully before buying-in. The occupancy agreement which residents sign before moving in is normally renewed automatically every three years—unless they have been given notice to leave by the board of Directors for some infraction of the By-laws.

Since all decisions are made by an elected Board, co-ops can be the most democratic form of group living. Members are each limited to one vote, regardless of the size of their respective living units or the number of these that they own. For this reason, cooperatives are well suited to many low and middle income housing developments. The residents, all with equal voting power, can get involved in energy conservation, the maintenance program and extra services, such as day care nurseries for children.

In some places, cooperatives can also be a very expensive form of housing. A good example is New York City, where a medium sized apartment in the better residential neighborhoods can easily cost over $250,000. These buildings are beyond the reach of many higher income buyers—to say nothing of those earning average incomes! At 50 percent down an apartment in this price range can require a down payment of $125,000, with the balance of over $100,000 to be financed through a high interest consumer loan.

In a cooperative designed for more moderate incomes the most important consideration is that you, as a resident, are financially dependent on your fellow members' ability to carry their share of the load. The By-laws make the total membership liable for any defaults by individual members. In the depression of the 1930's as economic conditions got worse throughout the country, it became common for more and more co-op members to fail in their payments. The other members would often stretch their resources to the limit in making up the difference. When they were no longer able to do this, mortgagees and other creditors foreclosed, converting the building into rental apartments.

Table V: COMPARISON OF SIMILAR TERMS

	COOPERATIVES	CONDOMINIUM
Mortgagor	The cooperative corporation	Each individual owner that borrowed money to purchase the unit
Mortgagee	The lending institution	Same
Monthly Charge	Proportionate share of all costs including mortgage	Percentage of common estate costs. Any mortgage payments on the individually owned unit are paid separately as are those assessed on the individual unit.
Real Estate Taxes	Assessed on the property of the cooperative corporation	Assessed on the individual unit
Voting	Each member has one vote.	Each owner has the number of votes representing the percentage of value of his unit to the total of all units.
Mortgage Term	Cooperative corporation usually has 40 years—member is not a mortgagor.	Owner usually has 30 years—condominium is not a mortgagor.
Closing or Settlement costs	Costs in addition to the price of the corporate property including mortgage service charge, title search, insurance and transfer of ownership charges paid when the cooperative first purchases the property. Only a small transfer fee is charged to transfer future membership in the cooperative.	Costs in addition to the price of a unit and its undivided interest in the common estate including mortgage service charge, title search, insurance and transfer of ownership charges paid each time the unit is resold or refinanced.
Equity	Increase in the value of a membership certificate over and above the initial or "downpayment" resulting from members monthly contribution toward payment of the corporate mortgage.	Increase in value of ownership interest in the unit as the owner pays off his mortgage and from market value appreciation.
Escrow Funds	Subscription or downpayments required to be held unused until the viable cooperative is assured. Transfer of membership funds are sometimes escrowed until the transfer is complete.	Subscription or downpayments required to be held unused until the condominium regime is recorded on the property and titles are conveyed to each buyer. Escrows are usually used in each resale situation. The deed is held in escrow until and conditions of the sale (including any prepayments) have been met.

Source: U.S. Department of Housing & Urban Development, 1976

Table VI: Commonly Encountered Condominium Regulations

1. 24-hour parking in designated parking areas is permitted. Overnight parking on streets or cul-de-sacs is not allowed.

2. The 20 MPH speed limit within the community must be observed and so must all STOP signs.

3. No resident may park a commercial vehicle or truck overnight at any place within the community. Boat trailers or recreational vehicles belonging to owners may only be parked in designated areas.

4. Bicycles used within the community will follow the same speed limits and observe traffic signs as other vehicles. If ridden at night they must have headlights and rear tail reflectors.

5. Motorcycles are not permitted within the community at any time. Mopeds shall adhere to state muffler regulations and the same applies to exhaust systems on all other vehicles.

6. No group games shall be played on streets, cul-de-sacs or common property lawns. Residents may use the playing fields, courts and other facilities provided for this purpose.

7. Residents are allowed to keep one pet on their premises. Prior consent of the Board of Governors is required in each case. If a pet dies or is lost, an application must be made and approved in order to obtain another pet. Pets must be kept within the dwellings and may not occupy the crawl space under them. Pets shall not be permitted to run free at any time, but must be kept on a leash not to exceed six feet while outdoors. Pets may only be walked on streets and not on the common lawns between the dwelling units.

8. No commercial business shall be conducted from any dwelling without the prior written consent of the Board of Governors.

9. After 10 p.m. all television sets, radios and hi-fi units shall have their volume turned down sufficiently so that they will not be heard outside the dwelling unit. No musical instruments may be played after 10 p.m.

10. Exterior television antennas are *not* permitted. Reception is provided by the community cable system.

11. After 7 p.m. power tools may only be used if they cannot be heard outside the dwelling unit.

12. After 11 p.m. any shouting or loud conversation which results in complaints from other residents shall be treated as a public disturbance.

13. Visible clotheslines are *not* permitted. Neither shall blankets, pillows or wearing apparel be aired in the open.

14. No exterior additions which would encroach on neighboring units shall be built without the express written consent of the Board of Governors. At present the following will be approved:
    * patios, not to exceed 200 square feet;
    * patio covers for above, which may not clash with the color or design of the dwelling. Screens or exterior walls between the patio and its covering constitute encroachment and are forbidden.
    * window awnings, provided they do not clash with the siding.

15. Installation of major appliances must be done by a licensed professional, in conformance with state and local codes.

16. Any exterior repainting or trim must conform to the original color scheme of the dwelling and requires the prior approval of the Board of Governors.

17. Visible trash containers or other receptacles are not permitted. Exterior toolsheds are not permitted.

18. If hoses are left lying on lawns, they will be considered an obstacle to the lawn mowing crews and these lawns will not be cut. If this situation recurs enough times to allow the grass to reach an unsightly height, the resident will be required to either remove the hose or have the lawn mowed at his or her own expense.

19. Fence-like boundary dividers of wood, brick or cinder blocks are prohibited. Neither shall hedges, shrubs or trees be planted for this purpose, or to screen off an open area.

20. A resident's nameplate, not to exceed 20 inches by four inches, is permitted above the dwelling's mailbox. Other signs of any kind, including "FOR SALE" signs are prohibited.

21. Planting groups of one or more shrubs or trees must be at least 12 feet apart. The mowing crews will not cut the grass in the area enclosed by a planting group.

22. Planting alongside the foundation and not to extend further outwards than three feet from the foundation is both permitted and encouraged. Vegetable plants are permitted in this area as long as they do not extend more than three feet outwards. Vegetable plots or gardens on the lawns, however, are *not* permitted.

23. Due to the possibility of damage to underground utility lines and TV cables, prior approval by the maintenance department is required before digging holes for trees or shrubs, even in authorized areas.

24. If the planting of any trees or shrubs adversely affects the drainage of the surrounding area, the resident may be required to remove these plantings and the area will be resodded at the resident's expense.

25. Children are not allowed in facilities reserved for adults. When using the swimming pool, children shall be accompanied by adults at all times.

CHAPTER 4

Rehabilitation: Wood Frame Houses

$\mathbf{A}$fter looking at both new and older homes, most house hunters have mixed feelings about modern construction. The majority like the appliances, fixtures, bathrooms, three-wire ground outlets, insulation and triple-glazed windows found in good developments and new single homes. But only small children would see the interiors of these houses as large. To many the modern home in the moderate price range seems cramped when compared with the larger interior living space of comparably priced houses dating back to the 1930's and earlier.

Buyers also find that they are paying a great deal more for new construction and getting less for the money than their parents got for theirs. If they break down the present average nationwide cost of a completed house and compare it to similar figures as recent as 1960, they will note startling increases, even when adjusted for inflation.

In places like Washington, D.C., or parts of California, a lot as small as one tenth of an acre can cost over $30,000. Hawaiian buyers could expect to pay $50,000 or more for a lot this size. Moreover, the house itself will cost more, since where land costs are rising the price of labor and materials will also rise.

The asking prices for good existing homes in desirable residential areas will be equally dismaying. Well maintained houses will be priced very close to new homes, and the only "break" a buyer can expect is to purchase mortgage money at below-market rates from an owner anxious to sell.

So if you have fixed on an attractive neighborhood, prefer not to share a house with singles or another family, and have a limited budget for housing, the options of a new or well kept up older house may be out of reach. There's a third option if you are reasonably handy with tools, a methodical planner and can learn to deal with sub-contractors: buy a run-down but structurally sound older house and restore it to tip-top shape. Such neglected houses are more common than people think and many don't look at all bad from the outside.

What to Look for in a Wood Frame House

If you decide to look for a restorable wood frame house, you'll find that these can be constructed in two ways, one of which is quite rare in the post-industrial age and the other quite common.

Post and beam framing. Existing post and beam houses will usually be very old, dating back to the 18th century and earlier. The exceptions would be houses recently erected from a kit. Compared to the structures you see going up on builders' sites today, a post and beam frame uses relatively large timbers. These thicker beams can span longer distances without supports, which gives the framework of the house an "open" look.

In older post and beam houses, the large sill beams (laid flat on the foundation to support the walls) and the vertical posts which stand on them can measure a foot square. Both the girt beams (which run horizontally between the exterior posts at ceiling height) and the top plate beams (on which the lower ends of the roof rafters rest) can measure 6 inches by 8 inches. Beams of this size and weight cannot be toenailed together at the butt joint—even large nails won't hold such heavy loads and will pull out, or else split the ends of the wood.

The old post and beam structural members were joined by mortise and tenon joints. The tenon was formed by cutting off the outer thirds at both sides of the end of the horizontal beam. A matching cavity, or mortise, was chiseled out of the vertical post to admit the protruding inner third of the beam. This "tenon" was then pushed into the mortise and a hole was drilled through both members, into which a round peg or "treenail" was hammered. Anyone doubting the strength of well made mortise and tenon joints should talk to people who specialize in taking down and restoring old barns. These folks say that pulling apart the old mortised joints is one of the hardest parts of the job.

Post and beam framing largely disappeared from mass housing with the advent of standardized building lumber. It then became cheaper and easier to put up a light frame structure, as compared to the higher cost of the heavier timbers and the amount of muscle and effort needed to man-handle them into place.

Platform framing. A platform frame uses the smaller standardized wood sections that you constantly see at lumberyards. The most common dimensions used are today's slimmed-down version of the 2 × 4 and 2 × 6.

Platform framing uses a large number of these eight foot high 2 × 6 vertical "studs," toenailed to the 2 × 6 "sole plates" on the sub-flooring and the "top plates" (both usually consist of a pair of 2 × 6's laid flat, one on top of the other). Most building codes have stipulated that stud centers be no more than 16 inches apart on load bearing walls.

Older homes will also have "firestops" horizontally toenailed between vertical studs, about halfway up the wall. The purpose of these was to block drafts which might help a fire spread inside the wall, and also to brace the upright studs. These firestops can be a real nuisance if you have to blow in loose insulation, or install new electrical wiring by "fishing" it up behind the wallboard.

The tops of window openings are formed by a horizontal piece of wood called a "header," whose ends rest on shorter supporting studs. These are nailed to the adjacent full-length studs, and nails are also driven through the long stud into the header. The horizontal framing member at the bottom of the window is the "sill," which is supported by short studs sometimes called "cripples."

The openings for the doors are made the same way, except that the open area extends clear to the floor.

The sub-floors are made up of "header joists" around the perimeter and "floor joists" which support the sub-flooring. In the center of the span, where the ends of two joists are "lapped" or joined side-by-side, these are in turn supported by a girder. Boards for the sub-flooring are now laid diagonally over the joists and covered with plywood. In many older homes, however, the sub-flooring can be a single layer of thick boards laid across the joists.

The roofs on platform frame houses are supported by "rafters" whose lower extremes rest on a "top plate" of two 2 × 6's and whose tops join a "ridge board" at an angle. At each end of the roof the rafters will be supported by "end studs" and every fourth pair of interior rafters may be cross-braced by a "collar beam."

Spanning the top plates, and usually lapped and supported at the center of the span by a girder, are the "ceiling joists" or "crossties." The laths or gypsum board of the ceiling below are attached to their underside and the attic floor—usually of ordinary boards—is nailed to their top.

The above is a brief and somewhat general description of the structure that supports the walls, floors and roof of a wooden platform frame house—which is also known as "light frame" construction. The rest of this chapter will deal with potential problem areas in restoring such a house to a state comparable to similar homes that have been well maintained and modernized.

First, those areas where any serious problems should mean rejecting a house no matter how much you like the neighborhood. If this is your first 'rehab,' hiring a building inspector now could save a lot of money later on.

Foundation. Older homes in most suburban areas usually have a full basement, rather than a crawl space over a concrete slab or perimeter of concrete blocks. This area was used to store coal before the arrival of oil heat and the old washtubs for the family laundry normally went in the basement.

The *floor* of the cellar should be at least four inches of concrete reinforced with a steel mesh, resting on not less than four inches of sand. The layer of sand is important in that it allows water to drain away and also acts as a cushion between the floor and the underlying earth. Soils containing clay can absorb considerable amounts of water and when this happens they expand. No residential rigid concrete floor can withstand such pressure.

The floor should be free of open cracks, although small hairline cracks are common in concrete walls and floors and don't indicate any problems. If you notice several wide cracks and water stains or rotted wooden areas up to about a foot above the floor, get the advice of a soils engineer familiar with the local water table and water runoff patterns.

Or, if you are able to visit the house during or immediately after a heavy rainstorm, check whether water is welling up through these cracks. This trickle can flood the basement with six inches or more of water in several hours. A high water table doesn't necessarily mean the foundation is unsafe, but it *does* mean the basement will be damp. Plans for the below-grade playroom or workshop will probably have to be scrapped.

If the floor not only shows open cracks but has also settled unevenly in a number of places, the building inspector will likely suggest that you reject the house. His advice should be followed.

The walls of the basement should preferably be of poured concrete. Also acceptable are walls of mortared concrete blocks waterproofed on the outside. Even if the basement looks dry during your inspection, check the walls for water stains or flaking and crumbling plaster. If present, these may be due to water seeping through mortared joints or cracks in the concrete. If you are able to visit the house during a downpour, check the walls as well as the floor for seepage.

The only way to stop water from seeping through walls is to direct it away from the foundation or else seal the exterior. The first thing to look for are broken downspouts or one which is discharging towards the house. Assuming the water table is low and the drainage good, directing water away from the house can mean a dry basement even if the walls are not entirely waterproof.

If the house you're looking at combines both evidence of wall seepage and poor drainage, getting a dry basement means sealing the outside. This involves excavating a deep trench around the foundation wall, applying two or three coats of waterproof cement or a coat of epoxy sealer, and often laying new perforated drainage pipe on a bed of gravel at considerable expense.

If you are house hunting in summer, you may notice a damp film of moisture on the surface areas of basements. Interior humidity is the cause, condensing on the cooler walls of the cellar. Ventilation or a dehumidifier will usually dry things out.

Finally, and most serious, the foundation may have settled unevenly. This condition has been mentioned last because you note its effects just by looking at the house. Sagging rooflines, warped eaves, out-of-square window and door frames, sloping floors and cracked chimneys usually mean a severely distorted structure which is either impossible or else not "cost-effective" to repair. No amount of remodeling will turn such a house into an appreciating investment.

Floor support girders. These are the heavy wooden beams over which the floor joists are laid. The heaviest loads bear on the girder or girders under the first floor. These are the beams you see supported by masonry pillars in the basement. They will always deflect to some extent and up to 3/8-inch sag over a 10-foot span is acceptable.

A sound girder with a greater deflection or sag can be straightened, and the floor above it levelled, with a heavy duty adjustable screw jack post. Ask the building engineer's advice: these girders must be raised *very* slowly, about one quarter turn every 24 hours. Turning the jack any more than this, or at shorter intervals, transmits a tremendous amount of force to the rest of the structure which could damage walls and floors throughout the house.

Should the girder be cracked or decayed, the building engineer may advise rehabbing some other house. The sag may have damaged other parts of the building; or, if only the floor above is affected, replacing such a basic support member without damaging the rest of the house would be an expensive operation requiring professional equipment.

Roof. If the ridge pole has a sag which is not due to settling of the foundation, the cause might be sagging rafters or inadequate support. Fixing a roof skeleton can be a major carpentry job—ask the building inspector's opinion.

When you look at the roof's exterior, worn shingles are to be expected in a house which has been allowed to run down. Most roofing contractors will quote less than $1 per square foot to install new shingling. However, if the underlying *sheathing* has been damaged by weather to the point where it needs replacing, this would be much more expensive and another house might be a better deal.

If the building engineer OK's the house as structurally sound, he may still point out areas which will need a lot of hard work or money, or both, to restore. A termite inspection is essential, and if you are taking out a mortgage to finance the purchase of the house, the lender will require this check and an inspector's certification that it is free of termites.

Outside Repairs

The exterior eaves, sheathing and siding may have suffered moisture damage and rot, due either to the absence of a roof overhang which allowed rain to run down the wall, or to lack of a vapor barrier which made it possible for moisture to flow outwards and condense inside the wall. If the sheathing under the clapboards is extensively damaged the siding must come off before it can be replaced. This job takes time and costs money: it would be a valid reason to reject the house.

It's usually not a big-ticket item to replace rotten eaves and pieces of siding. Probing with an ice pick at corners, around door and window frames, and where clapboards join end-to-end will reveal soft damp spots which have decayed or are likely to.

On the other hand, the siding may be solid but its "skin" of paint be flaking, peeling, blistered and generally in terrible shape. A new paint job will look better and last much longer if the old paint is removed down to the bare wood.

Porches. Unenclosed front or side porches are open to rain and melting snow, which can easily raise the moisture content of their structural members to the point where damp rot flourishes. The bases of posts or pillars are common problem areas, since the water gets into the joints between them and works its way into both members. On some porches, steps contact the ground directly, which is not a good practice with untreated wood that can absorb ground moisture through capillary action. When the wood gets moist enough, its cellulose becomes food for fungi.

If only a few sections of the porch are rotted, they can be replaced with new wood. A seriously deteriorated porch should be completely rebuilt, however, and if it is a large one you may have to call in a professional carpenter. Otherwise, there's the risk that the unpatched areas are moist enough for damp rot to spread. Damp beams are also preferred homes for colonies of carpenter ants, which will stake out the rest of your house as their territory.

Windows. Be prepared for problem windows if you buy an old wood frame house. If these don't fit tightly, they will let in cold winter drafts and each can leak out as much heat in a winter as half a barrel (21 gallons) of oil will produce. Fixing all windows should get a high priority: start by late spring if possible, so that these openings will be tight when cold weather arrives.

Double hung windows can require sealing around the casing—and dampness may have left the sills soft and in bad shape. If the house is so old that its windows are no longer standard sizes, a custom woodworking shop is about the only place that will sell you replacements.

In many older houses the main problem with windows is not damage but thick covering layers of old paint. As much of this as possible should be taken off with the electric paint softener (be careful not to char edges and corners). But the only way to get the remainder off is with liberal applications of a semi-paste remover and a lot of tedious scraping.

Cords for the sash weights will probably all need replacing. When the windows are fixed, reglazed and painted they should be weatherstripped with either sponge-filled tubular vinyl gaskets or spring metal strips.

Casement windows are sometimes warped—their tops and bottoms should be checked for straightness. If the old glazing compound has cracked badly, or if there are gaps in it, it will have to be pried out and new compound applied—not a job for cold weather since the compound then takes ages to set.

Finally, the storm windows should be examined and counted. They usually have little numbered buttons and there should be one for each window. If any are missing and the old windows are no longer standard, having new ones made can be expensive.

Doors. It is even more important that a door seal tightly, due to its larger area. If a door is frequently opened and closed, install the best possible weatherstripping and, if your climate has cold winters, consider enclosing the porch outside it to make a vestibule. Where there's a lot of traffic this will save a large amount of lost heat. A vestibule also protects doors on the north side from winter winds.

Doors in an old house commonly have two problem areas. A minor problem is that the door has warped enough so that it won't latch—adjusting the latch up or down will usually correct this. A storm door, or one exposed to rain, may have rotted wood in its lower part. It's best to replace such doors if you can.

The problem is much more serious when the door frame has leaned or been pulled out of square by settling in the house. The frame is now a parallelogram enclosing a rectangle; and planing the door may allow it to shut but will still leave openings. If the lean isn't serious, strips of wood nailed to the frame, flush with the closed door, may cover the openings. If the cracks are too wide for this quick 'fix,' the whole frame will have to be rebuilt.

Interior Repairs

Fireplaces and chimneys. You can do some research on chimneys before actually looking at houses. In addition to reading up on good chimney designs that 'draw' well (in many houses they don't, leading to one type of "smoke filled room") find out if the local building code prohibits setting fireplaces and chimneys on the structural support members of a house. If the code prohibits this practice, you won't have to worry about structural problems caused by a chimney and fireplace so installed by a previous owner. A fireplace with its chimney is heavy and should rest directly on its own footings.

The damper in the fireplace should open completely in order to draw up smoke, and close tightly when the fire is out to stop warm air escaping up the chimney. The flue of the chimney should be lined with fireproof brick, and its masonry or mortar be free of cracks. Many cracks may point to a settling foundation.

It's also important to look at where the chimney passes through the ceilings and roof. It must clear all wooden parts of the house by at least two inches—combustible wood members nearer than this are a fire hazard. These open areas around chimneys are covered by flashing, usually corrosion-resistant copper or aluminum embedded in mortar. If the roof flashing has pulled away from the mortar, have the gap cleaned out and resealed immediately—otherwise rainwater flowing down the chimney side will be guided under the roof and down to walls and partitions below.

The top of the chimney may have a wire mesh spark arrester over it and a conical tin or slab as a rain cap. Or, it may have a roundish rain and draft deflector looking something like the top of a mosque's minaret.

Floors. If the floors on the first story squeak but are otherwise fairly level, eliminating the squeaking is a simple job for two people. First, inspect all the 2 × 4 "X" webs between the joists above the basement and renail the ends of any that are loose. Make sure that the joists are solid and sound.

Then have your partner walk over the floor until it starts to squeak. This involves coordination and a lot of bellowing up and down—a portable 2-way intercom sounds like overkill, but it helps. Where you hear squeaking in the floor or notice movement in the sub-flooring, tap a wedge (cut from the tapered side of a piece of clapboard) between the joist and subfloor board. Have your partner walk over the spot again. Repeat the operation for the whole floor area until squeaking stops.

If the floorboards are humped or raised over a solid, levelled subfloor, special ridged flooring nails can be hammered down at an angle through the boards. Or, you can correct the problem from below by drilling holes through the subfloor, inserting screws and pulling the floor boards down with a screwdriver.

Finishing floors. Sanding down the old, worn finish often reveals nicely grained wood which can be sealed with two coats of a clear tough polyurethane liquid. Floor sanders can either be of the horizontal revolving drum type or else the smaller kind that uses circular sanding discs.

The circular disc machines are for sanding a strip along the walls and the heavier drum types for sanding the rest of the floor. Both machines should be equipped with dust bags and can be rented from tool rental stores listed in the yellow pages. You'll need to wear a mask for this job.

Stairs. One of the first things to examine, preferably with the help of the building inspector, is the framing of joists around the upper and lower openings for stairs. The floor in these areas should be level and feel solid. If you note a weak or sagging floor around stairwells the supporting joists may need careful leveling and reinforcing. This usually means calling in a professional carpenter. It's been estimated that as many as half of the wood frame houses in the country have inadequate joist framing around their stairwells.

In addition to the framing around the top and bottom stair openings, the "stringers" (which support the risers and treads of the steps) should be checked for straightness. A well built stair will usually have two or more wooden beams between the stringers to support the risers near the center. If the underside of the stair is covered with gypsum board or lath and plaster, cut a strip across this surface to see if such beams were used. If not, you may want to knock off the whole covering and lay 2 × 6 riser support beams along the stairway.

Non load-bearing interior partitions. These should be pointed out by the building inspector and you may want to mark them. Alternatively, you can ask him to indicate the *load bearing* partitions and mark *them*—taking down one of these by mistake will seriously affect the way load forces are distributed through the structure of the house. If you decide you need more room space, demolishing a partition (non load-bearing and no electrical wiring or plumbing inside) can be immensely satisfying.

Insulation. Unless you have done the job before, it's best to hire a professional contractor to blow loose insulation into the spaces within the outer walls. You don't know how many of those pesky little horizontal 2 × 4 "firestops" may exist between the studs, but insulation contractors usually have worked on similar homes and know just where to bore the holes for the hose nozzle.

Another reason to hire a contractor instead of renting an insulation blower is that blowing in loose fill means lots of small particles in the air which are not beneficial to your lungs. In fact, it's a good idea to work on projects well away from the house while this particular job is in progress, and give the walls and floors a good vacuum cleaning when it's over.

Regarding the rather complicated and economically vital matter of insulating a home, *"The Complete Book of Insulating,"* 1980, edited by Larry Gay, Stephen Greene Press, Brattleboro, Vermont is precisely that. A very thorough treatment of insulating materials, sealing against air infiltration, insulating new homes and the problems encountered in retrofitting older homes with insulation.

Plumbing and electrical wiring. It's one thing to install plumbing and wiring in a contractor-erected shell (see chapter 7). These people are using materials pre-selected by the manufacturer of the house package and can refer to his instructions and drawings. If they get into trouble, help is usually available from the builder who erected the shell. Exploring behind the walls and crannies of an old house to trace its original piping and wiring—and additions by subsequent owners—is a different story. This is a job for a professional who can draw on years of residential experience with similar old homes. If you are going to rip out wallboard and expose the inner walls, doing this first will make things easier for both electrician and plumber and reduce the hourly charge on their bills.

In many cases, when the original wiring is old and in poor shape, it will be easier to simply bypass it and completely rewire the house.

The plumber can judge the condition of fresh water and drainage pipes. He can point out rusted joints, pipes that have burst through freezing, bad shutoff valves, leaking bathroom connections which could damage—or have damaged—the ceiling below, and clogged drains. He should also be able to recommend the best way to connect your new kitchen and bathroom fixtures.

———

The areas generally evaluated up to this point are the major ones which would influence your decision to choose one house over another, or which might wreck your budget by requiring modification or structural repair work by highly paid building trades specialists. Whatever kind of older house you want to buy—wood, stone, or brick—it's a good idea to have it inspected by a qualified home inspections service. See chapter 10 for detailed information.

As far as tackling the multitude of renovating jobs around a house, it would take a separate appendix to list all the books dealing in depth with different phases of home repair and construction. Your best source of reference material is "Books in Print," available at all libraries, which lists currently available titles by subject or specialty. Make a list of the titles you could use, then check the library card catalog or nearby bookstores with technical or "craft and hobby" departments.

One excellent resource for helping you estimate how much your renovation will cost is the *Home-Tech Estimator*, a two volume manual designed for contractors, that breaks down each element of an alteration, remodeling or home improvement project and gives the cost of labor, materials and contractor's mark-up for each. You can also subscribe to Home-Tech's semi-annual area price updating service. Home-Tech Inc. is located at 7315 Wisconsin Avenue, N.W., Washington, D.C. 20015.

Acting as your own Prime Contractor

If you assign the entire renovation job to a general or "prime" contractor, he assumes management responsibility for bringing together tools, material and labor at your site. He schedules the start and completion of each job in a sequence to avoid long delays.

In theory the general contractor guarantees the job will be completed 100 percent to your satisfaction, in return for a fixed fee. In practice, homeowners should make sure that everything is precisely spelled out in the contract: each item that is to be done, how it will be done, and when it is to be completed. In the absence of such a specific contract, it is not unknown for contractors to depart from a job that is somewhat less than 100 percent completed to start on a new job elsewhere. The following are a few hints on job scheduling and dealing with subcontractors.

To begin with, a typical frame house rehabilitation should follow the sequence below (many of the operations will overlap and be going on concurrently):

1. Foundation or masonry work (but only if this is necessary to repair structural damage). Stone masonry and brickwork are slow, expensive and can be learned. Cosmetic patching, pointing and cleaning can be done later at great savings.

2. Demolition. Removing unwanted or damaged porches, vestibules, interior partitions, wallboard or laths, old fixtures.

3. Exterior and interior framing. This involves fixing problem windows and doors on the outside, and replacing

eaves, sheathing and siding which are damaged. Inside the house, partitions are erected for any extra rooms desired, stairwell framing and problem floor areas are fixed.

4. Roof. As soon as the roofing contractor is able to put up ladders, the repairs to the roof and chimney flashing should be started. When the roof is completed, any new gutters and downspouts should be installed.

5. Exterior paint removal, priming and repainting.

6. Roughing in plumbing and electrical wiring. New water and drainage pipes go in, old pipes and connections that you want to keep are fixed where necessary, sewage lines are cleaned out, the new circuit breaker switchboard goes in and the house is rewired. All this work will have to be inspected for building code compliance.

7. Insulation. Batts are placed between open wall studs and floor and ceiling joists, or else loose fill is blown into enclosed wall spaces from outside (in which case you might want to postpone exterior painting until the blower crew has left and the holes are sealed).

8. Wallboard. The drywall is installed, the joints are taped and sanded smooth, and any special areas are plastered. This job should start on time and be completed as quickly as possible. Steps 9-11 can't start until this contractor has finished.

9. Interior painting, wallpapering and trim. Cabinet work.

10. Electrical and plumbing fixtures.

11. "Mechanical" systems (heating, cooling and air cleaning).

12. Floor sanding and finishing. Laying tile and carpets.

13. Install large kitchen appliances.

14. Landscaping.

It will be much easier for you to schedule all these activities if you have a clear plan of what needs to be done and can communicate this to each subcontractor.

Make sure you limit yourself to telling the contractors *what* you want and not *how* to do it. This seems elementary, but quite a few of the handier homeowners get involved in procedural details and craft professionals generally don't like this. They do, however, discuss procedures with related trades and your plumber, electrician and heating contractor will want to coordinate their respective jobs. Try to arrange a meeting before the work starts—they can take it from there. They are used to working together.

You will have to provide two facilities at the site: functioning toilets and electric power. If you intend to replace the electrical system while other work is going on, talk to the utility company about providing emergency service until the new switchboard and wiring are installed.

Depending on the extent of your renovation and the firms available in the area, you could start your planning with either an architect or a building engineer. Most residential architects concentrate on new house design, but you may find one who does renovation work. Architects are very good at visualizing the way a completed remodeling job will look. They are less proficient at accurately estimating costs, as a rule, but have the experience to help you plan and schedule the project.

Drawings of each floor's interior layout are known as Plan Views. These do not have to include dimensions and details of areas that will be left "as is," but any modifications or structural restorations should be carefully drawn in. The building engineer may provide separate drawings showing electrical outlets and the plumbing and heating network—both existing and anticipated. The drawings may have insets showing cut-away cross sections or blown-up detail drawings.

If you must regrade your lot to improve drainage or have extensive landscaping in mind, the lot will have to be surveyed. This data forms the basis for Site Plans showing the contour lines, and a Landscaping Plan. The bank will require a survey of the lot in any event.

These plans will be necessary when you apply for a building permit at the local building office. This is a routine procedure, but for major interior changes they will likely want to look over the plan views of the interior—stamped and signed by the architect or engineer. They will want to see your site plan if you are going to add to the home's exterior. This is to make sure that the additions don't violate zoning setback limits or encroachment restrictions towards neighboring lots.

The engineer will also make up a list of Written Specifications which spell out by job category the materials and work necessary to carry out the changes illustrated in the plans. When everything has been clearly drawn and spelled-out in writing, down to the last detail, you are then in a position to communicate effectively with subcontractors.

Have a copy of the plans and specifications made for each category of work to be done. The building trades are organized along craft lines, and each contractor specializes in providing the labor, skills and materials to complete his type of work. A good set of drawings and specifications will clearly show what each craft has to do, and contractors who know their business will arrive at the site with all the materials needed to complete the job without running to the store for missing parts.

The contracts for each category of work can either be negotiated with contractors you select on the basis of interviews, or else you can solicit competitive bids. Experience and a knowledge of prices is needed to evaluate bids. You could try shopping around the wholesale outlets the contractors buy from and the building engineer might also advise you on what would be a fair price for each job.

When the bids come in, check each bidder's reputation at the Better Business Bureau. Check his credit rating at his bank. This is to make sure that he is financially capable of completing the job. In some parts of the country you, as prime contractor, are liable if he doesn't pay his creditors. Be sure to call the people on his reference list of jobs.

Also make sure that each subcontractor carries workmen's compensation insurance and also insurance against property damage and liability.

In selecting bidders it's not a good idea automatically to pick the lowest bid. First ask a contractor submitting a bid significantly lower than the others how he determined his price. Neither is the highest bid an assurance of quality. The

contractor may have less experience in estimating that particular job, or may be used to high profit margins. And it's
generally good business practice not to discuss one contractor's price with other bidders.

When you draw up the contracts have your real estate
lawyer or the bank that is lending you money check them out.
Each contract should specify exact start-up and completion
dates. On the job, you may be able to allow some leeway if the
contractor has labor problems or is slowed down by bad
weather. The actual contract, however, should include a
definite completion date and also a clause stating that left-
over material and debris shall be removed and the work area
swept before he departs.

You should also insist that contractors guarantee their
labor and use the materials indicated in the written specifications. If these stipulate "kiln-dried grade-stamped structural
lumber," make it clear in the contract that inferior sub-
stitutes are not acceptable: no green wood or 2 × 4s full of
knots. The same applies to material specifications on things
like paint quality and color.

Home Improvement Financing

HUD's Federal Housing Administration has two loan programs designed to provide financing for a renovation job.

The FHA Title I loan of up to $15,000 is available to those
who own their own property, have a satisfactory credit rating
and earn enough income to repay the loan over its term. The
money may be used for improvements "that will make your
home more livable and useful" (FHA). The agency adds that
it may not be used for luxury items like "swimming pools or
outdoor fireplaces," or to pay for work already done when you
apply for the loan.

Banks, thrift institutions and other qualified lenders are
allowed to make these loans, and the FHA insures the lender
against possible loss. The Title I loan will not affect any mortgage or deed of trust you already have on the house and borrowers are not required to live in any particular type of
neighborhood.

If you are making major structural improvements on a house more than one year old, you can qualify for a larger FHA 203(k) loan secured by a second mortgage on the house. .

Other possibilities would be refinancing your existing mortgage if you have been living in the house for some time, or taking out a construction loan at the current market interest rate. If a contractor offers to arange financing for his part of the project, do not allow this to be secured by a lien placed on your property.

CHAPTER 5

Rehabilitating a Row House in the City

$\mathbf{I}$f you picked this chapter instead of the sections dealing with suburban housing, the odds are that you're committed to urban living and like the variety of human activity that city life offers.

Urban dwellers generally come from two backgrounds: (1) people who have always lived in cities, like them and would think of living nowhere else; (2) people whose parents were part of the great 1950's and 1960's exodus to the suburbs and beyond, but who can't afford the high costs of commuting to work in the energy-scarce 1980's and move closer to their jobs.

City dwellers in the second category will have noticed a degree of spaciousness and craftsmanship in their friends' renovated town houses far superior to homes in the subdivisions where they grew up. Although many of these row houses are neglected and in seedy neighborhoods at time of purchase, they were originally built as substantial homes.

The original owners liked solid construction, high ceilings and large rooms. Although residential land was costly even back in the nineteenth century, resulting in houses built with narrow fronts and shared walls, the lots and buildings extend well back from the street. Urban row houses typically have long corridors, large public rooms and bedrooms bigger than most postwar living rooms.

With increased automobile commuting costs, there has been an increasing demand for these urban houses. Pioneering couples, usually childless (when children arrive they tend to sell out and relocate near good suburban schools) are the first to spot a rundown area with solid, restorable houses.

When the pioneering rehabbers have renovated the interiors of their houses and spruced up the exteriors, the other residents on the street notice that their homes don't compare too favorably in appearance. Many do some cosmetic work on their own houses, scrubbing the inside and painting the outside. The appearance of the whole street noticeably improves and other rehabbers arrive, look around and make offers. A number of the original owners are now able to sell their houses to renovators at reasonably good prices.

The renovation spreads to nearby streets, newspaper articles appear describing this activity and finally, when about a quarter of the houses look like they did when the community was prosperous, word gets around that the neighborhood is "in," and prices skyrocket. At this point, some pioneering renovators sell their homes, pocket a fat profit, and start over somewhere else.

For the average urban renovator, the time to move in is when about 10 percent of the houses are being refurbished. The pioneers will have already done their missionary work with the banks and mortgage companies. They may also be willing to give you tips on good lawyers, real estate agents, friendly banks and contractors to avoid.

Prices, however, should still be within reason, although within two or three years they will have increased considerably. If you buy at the optimum time, you will be in a position to sell and pay yourself well for your time and effort—or else enjoy the benefits of a pleasant residential street for far less money than the new families moving in are investing.

The transformation process is not as big a gamble as some might think, as long as the housing stock is sound, and mass transportation to offices is nearby. The same location factors that once made the area a desirable address can make it fashionable again if the houses have been well restored.

But there are problems. For one thing, you may have to deal with distinctly unpleasant speculators who withhold information about structural problems in order to get rid of an unprofitable building.

You can avoid direct negotiation problems by using a broker who will act as your agent, not the seller's. Try any well-recommended, licensed real estate agent. If one agrees to search for the house you want, he or she will probably insist that you deal exclusively with that particular firm. The broker's commission typically ranges from 3 to 5 percent of the asking price, which avoids any conflict of interest between broker and client in negotiating a lower price.

Check the house for building code violations. Your renovation will, of course, correct these, but existing violations of the code can be used to negotiate a reduction in the selling price.

In most cities a binder or "earnest money" purchase offer is normal when buyers decide they want a building. This takes the property off the market until the sales contract can be drawn up. Binder agreements in some urban areas are quite complicated and buyers can be sued if they subsequently try to withdraw from the agreement. It is good practice never to sign any binder without consulting a lawyer experienced in urban residential real estate. Never hand over binder money to brokers who are not licensed and thoroughly reputable. If you give a check to the other kind, you and the seller may never see the earnest money again.

Other good sources of information about houses for sale are the classified ads in newspapers. Most cities also have an Urban Renewal Office which handles the federally funded programs. This office purchases rundown or abandoned buildings and sells them periodically in public bidding. Rehabilitation of such houses may be financed through a low interest 20-year HUD loan under Section 312 of the National Housing Act. These are direct loans from HUD to moderate and low income people who would not otherwise qualify for a loan. The property must be part of a HUD-assisted urban community development block grant program in the municipality.

Renovating a Row or "Town" House

The first thing to watch out for in urban renovation is the dishonest contractor who bids low and then tells you that he needs an advance in order to complete the job. If you pay him he disappears, tries the same tactic at another job he's working on and leaves you in the unpleasant position of having to track him down to finish the job while you fend off his creditors.

A suburban contractor operating this way would immediately generate a flood of complaints to the Better Business Bureau. His reputation would also spread quite rapidly by word-of-mouth. These processes work more slowly in cities, where dishonest contractors can operate for years by collecting advances from trusting owners and then vanishing in a sea of humanity.

The initial inspection of a row house will be similar to the wood frame house inspection mentioned in the previous chapter. The difference is that you are buying a tall, narrow house four or five stories high which shares common walls with its neighbors. This type of house is often built of stone or brick and will be quite a bit older than the majority of wood frame houses—and so may its plumbing and heating systems.

As you and the building engineer go over such a house, keep in mind that one or more floors can be rented, which in turn could enable you to live "rent free." But you might not want the renters passing through the public areas of your own living space. Neither may you want to climb stairs to the top floors while renters live on the first and second floors. You could ask the building inspector if it's economically possible to build an enclosed space behind the front entrance, with one door leading to your own living space and the other leading to the rented portions of the house.

One convenient solution to the separate entrance problem is the raised front porch, or "stoop." The steps lead up to a front door which is raised several feet above street level. Under these steps, a side entrance leads to the ground floor room which formerly contained the washtubs, kitchen and servants' quarters. Below this there was usually a cellar for coal storage. This ground floor area is ideal for converting into a rental apartment.

The renovation job schedule for a row house is basically the same as for a wood frame house, except for these differences:

Plumbing. Urban row houses are often very old and four or five stories high. Ask the building inspector to make sure it has no old lead fresh water pipes. Lead is harmful to human beings and affects the nervous system. Many children have sickened from eating old lead paint, and some historians blame lead-lined water conduits along with slavery and the Visigoths for the decline of ancient Rome.

Old galvanized iron pipe should come out as well, since it corrodes in time. It will be badly rusted if copper or brass pipes and fittings have been connected to it: when two such metals touch electrons flow from the more active metal and speed up corrosion. You can note this effect in a tin can with a scratched or broken coating—the exposed steel rusts faster than if it had not been plated.

Also ask the building inspector to make sure the water pipes are large enough in diameter. They may originally have been designed to service one or two baths and the kitchen. If more bathrooms have since been added, turning on the first floor faucets could mean loss of water pressure on the upper floors.

In general, electrical systems in old row houses are the same vintage as those in old frame houses and the problems in rewiring are much the same. The plumbing in a stone or brick row house may not only be ancient, but has to service a lot of taps, showers and toilets at higher elevations. It cannot be emphasized too strongly that an adequate plumbing system should be installed at the "roughing in" stage. Otherwise, finished walls and ceilings could be damaged later, at which time a number of expensive visits by the plumber are likely.

Air quality. If you will be installing a central forced air heating/cooling system, consider adding an electrostatic air cleaner to it. Clean air is *not* among the city's attractions.

Duplexes: Where Rental Income Pays Mortgage

Not all prospective home buyers returning to urban areas choose the inner city. Some like to live in the renovated inner ring of older suburbs. A common type of building in these suburbs is the duplex, or two-family house.

Two reasons for living in these suburbs are affordable shelter and a short commute to firms who have left the city and moved further out.

Younger people see a number of advantages in starting off the way their grandparents did. Before the war it was common for people to save for years until they could afford to buy a duplex, and then use the income from the rental unit to pay back the lender and keep up the property. Today, the owner of a duplex not only gets the tax deduction benefits of any other homeowner, but can also deduct half the maintenance cost of the house and is allowed a depreciation allowance on the rental unit.

Although duplexes generally did not gain much in price during the suburban single-family mini-estate mania of the 1960's and 1970's, the current high interest rates have changed that. Most built-up areas have a shortage of good rental housing, and a duplex at a fair rent will not be vacant for long. Expensive mortgage money means that lenders will look favorably on mortgagors receiving rent income—prompt and regular monthly payments are that much more likely.

If you plan to renovate a wood-frame duplex, follow the same guidelines as in the preceding chapter. But schedule one extra category of jobs: redundancy. Each section of the house should have its own bathrooms, heating and cooling systems, and all other utility-supplied functions on separate meters. And if the two units are side-by-side, it's a good idea to install the heaviest possible soundproofing in their common wall.

Financing an Urban Renovation

The FHA Title I loan described in the previous chapter is equally available to urban dwellers. A problem is its fairly low limit: $15,000 will not buy much renovation in our major cities today.

There are also the federally financed urban block renewal programs. These funds are administered by the municipal authorities and the first place to contact for information is City Hall.

Another loan program is offered by HUD under the authority of Section 221(d)(2) of the National Housing Act. Under this program, HUD insures the lender against loss on a mortgage "to finance the purchase, construction or rehabilitation of low-cost one-to-four-family housing."

The key to whether or not applicants are granted a 221(d)(2) loan is the type of building they want to buy. Anyone within the income limits may apply (and families displaced by urban renewal get special terms), but the emphasis is on low-cost housing. Maximum loan amounts are currently $31,000 for single-family houses ($36,000 in high cost areas) and $36,000 and $42,000 respectively if the family is a large one of five or more persons. The mortgage limits on two to four family housing are higher.

Many urban renovators get government-backed loans through the Title 203(k) rehabilitation home mortgage program. This was briefly outlined in the previous chapter and here, in more detail, is how it works:

- The purpose of the program, states HUD, is "to promote and facilitate the restoration and preservation of the nation's existing housing stock."
- Rehabilitation, as defined for the 203(k) program, includes:
  (1) Repairs or replacement of windows, stairs, walls, floors, roof, plumbing, wiring, heating or other mechanical equipment.
  (2) Additions of solar heating equipment.
  (3) Any additions onto the outside of the building, such as an attached garage, carport or porch.
- Eligible rehabilitation expenses include material, labor, contingency reserve and overhead, plus related expenses such as permits, fees, licenses and payments to architects and engineers. Also included are the supplemental origination fee (up to the allowable limit) lenders charge when a mortgage involves rehabilitation advances, and that part of loan discounts or "points" (which the borrower is permitted to pay) applicable to the rehabilitation portion of the loan.

- The supplemental origination fee will be 2½ percent of the rehabilitation portion of the loan, or $350, whichever is higher.
- Appraisals. A 203(k) mortgage requires two of these: one at time of purchase to determine the "as is" value of the property, and the other to determine the dwelling's market value when rehabilitation is complete.
- A 203(k) mortgage is issued by a HUD-approved lender and HUD insures the loan. When the mortgage involves the insurance of rehabilitation advances, it is executed as a "Rehabilitation Loan Agreement" to which must be added the "Mortgage Rehabilitation Rider." This agreement sets forth the conditions under which funds are released for the improvement of the property.
- The maximum interest rate will be that currently in force for the 203(b) home loan insurance program. This interest rate will apply to the entire amount of the mortgage.
- The provisions of the HUD/FHA Section 203(b) one-to-four-family house mortgage program apply to any aspects of a home improvement mortgage not specifically covered by Section 203(k).
- To be eligible, the property must be a one-to-four-family dwelling over a year old.
- If the rehabilitation loan will be the first lien on the property, it can be approved for HUD insurance before rehabilitation begins. The money can be used to buy the house or refinance existing debts on it, to pay for closing costs and to pay for modifications and renovation.
- Section 203(k) mortgages which do *not* involve rehabilitation advances, refinancing present indebtedness, or the purchase of the property may be a second lien on it. However, they may be junior only to the first mortgage.
- Maximum amount of loan. This is determined by subtracting the borrower's existing indebtedness from HUD's estimate of the property's value. The latter will be the *smaller* of either (a) the computed total rehabilitation cost added to the purchase price of house and land, or (b) 110 percent of the estimated worth of the property after rehabilitation.

- The maximum amount of a 203(k) mortgage can be increased by up to 20 percent if solar energy systems are to be installed in a building. The actual increase will depend on HUD's estimate of either the solar equipment's replacement cost or its effect on the market price of the dwelling.
- The part of the loan allotted to rehabilitation is placed in an escrow account (an account that cannot be used for any other purpose) with the lender. This account will bear not less than 5 percent interest—paid to you monthly—and be insured by FDIC if the lender is a commercial bank or by FSLIC in the case of a savings and loan institution. The amount of money in escrow may not be less than 15 percent of the total loan.
- The funds in escrow may not be used to pay real estate taxes, insurance premiums, ground rents or assessments.
- After looking at the plans and specifications, and discussing the project with the borrower, the HUD Construction Analyst prepares an Inspection and Release Schedule, form 92004KS. This sets forth the schedule of inspections which the lender must adhere to before releasing funds from escrow. Before releasing any money, it is the lender's responsibility to see that the work is examined by the HUD-authorized inspector and approved.
- The lender may release funds from escrow when he receives a Compliance Inspection Report, Form 92051, from the authorized inspector. The inspector will check the work completed against the plans, specifications and materials list to make sure that their requirements and any applicable property standards have been met.
- A 10 percent "holdback" will be withheld from each release of funds in the Inspection and Release Schedule. Only after the final inspection of the job will the total of the holdbacks be released.
- If the renovation will be large and complex, the HUD Construction Analyst can decide to include a Contingency Reserve for possible cost overruns in the Inspection and Release Schedule. This reserve may not exceed 10 percent of the total rehabilitation portion. Before releasing any part of this contingency reserve, the lender must submit a written request to the HUD field office for approval.

Figure 1.

Purpose: The Inspection and Release Schedule establishes the conditions under which advances are to be released from the Rehabilitation Escrow Account. The lender is required to follow this schedule of inspections and releases.

Copy to borrower: Yes, as part of the Rehabilitation Loan Agreement.

U. S. DEPARTMENT OF HOUSING AND URBAN DEVELOPMENT
HOUSING - FEDERAL HOUSING COMMISSIONER

SUPPLEMENT TO FIRM COMMITMENT
SECTION 203(K) INSURED ADVANCES
INSPECTION AND RELEASE SCHEDULE

HUD Case Number

Not withstanding subsection (c) of the Mortgagee's Certificate, the Mortgagee shall deposit the rehabilitation mortgage proceeds for rehabilitation in a rehabilitation escrow account and shall not release such funds prior to receipt of a HUD Compliance Inspection Report, executed by a HUD-approved fee inspector, indicating completion of work to appropriate stage. Contingency reserve is not to be released without prior HUD approval. Any unused contingency is to be applied as a mortgage prepayment.

Part I - DISBURSEMENT OF MORTGAGE PROCEEDS

Mortgage proceeds for purchase or refinance	$
Mortgage proceeds for rehabilitation/improvement to be escrowed:	
HUD Cost Estimate	$
Contingency Reserve required by HUD	$
TOTAL MORTGAGE AMOUNT	$

Part II - INSPECTIONS AND RELEASES OF ESCROWED FUNDS

No.	Inspections During Rehabilitation	No.	Escrow Account Releases During Rehabilitation
			$
			$
			$
			$
	Final Completion Inspection		Final Release - to include total of holdbacks
			$
	Total Number of Scheduled Inspections		Total Number of Scheduled Releases ....

Part III - DESCRIPTION OF INSPECTION STAGES

No.	Description of work to be completed at inspection, by inspection number used in Part II above.

Prepared by:

(Date) (Construction Analyst)

HUD-92004-ES (4-86)

Source: U.S. Department of Housing & Urban Development

Figure 2.

Purpose: The Rehabilitation Loan Agreement between lender and borrower establishes the conditions under which the lender advances the 203(k) mortgage money. It is a format which the lender must follow.

Copy to borrower: Yes.

Rehabilitation Loan Agreement

This Agreement is made this _____ day of _____ 19___, between _____ (Borrower) and _____ (Lender) to establish the conditions under which the Lender will advance proceeds of a loan to be used to: purchase and rehabilitate, refinance and rehabilitate, rehabilitate the property described below. The property is located in the County of   , State of   , and is described as:

1. The loan will be in the principal sum of Dollars ($_____) to be advanced by Lender to Borrower as provided in this agreement and will be secured by a mortgage or deed of trust ("Mortgage") which will be a first lien on the property.

2. Payments required under the mortgage or deed of trust must be made by the borrower on the date specified, even though the proposed rehabilitation or improvement may not be completed, or the property may not be suitable for occupancy, on the anticipated date.

3. The Lender intends to request the Federal Housing Commissioner ("Commissioner") to insure the loan under the provisions of Section 203(k) of the National Housing Act; therefore, Borrower agrees to conform to, and to cause improvements to be constructed in conformance with, all requirements of the Commissioner.

4. The Lender will place that portion of the principal amount of the mortgage allocated to rehabilitation in an interest bearing account, trust or escrow for the benefit of the Borrower. Lender shall release these funds by check, payable to the Borrower (or at Lender's option, to Borrower and appropriate payee who performed the work and supplied the materials in connection with this contract) at such times as the stages of construction are completed as follows:

Lender to Incorporate Inspection and Release Schedule

5. The principal amount of the loan specified in paragraph 1 may contain a contingency reserve. If the actual cost of rehabilitation exceeds the estimated cost of rehabilitation, the contingency reserve or any part thereof may, with the consent of the Commissioner, be paid to the Borrower or contractor. If the contingency reserve or any part thereof is not so paid, the remaining balance will be applied as a partial prepayment of the loan, but such prepayment will not extend or postpone the due date of any monthly installment due under the note, nor change the amount of such installments.

6. The Borrower will complete all improvements on the property in accordance with Drawings and Specifications as approved by the Commissioner.

7. Changes in the Drawings and Specifications, or the Inspection and Release Schedule must be approved in writing by the Lender and the Commissioner.

8. Borrower will cause all improvements to be made in a workmanlike manner and in accordance with all applicable statutes and regulations. All licenses, permits and privileges required by local governmental authorities to rehabilitate the property will be obtained by the Borrower or Borrower's contractor.

9. Representatives of the Lender and of the Commissioner shall have the right to enter upon the property at all times during the period of construction and on completion of construction to determine whether the work conforms with this agreement and to determine the amount of the loan to be released by the Lender.

10. Borrower will furnish such records, contracts, bills and other documents relating to property and improvements as the Lender or the Commissioner may require.

11. Without prior, written consent of Lender, no materials, equipment, fixtures or any other part of improvements financed with this loan shall be purchased or installed subject to conditional sales contracts, security agreements, lease agreements or other arrangements

whereby title is retained or the right is reserved or accrues to anyone to remove or repossess any item, or to consider it as personal property.

12. The Borrower shall cause either this instrument or the construction contract under which the improvements are to be made to be filed in the public records, if the effect of recording will be to relieve the mortgaged property from mechanics' and materialmen's liens. Before any advance under this agreement, the Lender may require the Borrower to obtain acknowledgement of payment and releases of lien from the contractor and all subcontractors and materialmen dealing directly with the principal contractor. These releases shall cover the period down to the date covered by the last advance, and concurrently with the final payment for the entire project. Such acknowledgments and releases shall be in the form required by local lien laws and shall cover all work done, labor performed and materials (including equipment and fixtures) furnished for the project.

13. Borrower shall cause work to begin within 60 days following the date of this agreement. Borrower shall have work completed within 18 months following the date of this agreement. Work is to be performed with reasonable diligence, therefore, work is never to cease for more than 45 consecutive days. Should Borrower fail to comply with these terms, the Lender may refuse to make any further payments under this agreement. Any funds remaining in the Rehabilitation Escrow Account shall be applied as a prepayment to the mortgage.

14. In the event any Stop Notices, Notices to Withhold, Mechanics Liens, or claims of lien are filed against property, Lender, after five (5) days' notice to the undersigned of its intention to do so, may pay any or all of such liens or claims, or may contest the validity of any of them, paying all costs and expenses of contesting the same.

15. Failure of the Borrower to perform under the terms of this rehabilitation loan agreement shall make the loan amount, at the option of the lender, due and payable.

Source: U.S. Department of Housing and Urban Development

Figure 3.

> *Purpose:* The 203(k) Mortgage Rehabilitation Rider modifies the mortgage instrument to allow releasing HUD-insured advances from the escrow account.
>
> *Copy to borrower:* Yes, as part of the Rehabilitation Loan Agreement.

Rehabilitation Rider

1. Loan proceeds are to be advanced for the rehabilitation of the premises in accordance with the rehabilitation loan agreement dated _____, 19____, between borrower and lender. This agreement is incorporated by reference and made a part of this mortgage. No advances shall be made unless approved by the Secretary of Housing and Urban Development.

2. If the rehabilitation is not properly completed, performed with reasonable diligence, or is discontinued at any time except for strikes or lockouts, the lender is vested with full authority to take the necessary steps to protect the rehabilitation improvements and property from harm, continue existing contracts or enter into necessary contracts to complete the rehabilitation. All sums expended for such protection, exclusive of the advances of the principal indebtedness, shall be added to the principal indebtedness, and secured by the mortgage and be due and payable on demand with interest as set out in the note.

3. If the borrower fails to perform any obligation under the loan, including the commencement, progress and completion provisions of the Rehabilitation Loan Agreement, and such failure continues for a period of 30 days, the loan shall, at the option of the lender, be in default.

Source: U.S. Department of Housing and Urban Development

Figure 4.

Purpose: The HUD Contingency Notice informs the lender that the mortgage will include a specific amount as a contingency reserve. It states what the lender must do to get these funds released.

Copy to borrower: No.

Section 203(k) HUD Contingency Notice

(To Mortgagee)

203(k) Case No. _____

_____

_____

The HUD Field Office processing of your application for Section 203(k) mortgage insurance on this case has included an amount of $_____ as a reserve for contingencies. This amount must be set aside and used only if and when the borrower and/or his contractor needs additional funding resulting from unanticipated cost in connection with the approved rehabilitation work.

Any request for use of all or any part of the contingency reserve must be in writing and must specify the item of work to be covered. The request must be sent to the HUD Field Office for inspection of the property to determine if the request can be approved. We will notify you of our approval or rejection of the request before any of the reserve funds may be released.

Any remaining unused portion of the Contingency Reserve Fund at the time of final inspection is to be applied to reduce the mortgage balance.

Chief, Mortgage Credit Branch

Source: U.S. Department of Housing and Urban Development

Figure 5.

Purpose: The HUD Contingency Release Letter tells the lender whether his request for contingency funds has been approved or disapproved.

Copy to borrower: No.

HUD Contingency Release Letter

(To Mortgagee)

203(k) Case No. _____

Property Address _____

_____

We have received and reviewed your request for release of $_____ of the contingency reserve for subject 203(k) mortgage. Your request is approved/disapproved, for the amount of $_____.

_____

Chief, Architectural Branch

Source: U.S. Department of Housing & Urban Development

Figure 6.

Purpose: The Morgagee/Mortgagor Completion Letter is a format by which the lender notifies HUD that the work is complete and that a final inspection has been assigned.

Copy to borrower: Yes.

Mortgagee/Mortgagor Completion Letter

203(k) Case No. _____

Property Address _____

_____

Mortgagor

The rehabilitation construction and/or addition construction as outlined in the Rehabilitation Loan Agreement has been completed in a satisfactory manner.

_____   _____

Date

_____

Signature(s) of Mortgagor(s)

Mortgagee

The rehabilitation construction and/or addition construction has been completed in compliance with the Inspection and Release Schedule. The final inspection has been assigned to _____, a HUD fee inspector, who is to forward directly to HUD Form 92051, Compliance Inspection Report.

_____   _____

Date   Signature of mortgagee

_____

Title

_____

Source: U.S. Department of Housing & Urban Development

Figure 7.

Purpose: The HUD Final Release Notice: (1) informs the lender that the work is completed to HUD's satisfaction; (2) authorizes the lender to make the final scheduled payment along with all the amounts held back; (3) tells the lender to apply any money remaining in the escrow account against the mortgage principal.

Copy to borrower: Yes.

HUD Final Release Notice

203(k Case No. _____

Property Address _____

_____

(Mortgagee)

We have reviewed the final inspection of the improvements made to the subject property.

Based on our findings and the documentation in the file, you are hereby authorized to release the final draw along with the holdback.

The mortgage must be prepaid in the amount of $_____ which represents the balance of the contingency reserve not approved for release.

_____

Chief, Mortgage Credit Branch

Source: U.S. Department of Housing & Urban Development

CHAPTER 6

Buying a Lot and Siting Your House

$\mathbf{I}$f you've decided that the most economical way to get your dream house is to buy a lot and put your house on it—consider the lot as your first important investment.

Private lots. If you plan to buy a lot in a settled area, you may find most of the best land already occupied by houses. The unimproved land still available may be heavily wooded and, in many cases, quite steeply sloped. These are not necessarily disadvantages.

For example, in a wooded lot you can carefully select and mark the trees that will be left standing. Try to retain the trees in clumps, or else contact the Forestry Department of your nearest university, since woodland trees are often interdependent and not all can stand alone. To make sure that the trees and their roots will not interfere with construction, you will have to consult with your builder or the contractor pouring the foundation for your factory-built house. A tree will often die if excavation destroys some of its roots.

Whether a sloping lot is a problem depends on (a) the direction in which it slopes downwards, and (b) whether this slope continues upwards beyond your property line. If the lot slants downward in a northerly direction it's best to forget it, unless you live in the sunbelt.

Houses on lots which slope down towards the North gulp fuel in winter—their walls and foundation are exposed to heat-robbing cold winds, while other homes or trees on the slope above them block the winter sun. Even if the lot slopes away to the South, its decline should be *towards* the street and not away from it, otherwise you'll need tire chains to get out of your driveway in a snowfall.

It's a good idea to take along a compass when looking at building lots. Once you've narrowed your choice to one or several, they should then be looked over by a soils engineer experienced in residential housing.

If there is higher ground behind your land, water runoff could be a serious problem, flooding your basement and eroding your topsoil away. It pays to visit any lot during a rainstorm, to find out how the soil absorbs water and drains. And if you see a number of rivulets converging on it from higher ground, the only way to keep things dry in wet weather would be to build the house off the ground on piers or pilings! Your land should also be above the flood high water mark—you can verify this at the municipal or county surveyor's office.

It's important that the soil on a sloping lot drain well and have enough strength or bearing capacity to support the foundation and weight of the house. Good soils will consist of gravel, sand and some clay. Get test cores from *all* areas covered by your foundation, since if this rests on different types of soil it will not settle evenly unless each part is designed to compensate for the ground under which it stands.

One should also be very careful with clay soils of high plasticity on sloping lots. Clay is made up of very fine particles and can absorb large amounts of water. In a heavy rainstorm the whole muddy mass can start moving—some of the more spectacular landslides have occurred in clay soil during and after heavy rains.

For obvious reasons, avoid underground springs and a high water table. And if there are no municipal water or sewage facilities in place, it's a good idea to ask neighbors about their experience with wells they've drilled and have a sample of the water analyzed.

If you can't hook up to municipal sewer lines, your soil will have to be suitable for a septic tank. If there is a possibility of future municipal sewer service, it's important to locate the septic tank connections close to the street, either at the front or the side of the house.

Finally, avoid any lots on landfills. For one thing, organic matter and loose fill are not stable and won't support the weight of a house—building on this stuff will almost certainly mean a cracked and buckled foundation. If the landfill has reclaimed a wet area such as a marsh, the soil will not drain and moisture problems in the basement will bedevil the owner. Even if the filled area is on higher ground and already has some houses, you still don't know what was filled in or covered—there could be some nasty toxic surprises just a few feet below your home.

After you have picked a lot, get a residential architect's opinion before you buy. If he OK's it, ask for a site plan showing all the contours. Also ask the architect's advice on the type of house which best suits the lot with the least amount of expensive earthmoving. These services will all involve a fee, but could save you a lot of money when the building starts.

Buying a Lot from Developers

Due to the scarcity of unimproved land in established communities, many people who want the full range of municipal services are buying their plots of land from developers. Here, as with condominiums, the buyer must be very careful and the services of a lawyer are strongly recommended.

Today's buyers are better protected against the more flagrant forms of dishonesty by a federal entity with the curious acronym of OILSR. This is the Office of Interstate Land Sales Registration, a department of HUD, which came into being when Congress passed the Interstate Land Sales Act in 1968.

This Act is a "full disclosure" law which requires the seller of more than 50 units to register the development with OILSR and disclose the HUD-specified facts about the land offered for sale. Its purpose is to give you some measure of protection by making available the information you need for what HUD calls a "sensible, unhurried land purchase." How consumers use this information, HUD continues, is up to them and their booklet on the subject begins with the words "Caveat Emptor" [Buyer Beware]. So in spite of OILSR's existence, you still need a good real estate lawyer when dealing with developers of single family home subdevelopments.

For example, HUD does *not* inspect the lots, prepare the property reports *or* verify the statements in them. HUD *does* require developers to include specified information in their property reports and to deliver that information to prospective buyers. If you buy a lot on the basis of information which has been misstated in a property report, you have solid grounds for a lawsuit. HUD goes on to say:

> "If the Statement of Record and the Property Report contain misstatements of fact, if there are omissions, if fraudulent sales practices are used, or if other provisions of the law have been violated, the purchaser can also sue to recover damages in court against the developer. Damages may include the amount of the purchase price of the lot plus reasonable cost of improvement and court costs."

Purchasers are warned, however, that although they have the right to void the contract with the developer under these conditions, they may still be liable for payments to a third party.

Exemptions from the 1968 act. If the property meets the following conditions set forth by HUD, the developer does *not* have to file a Property Report and buyers are on their own.

Sale or Lease of:

- Tracts of fewer than 50 lots which are not part of a common promotional sales plan.
- Lots where *every* lot in the subdivision is 5 acres or more in size (HUD's main interest is to protect lower and middle income buyers).

- Lots containing a residential, commercial or industrial building, or where the seller is required by the sales contract to erect such a building within two years.
- Real estate subject to court order.
- Real estate by government agencies.
- Lots sold for less than $100 (including closing costs), provided the purchaser is not being required to buy more than one lot.

Lease of—Lots for terms of five years or less, provided the lessee is not required to renew the lease.

Resale of—A note originated by a land sale (or other evidences of indebtedness secured by a mortgage or deed of trust).

Other exemptions—These apply to sellers promoting their lots to buyers who are located close enough to inspect them personally.

Tracts for which HUD's secretary issues an exemption order which waives OILSR enforcement as unnecessary to protect buyers. To qualify, the seller's request for exemption must apply only to a single transaction, or involve a subdivision of fewer than 300 lots located, offered and advertised *within one state,* and with no more than 5 percent of the lots sold to non-residents of the state in any given year.

Lots sold "onsite, free and clear of liens." To qualify for this exemption, the seller must file a claim with HUD and prove he will sell only to buyers who make on-site inspections. He must also prove that all restrictions are beneficial and enforceable by lot owners. He must furnish buyers, before they sign the sales contract, a HUD-approved statement which sets forth any reservations, taxes, assessments and restrictions on the lot. The sales contract must include a clause which requires him to give the buyer a deed within 120 days of its signing. He must get a receipt for the HUD-approved statement from each buyer and file these receipts with HUD once a year.

Here are the seller's obligations on lots on developments not covered by the exemptions above:

1. He must file a *Statement of Record* with HUD, and provide you with a copy of the *Property Report* which
   describes the property. If he fails to do this he can be
   fined up to $5,000 and jailed for up to 5 years. The State-
   ment of Record, which is reviewed and retained by HUD,
   must include:

- A copy of the developer's corporate charter and financial
  statement.
- Information about the land, including the title policy or an
  attorney's title opinion, copies of deeds and mortgages.
- Information on local ordinances and health regulations.
- Information about nearby facilities such as schools,
  hospitals and transportation systems.
- Information about the availability of utilities and potable
  water.
- Information about sewage disposal.
- Projected roads, streets, recreational facilities and other
  development plans for the property.
- Maps, plats showing the lot subdivisions, letters from uti
  lity companies and other supporting documents.
- A statement swearing that all the information submitted is
  correct and complete.
- HUD's fee.

If HUD considers the Statement of Record to be in-
complete, inaccurate or misleading, they will inform the seller
within 30 days. They will also withhold OILSR registration
of the development until they get the necessary additional information. Once HUD is satisfied with the information submitted, they will have the Office of Interstate Land Sales
Registration assign a number to the statement. HUD retains
the Statement of Record and makes copies available to the
public for 25 cents a page.

2. The Property Report contains excerpts from the more
   detailed statement of record, and HUD strongly sug-
   gests that you read it carefully. Although the seller may
   give this report to buyers ahead of time, he is not required to do so until the signing of the purchase agreement—this can make an unhurried perusal of the report
   difficult.

If the seller won't give you the report until the signing, and you still want to buy into the development, you can get a copy of the Property Report from HUD for $2.50. Write to HUD/OILSR, 451 Seventh Street, Washington, D.C. 20410, and include the developer's name, the name of the development, and the location within it of your subdivision.

Furthermore, if you receive the copy of the Property Report from the seller—as required by law—less than 48 hours before you sign the contract, you then have a "cooling off" period in which you can void the contract. You must do this by written notice to the seller up to midnight of the third business day (all calendar days except Sundays and official business holidays) following the transaction.

It must be emphasized that OILSR cannot act as your attorney—the department is only concerned with full disclosure of the facts affecting the transaction. It is not involved in zoning or land use planning and has no control over the quality of the subdivision. OILSR cannot dictate what land can be sold, to whom, or at what price. The department will, however, advise you on securing the rights provided you by the Interstate Land Sales Full Disclosure Act.

The U.S. Department of Housing and Urban Development can, on the other hand, go after the "baddies." HUD is authorized by law to conduct investigations and public hearings, to subpoena witnesses and secure evidence, and to prevent violations of the law by seeking court injunctions. If necessary, HUD may also ask for criminal indictments.

The Department's booklet concludes with these warnings to prospective buyers:

1. Ask the developer if he is registered with HUD or else entitled to an exemption.
2. Ask for a copy of the Property Report. If you can't get one from the developer, order it from HUD and take the time to read it carefully.
3. Compare the going prices in the area by visiting other independent real estate brokers.
4. Talk to other people who have bought lots in the development.

5. Check the seller's reputation at the local Chamber of Commerce, Better Business Bureau and consumer protection groups.

6. Ask the county and municipal authorities about local ordinances and regulations which will affect your property.

7. Ask how large the development will eventually become. What will be the zoning controls?

8. Confirm the provisions for sewer and water service set forth in the Property Report. What about garbage and trash collection?

9. If the developer has placed funds in a special escrow account earmarked for a sewage plant or other facility, how soon will the administering authority be formed? Who will be members of the authority? When will construction start and when will the facility be in operation?

10. Will there be access roads to your property? How will they be surfaced? Who maintains them? What will they cost and how much of this amount will you have to pay?

11. Will you have clear title to the property? What liens, reservations or encumbrances exist on it?

12. Will you receive a deed or recordable sales contract on purchase?

13. There can be special problems if the development is on a waterfront or man-made lake. Is the lake completed? How many lot-buying families will use it? Who maintains the dam and pays insurance on it? How is the lake kept free of sewage and other pollution?

14. Are there any annual maintenance fees or special assessments charged to property owners? What do they include? Do they accurately reflect costs, or are they set artificially low to attract buyers?

15. Will you be charged these fees immediately on purchase, even if you don't plan to build on your lot or use it for several years?

16. Don't be high-pressured by salesmen—delay any commitment until you have investigated unanswered questions.

Zero-Side Yard Developments

If the high cost of land is a major reason for high house prices in your area, savings of between ten and twenty percent are possible by building on a narrow lot. This arrangement works best if all houses on one side of the street are similarly located, so these "zero-side yard" layouts are normally offered by developers of subdivisions.

In real estate terminology, zero-lot line siting means that one wall of a building is located right on the boundary line of the property. In commercial buildings, an example would be a retail store whose front adjoins the sidewalk.

In suburban zero-side yard developments, one wall of each house is built on the same side boundary line of all the lots. This location allows the largest possible yard on the other side of the houses, whereas a central location would mean narrow strips of land on both sides of a house. The wall on the boundary overlooking the neighbors' garden generally has no doors or windows, light being admitted through clerestorys near the ceiling. These shut out noise and increase privacy—for the same reason, air circulation is often handled by installing special vents on this wall. Zero-side yard subdivisions originated in California and have spread to other areas where residential real estate is expensive.

Siting your House

Before selecting a house design and siting it on your lot, consider these two sets of guidelines which—depending on the home's layout and the topography and features of the site—will often conflict.

Siting for convenience and life style. Here, you will want to analyze your lot in relation to your neighbors and the street. For example, a large front lawn will look impressive to passers-by and also set your house further away from the street's traffic. But the farther back you are from the street, the smaller will be the back yard area which you can screen for privacy in your outdoor activities.

If your lot is a small one, you can get the best use of it by locating the house fairly close to the street and placing the driveway and trashcan storage area at one extreme of the front lawn. This will provide more land in back of the house for a patio, greenhouse, swimming pool or anything else that fits your lifestyle.

Siting for passive solar heating and cooling. While you can orient your home's window area to minimize heat gain in summer and heat loss in winter, the relatively light materials used in wood frame houses prevent your storing much heat from the sun's rays in winter.

When orienting a house to get maximum use from the sun, remember that in this hemisphere the winter sun is south of you all day long. Your north wall gets little or no heat, and should have good insulation and the fewest possible windows. Your east and west walls also receive much less heat than in summer.

When the days get warmer and longer, the reason is that the sun's arc has shifted upwards toward the north. Now, your east and west walls get a considerable amount of heat and even the north wall may get a bit. This is where you need shading: the bare deciduous trees which let sunlight through in winter are now in full leaf and block out most of the rays. They can also lower the temperature of the air under them some 10° F through transpiration.

To shade the sides of the house against morning and evening sunlight, you can use shorter trees or shrubs with a wide spread of foliage closer to the ground.

Active solar heating and cooling is a rapidly-developing technology which has probably progressed to a level comparable to that reached by electric heating in the early 1950's, before warming a house with Reddy Kilowatt became standardized and widely accepted. There is still a lot of sorting-out to be done with most active solar systems.

CHAPTER 7

Factory-Built Frame Houses

Some buyers incorrectly view all factory-built homes as an assembly line substitute for homes put up by a builder. But, as far as most of the manufactured housing industry is concerned, their best customers are local builders who offer "custom built" homes.

Factory-built houses and the home builder. Consider a typical builder's problems if he follows traditional methods:

- He builds or pours the foundation (although he may have more leeway here—the foundation dimensions for a manufactured house must be *exactly* as specified in the factory's drawings).

- He orders lumber and other materials, which are stored on the site and exposed to weather, theft and vandalism.

- These 2 × 4, 2 × 6, 2 × 8 and 2 × 10 "sticks" must then be sawn to the required lengths. If they can't be used with square-cut ends, the resulting studs, rafters, crossties, braces and posts must be cut on an angle (mitred), dadoed, rabbeted, dovetailed and lap-jointed as required. The pieces then have to be drilled and nailed together.

It can take as much as six months, from the time work starts on the foundation, for a builder to finish a house in this manner. And since the skilled workers he needs are hard to find in many parts of the country, some of the work may be substandard. Should a builder short in skilled workmen hire a subcontractor to do some of the work, he may still have a quality control problem.

A builder using traditional methods is also dependent on reasonably good weather. Although there are special techniques for keeping construction going in very hot or below-freezing climates, the possibility of inferior workmanship remains greater.

Because materials must be purchased and the work crew paid while the house is being built, the builder may have to take out a construction loan to meet the payments. If he does take out a loan, he will pay a higher interest rate than the one you would pay on your home mortgage. These financing costs are added into the price of the house, which is another reason traditionally-built homes cost so much.

Most builders now rely in varying degrees on manufacturers to cut their costs and improve the quality of their product. There are several reasons why they use these suppliers and why you, too, can save considerably on a manufactured house:

More buyer appeal. Just as it pays factories to use good materials to turn out durable sections as fast as possible, it also pays them to make their products as appealing as possible by retaining architects with good residential track records. The design input from these professionals shows in the finished homes—although not all styles offered may be to your taste.

Many builders, on the other hand, don't use architects but rely on their own "eye" for the lines of a house, developed through experience. The result sometimes shows it.

On the inside of a house, the on-site builder has a freedom of layout which factories are just beginning to try to match. Traditionally, a factory-built house's floor plan has been governed by shipping limitations. All of the states in the U.S. impose a maximum width of 14 feet on loads which travel over their highways, and housing sections will have to make all or part of their journey to the site by truck. Now, some manufacturers are beginning to use "double wide" modules, where the two halves are finished facing each other as they would before being mated at the site. When the two half-sections are joined, the buyer can get interior rooms as wide as 28 feet.

Factories are also varying their floor plans to give you other options besides rectangles. Many now offer modules or panelized design that can be joined in "L," "T" or "U" shaped layouts.

Energy efficiency. The factory-built house which must meet standard specifications is much less likely to lose heat through cracks. Many manufacturers also insulate the exterior sides with Expanded Polystyrene (EPS) board. Before arriving at a framing table, these sheets will have been pre-cut to fit together snugly, without gaps. The joints will then be sealed with caulking compound and the whole panel inspected for airtightness.

Generally speaking, a conscientious on-site builder who uses pre-cut "sticks"—or cuts his own—will have to use large quantities of caulking compound to ensure a tight draft-free house.

Mortgage financing. It is sometimes easier to get a mortgage on a factory-built house, since the lender may have previously evaluated the model. He also knows that if the factory has been selling the model for over a year, the chances are good that any small design deficiencies have been corrected.

In addition to meeting state codes, almost all factories build their homes to meet FHA standards. This allows mortgages on them to qualify for FHA insurance, VA guarantees and—in the case of some models at the lower end of the price range—for low interest Farmer's Home Administration (FmHA) mortgages. Although FHA standards will only assure you against poor construction, a factory-built house conforming to these standards will often get faster approval for a conventional mortgage than a more expensive site-built house not aimed at FHA buyers. The reason is that many lenders still base their home appraisal criteria on FHA standards.

Component Manufacturers

You wouldn't normally notice manufactured components in a house unless you actually entered the attic and crawl space and looked around. Component manufacturers affect you mainly by lowering the cost of the house—they mass-produce certain structural assemblies which allow builders to cut labor costs and speed up construction time.

Manufactured housing components are pre-built sections used by home builders. Not only do they use them in fairly standard houses but often in expensive one-of-a-kind homes designed by architects. Developers and builders specializing in condominiums and commercial real estate are also large users of manufactured components.

Most component manufacturers concentrate on standardized units which they can produce in large quantities. This allows them to invest in the specialized high-speed equipment which can turn out top-quality assemblies at very competitive prices. A component factory will usually limit itself to roof and floor trusses, and in some cases may also make wall panels.

A *roof truss* simply provides a way to support the weight of the roof with less expensive 2 × 4 lumber—these pieces are joined into a rigid framework of triangular shapes. When a load is applied to the truss framework, the nearest "web" of interior 2 × 4's absorb this weight along the direction of their length—not as a sideways bending stress which could easily break them. To handle its design load, it's important that all of a truss' wooden members be very accurately cut to the right length and angle, so that they will fit snugly without gaps where they join together.

You won't usually find trusses in the attics of older homes. Instead, the roof will be supported by large 2 × 8 or 2 × 10 rafters which allow a clear space to the top. Rafters are still used in homes whose owners want a clear full-size attic.

Today's almost universal use of the roof truss was made possible by a fastener known as a Truss Plate Connector. This is a metal plate with many small teeth protruding from one side. When the wooden truss frame members are aligned in a jig, a metal connector plate is placed teeth-down over each joint and pushed into the wood with a powerful press. This connection at the joint is stronger than the wood itself.

The purpose of a *floor truss* is to give you a large family room in the basement. It is designed and constructed to span wide areas without the need for support columns, as are found in the basements of most older homes. Both roof and floor trusses are designed by engineers to meet or exceed the load limits that will be placed on them in the houses for which they're intended.

Many component manufacturers also make *wall panels*, of the same type as those made by panelized factories. The difference is that they build these to order, to a builder's specific design, and do not sell them as components in houses of their own.

Panelized Home Manufacturers

Panelized home packages are the most popular and versatile form of manufactured housing. The wall panels, usually 8 feet high and ranging from 20 to 40 feet in length, consist of 2 × 4 vertical studs fastened to 2 × 4 top and bottom plates. A panelized home package normally includes roof trusses and a floor system.

The wall panels for the outside of the house will come with factory-installed insulating boards (where specified), sheathing and siding. Exterior windows and doors are also usually installed at the factory.

Panelized homes can be 1-story, 2-story or split level (apartments, mid-rise office buildings, churches, schools, clinics and hospitals can also be built of panelized sections). Most panelized packages are designed so that a builder's four or six-man crew can erect the structure in one day. They will conform to state codes and are likely to be more solid than a local code would require.

When the package arrives at the site, it will have been loaded in such a manner that the builder has to handle each item only once. First off the truck is the floor system, which is installed on the foundation. This is followed by the wall panels, which will have been stacked in the order needed to complete the building in the least amount of time. The last items to be unloaded are the roof trusses, sheathing panels and roofing needed to complete the house.

By erecting the house so quickly, the builder avoids the losses due to bad weather and vandalism described earlier. And by having the major portion of the work completed in the factory, which will have quoted a firm price and delivery, the builder also gets better control over building costs. The manufacturer may also finance the package at a rate lower than the going interest for commercial construction loans.

Panelized homes are available in two types of wall panels: "open" and "closed."

In an *open wall* panel, at least one surface is uncovered and it usually does not include electrical wiring or plumbing. If a local building inspector wants to check the interior structure, it's easy to do this with an open wall panel. Most open wall packages come with pre-cut floor joists, although some may include floor truss panelized sections instead. In some packages only pre-cut 2 × 4's may be supplied for on-site assembly of the interior partitions. Most packages will include nails, bolts and other fasteners, stairs and railings, and the trusses, sheathing, underlayment, rolls of shingle, flashing and gutters to complete the roof. Kitchen and bathroom fixtures, doors, interior trim and paneling are optional—builders, in fact, usually have the option of excluding any of the above items that they prefer to supply themselves.

If a builder erects a panelized shell for a customer, it's likely to be an open wall package.

By comparison, *Closed Wall* panels contain factory-installed electrical wiring and outlets, plumbing, insulation and interior wallboard. They are closed on one side by the exterior siding, and on the other side by interior paneling or sheetrock board. Once they are joined together it's only necessary to finish the interior walls, which saves the builder even more time and money.

The "mechanical core." An important component in most closed wall panelized packages is a single modular unit, often

10 by 15 feet, which on one outer side will have the necessary plumbing and equipment for the "wet wall" of the kitchen. This includes the sink, disposal, dishwasher and anything else which has to be connected to water and drain pipes.

On the inside of this module's wall will be one bathroom for the house, and usually a utility room containing a hot water heater, furnace, clothes washer, dryer and electrical service box. Additional bathrooms can either be supplied as modules or else put up by the builder on-site.

Modular or Sectional Homes

In the homebuilding industry both "modular" and "sectional" mean the same thing.

Modular housing manufacturers show considerable ingenuity in designing a relatively small number of modules that can be connected in many different ways to produce a great variety of house styles. If, as a buyer, you would like some changes in a model's interior layout the factory may be able to provide this by reshuffling the modules. These changes will usually add to the cost of the package, however.

When they leave the factory the sections of a modular home are advertised as 95 percent complete. This makes for very fast assembly at the site, but does make this type of housing the most expensive to ship. You probably have seen a number of these "wide loads" being transported along the highway.

A modular home can be ordered in three ways. Some manufacturers will only sell to you direct—assembling and completing the home to their own standards with their own trained crews. Before shipping the units, the factory will send a representative to your site to measure the foundation and confirm that it and the utility connections will be matched to the sections when they arrive.

The manufacturer's representative will also check the condition of the access road to your site. If he has not checked out the delivery route on his way down, he will retrace it on his way back to the factory, noting all bridges over the road for height clearance and all bridges under the road for weight limitations. He will make a record of any overhead obstructions such as low wires or tree branches, and the drivers will be informed of these before the shipment leaves the plant.

The buyer has to make a number of important decisions before a factory can schedule a modular house for production. He or she will have to select:

- The carpeting, tile or wood covering for the floor,
- The paint colors or wallpaper patterns for the interior walls,
- The desired light fixtures and bathroom fixtures,
- Kitchen equipment and cabinets,
- Windows and doors,
- The type and color of roofing shingles,
- The color and type of siding and exterior trim,
- Whether to specify the optional extra insulation package,
- The type of heating and air conditioning units desired.

All of these items will be installed or built into the home before the modules leave the factory. As you can see, the houses are far from standardized and most firms consider themselves to be in the *customized* modular home business.

Once the factory schedules a home for production, the modules typically take shape as follows:

Station 1. The flooring system is built and laid across the assembly line tracks. This rectangular platform will be quite strong—not only does it have to withstand the bumps and bounces of traveling to your site, but it must also keep the whole module rigid while it is being lifted or pushed up over a greased rail into place. Highest quality kiln-dried lumber will be used throughout and, depending on the size of the house, this 14-foot wide platform can be 24 to 60 feet long.

First, 2×10 structural lumber will be used to make the platform's perimeter frame. Into this go the 2×8 floor joists, spaced either 16 or 24 inches apart. The subflooring, usually either ½- or ¾-inch plywood, is then both glued and nailed to the frame—and often screwed down as well to give it maximum rigidity. Nails and screws are precisely spaced according to a predetermined nailing schedule. After the platform is inspected to make sure it is solid, level and square, it moves on.

Station 2. Here, a subassembly line on which wall panels are built joins the main assembly line. The interior partition walls are the first to be positioned, followed by the exterior walls—complete with insulation, sheathing, siding, windows and doors. The location of the wall panels is inspected and also the way they are fastened together and to the platform.

Station 3. The plumbing and electrical wiring for the panels are installed. The work is inspected.

Station 4. Interior wallboard is fastened to the panels. The joints are taped and finished smooth. Heating outlets and cooling vents are installed. All this work is inspected.

On the modules which require them, kitchen equipment and cabinets, bathroom fixtures, furnace and air conditioning units, water heater, electric switchboard and any other mechanical items are often installed at this point. The correct installation of each item is checked on the list after inspection. The exterior hookups are sealed and will be uncapped at the site.

Station 5. Another subassembly line will join here, on which the ceiling sections and roof rafters or trusses have been built. If the module must pass under bridges and low overhangs enroute to your site, the roof rafters or trusses will often be hinged so that they can be folded down flat while traveling. In order to keep the module's width inside the 14-foot travel limit, the eave overhangs may also be hinged and folded up over the top of the ceiling section. After inspection, the module moves to the last station.

Station 6. Here is where the module's interior takes on the appearance of a finished home. Wallpaper and paint are applied. The floor covering you specified is laid down, fitted and fastened. The final trim goes on and outlets, switches and lighting fixtures are installed. The module is cleaned up, given a final inspection and made ready for shipment.

The factory will retain the comprehensive inspection checklist covering all stations, for examination by state building inspectors or licensed independent third party inspectors hired by the state.

Local Dealers

A more common way to order a factory-built house is through a local dealer. Depending on the way the housing packages arrive at the site, the dealer's work on the house can range from those performed by a factory's erection crew to those of a large-scale builder of houses. In all cases, a good dealer will advise and help with modifications you want, selecting a lot (and checking its suitability for a well and a septic system if necessary), the foundation, building code certification, financing and the other details that must be taken care of before you can move in.

Pricing will vary according to the manufacturers' policies. Some companies set the prices and hold their dealers to them. Others leave the retail pricing up to the dealers, so that prices on the same model may vary from place to place. Most manufacturers and dealers will be happy to discuss the price of the house itself and its options. Unless you've already made a firm decision on where you are going to buy your land, however, don't expect an early estimate of shipping costs. These are quite high on a per-mile basis and the closer the site to the factory, the cheaper will be the home's delivered cost.

Independent Builders

The third way to buy a factory-built house is through a builder who, in effect, chooses to carry on his business without the problems of on-site construction. The factory constructs the houses to the builder's specifications and the homes will often resemble the ones he used to erect piece-by-piece on the site.

This type of builder is not a dealer. He calls the tune and the factories supply the components as specified in his purchase order. Essentially, these builders have substituted a factory work crew for most of the on-site building trades workmen they used to employ. And as previously mentioned, they are less affected by weather, can build houses of a more uniform quality, don't have to worry about on-site storage of materials, can erect a house in a matter of days, and can cost out each job on the basis of firm price quotations and delivery.

Whether all this means a subsequent saving to you depends on the builder. It's normal to charge what the market will bear, and this often means he prices his homes to match the selling prices of those being entirely built on-site. It will pay you to shop around—and if you can, find out how far away each builders' suppliers are located. One building expense that does *not* go down with factory-built houses is shipping costs to the site, and the closer the factory the less the builder pays for transportation. Some builders might pass this saving along to their customers.

Shopping For Factory-Built Houses

As a first step, send $6.25 to the Home Manufacturers' Council of the National Association of Home Builders, 15th and M Sts., NW, Washington, D.C. 20005 to get your copy of their color booklet, "Guide to Manufactured Homes." This booklet lists the market areas for each member company on a state-by-state basis. You can check the names listed under your state against the names listed in the "Product Classification."

You can then start preparing your shopping list. For example, if you want a panelized or modular package, the names that appear both under your state and under "Panelized Homes" and "Modular or Sectional Homes" are the ones to contact. By going to the alphabetical directory, you can get each company's address, phone number, the person to call and whether or not there is a charge for their literature. These companies will let you know if they deal direct, or else give you the name of their nearest dealer.

The types of descriptive literature you get will vary from small folders with a dealer's card attached, to packets with color catalog, artists' renderings of the different models, floor plans, specifications and prices. Many firms, however, charge for their full-color catalogs and also for their floor plans. The ones that do charge are noted in the alphabetical directory and the catalog prices listed.

It's important to review as many models and floor plans from as many different firms serving your market area as you can. Although a company will usually make certain modifications in their house plans, these complicate and slow down their operation and you will be charged extra for them. On the other hand, another company may have a similar style at a similar price with just the room layout you want.

Poor construction. As in any industry, there will always be a few manufacturers who cut corners, or the occasional home with defects. But the probability of your being stuck with a housing headache is very small if you do business with reputable manufacturers and dealers—and much smaller than if you were to have your home built entirely in the relative chaos of a job site.

If you regularly read newspaper or news magazine real estate sections, you are likely to come across an article about some housing manufacturer who is exporting homes all over, from the Middle East to the south Pacific. This is a good testimonial to the industry and the regard in which overseas customers hold their products—the landed cost of a housing package in New Guinea is a *lot* more than your delivered cost at the site.

Shell Homes

Shell homes are for the do-it-yourselfer who wants to invest less money and more time and effort in a home without inheriting the problems that plague on-site builders. Shells can be erected from kits of pre-cut lumber or open wall panelized packages. If a builder erects them on your own land, there's a possibility he will finance you or that you may qualify for mortgage with a large down payment (provided you can show proof of your ability to finish a home properly.)

Generally, any panelized shell should be erected by a professional contractor who knows these packages and has the necessary lifting equipment. Considerable muscle is needed to raise the walls and roof of these homes—indeed, of any home. If you have enough handy friends that you can *rely* on you might tackle the erection, but don't try to do it singlehanded.

A pre-cut kit of more than one story is also best left to a contractor, especially if you need financing. The outer walls of a frame house must be strong, square, true and plumb (absolutely vertical). The first three criteria also apply to the roof. If the erected house doesn't meet these standards, you could be living in a low equity nightmare instead of an appreciating investment.

A builder who puts up a shell is erecting a house that is closed-in and weatherproof on the outside. The windows, doors, sheathing and siding will all be in place. The inside, on the other hand, will bring a glow of pure joy to dedicated amateur craftspersons and also show them who their true friends are—the ones who haven't vanished.

The first challenge is the plumbing: to install it out of sight means sawing and chiseling many notches and drilling innumerable holes. Since these holes are of fairly large diameter and must be drilled at slow speeds, start off by investing in a $^3/_8$- or $^1/_2$-inch professional quality electric drill from an industrial supply house. The consumer line tools offered by hardware stores and lumberyards have cheap motors and bearings, which overheat under slow-speed loads. One of these will have to be replaced several times over. Buy your hole saws, spade bits and twist drill bits from the same source.

Soldering plumbing is easier than most people think, but be careful when placing a hot torch directly on plywood sub-flooring—use some sort of metal or asbestos pad. The plumbing will have to be checked by the housing inspector, so make sure you install it according to the code.

Like the plumbing, the electrical wiring is not that difficult to put in. There are a number of good reference works available, and you should know about current flow, circuits, grounds and how to use a test light. It's best to do this work with the main switch at the circuit breaker panel off, since a mistake could not only set fire to the house but could fry the occupant. Here again, the important thing is to do all work by the code so that the inspector will approve it.

And now for the real "sweat equity." Rolls of insulation must go in. Wallboard is nailed-on, and the nailheads covered with putty and smoothed. Wallboard joints—there will be many of these—will need taping and smoothing with a sander. Make sure the edges of the tape are beveled flush, so that it won't show through the paint or wallpaper. The windows, trim, doors and stairs must be sanded smooth and sealed.

When the finished area of the walls and ceilings is all ship-shape, it's down tools and up with cans of paint, rollers for the walls and brushes for the trim. Or you may prefer the joys of wallpapering instead and use panelling in the den. Acres of wood cabinets to be stained and varnished. Time out to install light fixtures on walls and ceilings, and put in electrical switches and outlets (make sure the master switch is off).

Next, the sub-flooring awaits the covering of your choice. Tile and linoleum to be precisely cut and laid perfectly square. Heavy, long rolls of carpeting to be hauled in and accurately unrolled, trimmed and laid over tackless fittings or tacked in place. Or, if wall-to-wall fuzz isn't your thing, rolls of underlayment to be unrolled and cut, stacks of tongue-and-groove floorboards to be cut to the exact length, laid absolutely straight, sanded perfectly smooth, and stained and varnished to a gloss or semi-gloss.

Post and beam shells. Catering to many peoples' wish for more massive walls than are possible with 2 × 4 and 2 × 6 "scantling lumber," several manufacturers are offering post and beam shells. Their erected price is surprisingly affordable, since a properly trained and equipped small crew can lift these big "sticks" into place in less time than it takes to hammer the numerous smaller structural members of a light frame house together.

For cost reasons, a modern pre-cut kit will probably not employ mortise and tenon joinery. Instead, horizontal beams will typically be laid over vertical posts and plates, being then secured at the joints with thick hardwood pegs driven into holes drilled through both members.

One successful home manufacturer is Maine Post & Beam Company, which freely admits it is no purist when it comes to traditional timber framing. Being more concerned with the on-site price of an affordable, solid, energy efficient completed shell, the company uses post and beam framing to reduce both shipping costs and on-site erection man-hours. A trained 3-man company crew can put up a timber frame very quickly: on average, it takes 25 days to complete the shell of one of the company's 2,160 square foot 1½ story Cape houses, for example. The completed structure will be weathertight, with doors and windows locked against vandals.

You may be interested in this manufacturer's "Home Building Partnership" philosophy. The homeowner is the overall project administrator and is involved from the start. The company, through its local offices, acts as a flexible "technical partner" which can assist in house design and layout, land acquisition, excavating, building the foundation and—if necessary—obtaining a construction loan or long term mortgage financing. When the house model has been selected, Maine Post & Beam assigns a project manager to the owner-prime contractor as technical partner. After the foundation is built, the house components are delivered and the company crew completes the shell. Owners may finish the interior themselves or hire subcontractors to do this work—if they run into problems, the company is still available for technical counseling.

The company's quoted prices for their different models include free delivery within a 50-mile radius from its local offices—beyond this point a typical shipping charge for a 1,600 square foot home in 1981 would be about $1.50 per mile, up to a maximum distance of 1,000 miles. At time of writing, the company's erected shells ranged in price (not including land and with door and window options still to be selected) from $14,888 for a 744 square foot Cape cottage to $34,993 for a 2,880 square foot two-story colonial.

Fig. 8 Modern post and beam construction, showing a 28' × 36' Cape model adapted for passive solar heating.

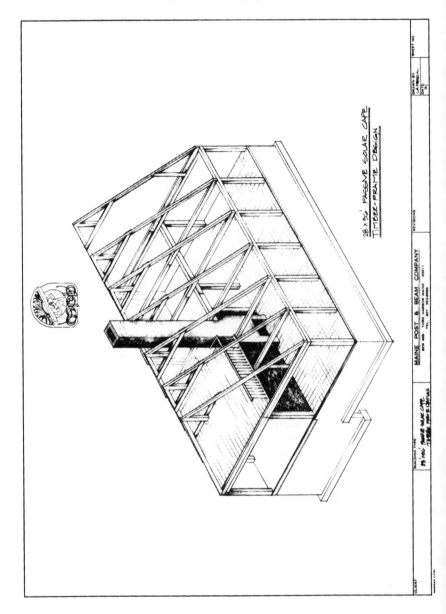

Courtesy: Maine Post & Beam Company, York Harbor, ME 03911

The company advises that the model shown in Fig. 8 might typically price out as follows:

28' × 36' Modified Cape Passive Solar

28 × 36 Cape model with 6 × 12 airlock entry, four skylights, one sliding glass door, two overhangs on South side	$25,000 approx
Foundation (half basement, half insulated slab) including excavation and site preparation	$ 4,800 approx
Operating double-glazed door and window units	$ 5,500 approx
Internal masonry thermal wall for direct-gain heat storage	$ 1,000 approx
Approximate total for completed shell	$36,300
Estimated costs for finishing the interior	$15,000 to $25,000
Estimated finished cost (excluding land)	$51,300 to $61,300

100% Manufactured "Mobile" Homes

The distinction between mobile homes and modular housing is very confusing to most buyers. The word "mobile" really only applies to the industry in the socioeconomic sense: many firms abandoned their old trailer camp clientele years ago and have moved into higher price markets.

Today, they offer houses of up to 2,000 square feet of living area, varied and attractive exterior trim, cathedral ceilings, 2½ bathrooms, state-of-the-art kitchens and Jacuzzi's. They come in "double wide" or "triple wide" assemblies of two or three sections. Once these sections are joined and anchored to the foundation, the house is about as mobile as an M60 tank with broken treads and a seized engine.

The differences between the two types of housing, as they affect you, have little to do with product quality but are very much influenced by history and social factors.

Modular housing factories are an economic development which came into being when on-site building costs got out-of-hand. The factories could make all or part of the house better and cheaper. The main thrust of their marketing and public relations efforts is to convince the more tradition-bound builders to accept their product, and to convince state authorities to allow their houses to be erected.

Manufactured or "mobile" home companies are still primarily trying to rid themselves of an unfavorable image in the eyes of communities and the buying public. Most got started as manufacturers of recreational trailers, or as makers of the equivalent to the restaurant industry's road-side diner: cheap boxes on wheels which served as shelter of last resort for low income families. Suburban communities quickly passed zoning laws against this type of housing, which then became segregated in trailer parks. There, the units were usually placed in rows on rented lots and became the suburban version of "the wrong side of the tracks." This industry is regulated by the National Mobile Home Construction and Safety Standards Act of 1974. The manufacturers must meet HUD minimum standards, whereas modular housing manufacturers conform to state laws.

Before going into the differences between modular and "manufactured" housing, it's worth mentioning one attribute they both share: both groups of manufacturers are intensely disliked by most of the building trades movement. In many metropolitan areas where these unions are entrenched it will be impossible for you to put up either type of home on your lot—if you live in or near a city, this is the first thing to check before buying one.

It's a sad situation, since both modular and 100 percent manufactured "no frills" units could be a low-cost answer to affordable housing in declining urban areas. States are slowly forcing their major cities to allow this type of housing, but the building trades will fight this particular battle to the end.

The following differences between "95 percent complete" modular and "100 percent manufactured" houses are the ones that make sense to buyers.

1. As of this writing, all "mobile" homes are 1-story and will appeal to those who like ranch-style houses. A modular house *may* have just one floor (most factories offer a range of 1-story models) but may also be split-level or two stories high.

2. A single-section mobile home is 100 percent completed at the factory. It can then either be shipped to your site or to a dealer's yard for storage. (This has led to warranty disputes between dealers and manufacturers in the past, with the owner caught in the middle.) The delivered price of a mobile home includes dealer set-up and anchoring to the foundation, hookup of utilities, complete furnishings, name brand appliances and a one-year guarantee. The cost of the land, foundation and any wells or septic tank facilities are extra.

A modular home which is "95 percent complete" when it leaves the factory undergoes the remaining 5 percent completion by the assembly crew at the site. (The same could be said for double-wide or triple-wide "mobile" homes, which arrive in two or three sections.)

3. A modular house is built to conform to the statewide building codes for the areas in which it will be sold. A manufactured or "mobile" home must by law meet a single federal code: the standards imposed by the National Mobile Home Construction and Safety Standards Act of 1974. (If the manufacturer also built his homes to conform to state building codes, they would then be modular houses and no longer fall under the legal definition of a mobile/manufactured home.)

The 1974 Act, which was first implemented in 1976, came about as a result of complaints that many "trailers" were poorly constructed and were firetraps. Also, after tornadoes touched down in some Midwest parks, and during the East coast hurricane season, the TV news carried stories of devastation among relatively flimsy and poorly anchored trailer homes. The HUD-enforced 1974 standards have greatly improved quality and safety.

Today's mobile/manufactured homes have a HUD seal permanently attached to their lower back panels. Be careful when buying older units that don't carry this seal. Mobile homes sold today must have:

- Not less than two easily accessible exits;
- Walls and ceilings of flame-retardant non-toxic materials;

- Interiors of furnace and water tank enclosures, kitchen cabinets and counter tops, interiors next to the stove, furniture materials, plastic bathtubs, shower units and doors must meet these same flame-retardant standards.
- Smoke alarms in each sleeping area;
- Emergency exit windows in all sleeping areas that can be quickly pushed out.
- The house must meet HUD limits on heat loss in winter and heat gain in summer. Heat loss level requirements are posted inside each home to inform buyers of the fuel bills they can expect. Homes for the snowbelt are required to have storm windows and storm doors, plus heavier insulation in walls, floor and ceiling.
- All appliances furnished with the home must meet HUD energy-efficiency standards.
- The heating and cooling system, as well as the water heater, must meet HUD energy-efficiency standards.
- The venting of clothes dryers, design of fireplace air inlets, and ventilation of the cooking area must meet HUD requirements.

As you can see, the government decreed in 1974 that any mobile home sold on the market must: allow a quick exit; allow you time to get away if it catches fire; be constructed so as not to go up like a torch; be energy-efficient. Like factory-built houses conforming to state standards, mobile homes are also built very tightly to reduce air infiltration. It is also less likely than most homes to start you coughing from fireplace smoke or make you spray away cooking odors. And, of all the housing options available to you, this is the only one that must meet a federal code in its entirety.

At present, 44 states allow mobile homes to be treated as real property if they are sold together with the land on which they are placed and anchored to their foundation. Having his or her home legally classified as real estate is important to the buyer. If the home is legally classified as a vehicle, it will not qualify for a long-term self-amortizing loan, cannot be used for the tax deductions that apply to other homes, and will depreciate instead of appreciating in value.

Communities also object when they have to supply mobile homes with essential services only to see the tax revenue on them go to the state Division of Motor Vehicles. This is one valid reason for a community to zone against these houses—acceptance comes much more quickly if mobile homes can be taxed like other forms of housing. And well planned subdivisions of attractive mobile homes are the most affordable type of housing in today's market. A community which encourages these attracts large numbers of middle-income owners, who in turn contribute to the tax base.

There's one other difference between modular and single-section "mobile" homes. The sub-floor frames of the latter still include a steel chassis to which the wheels are attached, before these are removed at the site and brickwork skirting installed around the openings. These steel chassis beams make for the strongest floor in the manufactured housing industry.

Buying A Mobile Home

Just as with a modular house, the first step is to find out which companies serve your area—the large ones will have factories in different parts of the country. You can get a list of manufacturers by calling either *Manufactured Housing Dealer Magazine,* (219) 295-7820 or *Mobile/Manufactured Housing Merchandising Magazine,* (312) 236-3528.

Then contact the firms nearest you. They will usually reply with a brochure and the name of the nearest dealer. In the case of the large double and triple width models, however, they may send their own personnel to help dealers with the assembly. If the price is high enough, the higher profit allows a manufacturer to invest more time on installations for individual owners.

If possible try to visit all the factories serving your area to see how the units compare and are put together. When it comes to buying, however, you will be involved in one of the last remnants of the industry's "trailer" days—buying a home through a dealer is much like buying a car or recreational vehicle. Start, as you would with other major purchases, by calling the Better Business Bureau and getting their OK on the dealer's business reputation.

Depending on your finances, you may want to steer clear of the bottom-of-the-line models. HUD standards prevent these from being shoddy, but they won't be as good in appearance, layout and convenience as the higher priced and multi-section units—which can still be a bargain in today's market at $25 per square foot, less than half the figure for a site-built house. You won't have any trouble avoiding the cheaper units, since most dealers will try to sell you the best model they think you can afford and also load it up with extras (sound familiar?). Be firm at this point, especially if the home is in the dealer's lot. These are often "loaded" and you can install your own lighting fixtures and decorations for far less money.

Financing a mobile home. In some areas you may still have to take out a higher interest 8 to 12 year chattel mortgage, particularly if you don't or can't own your land and have to place your home in a rental development.

If you can buy your own land, and can qualify for VA or FHA mortgage underwriting, you may be able to get a 20-year mortgage on the completely furnished unit plus the land. The VA will require no down payment, while FHA specifies 3 percent of the first $3,000 and 10 percent of the balance down. Since both VA and FHA currently set interest rate ceilings at around 15 percent, you will have to pay the lender "points" to make up the difference between this and the market rate (see chapter 11).

There are some major changes underway, in addition to having them classified as real estate, to make mobile home financing conform to the financing of other types of homes. These changes will affect mobile home buyers in three principal ways.

First, the federally-chartered thrift institutions are being permitted to increase their portfolios of mobile home loans. This authority comes from the Federal Home Loan Bank Board ((FHLBB) which has recently permitted federally-chartered savings and loan institutions to place up to 20 percent of their assets in mobile homes and lower the minimum down payment from 20 percent to 10 percent. FHLBB has also clarified the rules for its savings and loan institutions so that they can consider a mobile home mortgage as a real estate loan, regardless of any ambiguities in state laws.

Second, the people who insure mobile home loans will have to set maximum loan amounts comparable to other types of housing. You saw that FHA requires a low down payment but limits the loan term to 20 years (other types of homes qualify for 30 years). It also places an upper limit of $27,000 on the amount it will guarantee on a multi-section house.

This doesn't necessarily mean that people will never be able to get long term mortgage financing on the $100,000 California "mobile" ranch house of their dreams. Private mortgage insurors usually move in after FHA has brought some order to a chaotic situation and their loan limits are much higher. The FHA's interest is primarily in good, affordable moderate-income housing.

Third, the large secondary market investors, such as the Federal National Mortgage Association (FNMA) and Federal Home Loan Mortgage Corporation (FHLMC), are willing to buy large packages of these mortgages from the lenders who originated them.

FNMA recently announced that it will buy mortgages on mobile homes if they comply with their state as well as the HUD building codes, be firmly attached to their foundations with all wheels removed, be sold as a package with the land and be comparable to site-built housing in the area.

After all these agencies have made their enabling moves behind the scenes, the lenders may start to write mortgages. These can now be very similar to the ones they originate for other types of housing. Since all or part of these loan amounts can be insured, the lender can lower your down payment without risk. Since the mobile home is legally classified as real estate, it will appreciate in value like other houses and not depreciate like a camper. Finally, they can sell a mobile home mortgage to an investor and use the money to write other mortgages.

At this point, it becomes worthwhile for you to shop the federally-chartered thrift institutions in your area, and also the mortgage companies, who have traditionally done a large business in FHA/VA mortgages which they then sell to investors.

If mortgage money remains tight, many people can get their start by buying a used home (preferably with a HUD emblem) and finance it with a chattel mortgage until interest rates go down.

Mobile Home Parks

If you are unable to put a mobile home on a private lot in your area, buy a copy of *Woodall's Mobile Home and Park Directory*. Bookstores in smaller towns may carry it and in larger urban areas you may find it at news stands. It's the best source for up-to-date information on the parks nearest you.

Years ago, people who moved into a mobile home park did so because of economic necessity and did not expect to encounter the gracious suburban living featured in magazines directed at homeowners. Today's mobile home buyers still pay less for their shelter per square foot than for other forms of housing, but many of the parks available to them look more like landscaped residential developments. In them, they can buy the foundation and pay property taxes instead of rent. Their homes are classed as houses, not as vehicles. They often end up liking the community better than the one where they had hoped to buy a lot.

If you decide on a rental park, visit as many of these as you can and talk to the residents. Compare the monthly site rentals against each other, and the rental amounts to what you get. Are there fees for moving-in and connecting the utilities? How much? If you plan to stay for more than a few months, ask for a lease to protect you against eviction.

If you think you might have to sell your home for any reason, make sure the park rules allow you to show buyers the unit on its site. And if the park insists you buy a home from a certain dealer, or from them, try elsewhere.

If you have small children, finding a park which will take kids can be a problem. If your children are teenagers finding a park is almost impossible, since "young adults" are synonymous with vandalism in most people's minds. Some parks, however, get around the generation problem by having separate family and "adults only" sections.

In parts of the country where many mobile homes are sold, the parks are mostly full and not enough new ones are being developed to keep up with the demand. However, since this form of housing is obviously popular in the area, there may be more residential communities willing to allow mobile homes on private lots.

CHAPTER 8

Log Houses, Domes And Others

Log Houses

Buyers attracted to the outward appearance of a log home and its natural wood interior should note that this type of shelter is usually known as a log *house*, although U.S. makers of kit log homes describe their smaller vacation models as "cabins."

Webster's 'obsolete' definition of cabin is "any covered space for a temporary residence." Our forefathers used the word to describe the temporary shelters they put up as they settled the wilderness. On established farms well behind the frontier, the term continued to be used for storage sheds, the old pioneering shelters still standing and in the old South—regrettably—slave quarters. Some of our past presidents may have reminisced at election time about their humble beginnings in log cabins, but the generation that built these looked forward quite unsentimentally to the day when they could move up to a larger log or post and beam house.

In Canada, where log houses have traditionally been very popular, "cabin" is seldom used. If you should have questions about small and hastily built log structures while visiting north of the border, mention the "hut," "shed" or "shanty" and your hosts are more likely to understand.

An early buying decision is whether to choose a house of round logs or one of "hewn" (squared) logs. Many of the early British settlers considered hewn log homes more genteel and laboriously squared each log with a broadaxe, finishing it smooth with an adze before placing it in the wall.

Squared logs were long used for the better houses in Appalachia and other regions. Today, a number of people are actively restoring these older houses and are relearning how to square logs the old way. The owner-builder of average handiness should be careful, however, of books explaining how *most* folks can acquire these skills with a little effort. "How to" books in this field will likely include statements such as, "I never learned how to really handle an axe until age eleven. . . ." For these writers, building hewn log houses is a lifetime love affair and they are usually very, very good at it. Those who have reached this level of skill seldom understand why laymen simply can't carry out straightforward, uncomplicated projects.

Most people who like squared logs will have to buy a kit. These logs will be squared by a circular saw and giving them a hand-hewn appearance will involve considerable touching up with an adze.

Unlike the eighteenth century, in today's machine age most houses and buildings have smooth sides and a house of rounded logs is pleasingly different. To many it evokes memories of rustic retreats and vanishing woodlands. The whole natural log is a much better insulator than sections of lumber sawn from it—it is quite effective in slowing down heat transfer if its cross section is large enough.

In contrast, a wood frame house has very little heat storage capacity. At sunset it quickly loses its heat to the surrounding atmosphere unless walls and ceilings are heavily insulated. This heat loss is much slower in a properly built and tight log house. The latter is like an adobe: in summer the walls take a long time to heat up and the interior stays cool. In colder weather the walls retain internal heat and at nightfall will slowly release heat they have received from the daytime sun.

If you are interested in having a log house kit erected, a first step in locating manufacturers is to get hold of the National Association of Home Builders *Guide* and use the directory as described in Chapter 7 for panelized and modular housing manufacturers. It is also a good idea to read books intended for owner-builders—not so much the sections on log house construction, since most factories design their kits well, but rather their advice on what kind and sizes of logs to keep in mind when selecting trees.

Depending on the manufacturer, kits can be offered in any of four ways:

1. *Log wall kit.* Contains the pre-cut logs for exterior walls. Some interior partitions may also be included, along with spikes, dowels, splines and sealants necessary to complete the basic shell.

2. *Structural shell.* Contains all the items in a log wall kit, plus log beams, rafters, purlins, trusses, window and door frames.

3. *Weather-tight shell.* Contains all the items in a structural shell, plus flooring, roofing materials, insulation, doors, windows, all interior partitions, second floor materials, stairs.

4. *Complete log home package.* Includes all the above, plus electrical wiring, plumbing and mechanical equipment.

Log house buyers should know their building materials, since this is one type of kit where the "sticks" are *not* necessarily better than those which do-it-yourselfers could obtain. The big advantage of a log house kit is that it saves a staggering amount of work in preparing the basic building materials, and allows the owner-builder to erect it in a reasonable time, or a private contractor to complete the shell at a cost comparable to wood frame housing.

Remember that there is presently a big demand for log houses. A number of phone calls to different manufacturers produced delivery estimates of several months. Faced with such a backlog of orders, panelized or modular housing manufacturers would not normally need to go to less seasoned wood. Their lumber arrives kiln-dried and stable, and attempts to use material prone to warpage and cracks generally mean trouble on the production line.

The logs used in house kits are usually trucked to the manufacturer directly after felling. In seasoning, the whole log will shrink slightly: it can be processed through the factory, but will settle a small amount in the completed house. It's unreasonable to expect a log house manufacturer to lose business by keeping urgently needed raw material stacked in the yard to slowly air-dry. Rather, the logs will be peeled, cut to length, milled, dipped in preservative and shipped out in kits as fast as possible. This does not necessarily mean that a kit log home will settle unevenly. The factory usually designs the kit so that all logs will "set" together in alignment. It does mean that if a newly delivered kit is stored for any length of time, the logs can shrink according to their stack arrangement in ways that make it harder to fit them into their numbered locations in the assembled structure.

It's strongly recommended that buyers of log kits have the foundation in place and be ready when the trailer arrives. The sooner each log goes into its place in the shell, the better.

Much as you may love your completed log house, expect some fall-off in enthusiasm if you ever return from a tour of Scandinavia. The old Norse had a number of ways to cure trees in place, before felling, and fine old log buildings dating as far back as the Middle Ages seldom fail to impress visitors.

Fire. If you are worried about a log house being a firetrap, try to start a fire using well-seasoned logs alone in the fireplace. It's almost impossible to do, since the rounded shape presents a uniformly massive surface to the flame. Even in a fire, logs will mostly char and are much less apt to ignite than the lighter structure of a frame house.

Damp rot. Decay is a vital part of a forest ecosystem, being the process by which fungi convert dead wood into nutrients for living plants.

Log houses can remain habitable for a long time if their structure is kept free from the fungi which attack them. In the case of softwood logs, the busy recyclers are mostly brown rot fungi. These decay organisms feed on the cellulose in the cell walls of the wood, converting it into sugars. Since wood gets most of its strength from cellulose, brown rotted logs and beams lose strength rapidly quite early in the decay process. Wood affected by brown rot will have a dark brown color, and in drying will check or split across the grain, shrink and collapse.

Brown rot fungi need moisture for their work. A danger sign is often the appearance of Sapstain fungi which can be bluish, gray, brown, purple or reddish depending on the type of wood infected. Sapstain decay does not seriously affect the strength of wood, but does make it more porous. The greater porosity can increase the wood's moisture level above the fiber saturation point. This allows brown rot to flourish, even if it has remained dormant in air-dried lumber. The fiber saturation point is the maximum amount of moisture vapor that wood can absorb from the air. Wood reaches this state when its cell walls are saturated, but there is no free water in the cell cavities.

The fiber saturation point for most species of wood native to North America ranges between 28 percent and 32 percent. This is the minimum amount of moisture which will support the growth of wood decay fungi. The wood will not decay if its moisture content is below this point.

Preservatives. Creosote has long been used to protect telephone poles from decay and insects. It has one drawback for use on or in a home: a strong, long-lasting odor which many find unpleasant and which will be picked up by food sensitive to such vapors. The other oil-based preservatives for exterior wood finishes are the pentachlorophenols.

The penta WR sold by hardware stores and lumberyards for brush application is a 5 percent solution plus a water repellent in mineral spirits. It is strong-smelling, and the manufacturers' instructions warn that it must be used in well ventilated areas. After the volatile spirits evaporate, the wood surface is clean and can be painted. For indoor applications, people usually use a water-based solution of a copper-arsenic salt, and the wood so treated is clean, paintable and free of objectionable odors.

Logs dipped in a penta solution such as Cuprinol® will usually be protected from rot and insects for about five years. After this period another coat of preservative should be applied, both inside and out.

Much more effective is pressure-treating, using penta dissolved in either liquefied petroleum gas or methylene chloride. This method requires expensive equipment: large cylinders which can be sealed tightly for the logs, heating equipment, vacuum systems and compressors. The wood is impregnated to a greater depth under pressure, and when this is released the solvent quickly evaporates. As far as logs are concerned, the primary beneficiary of the pressure-treatment process is your telephone company.

Those interested in reading up on log house construction will want the following books:

- *Build Your Own Low-Cost Log Home,* Roger Hard (Garden Way Publishing, 1977). This is probably the most informative book for the U.S. buyer and will be invaluable either for those planning to have a contractor erect a pre-cut package or for owner-builders.
- *The Complete Log House Book,* Dale Mann and Richard Skinulis (McGraw Hill, 1979). This is an excellent book by two Canadian authors. It includes a section on restoring hewn log houses, this style having been popular with French settlers as well as British.
- *Building With Logs,* B. Allan Mackie (Log House Publishing Company Ltd., Prince George, B.C., 1979). This is not only a "how to" book, it is also an intensely personal statement by the author. Mr. Mackie has dedicated a major part of his life to not only preserving the British and French Canadian traditions of building log houses, but also to preserving the environment in which Canadian owners have customarily enjoyed these homes.

Dome Houses

Another form of housing, very popular in the West and spreading to other parts of the country, is the dome home.

The larger geodesic domes that have made the headlines since World War II are free-standing, open structures without load-bearing interior walls. Their spherical shells are divided into many small triangles which are exactly joined together. The reason for using the triangle as the basic building unit is that it is the most rigid construction form known.

For example, suppose you want to build a light perimeter frame for a large pegboard display panel. If you build it as a rectangle and tack on the pegboard, the whole panel will twist and sag since a rectangle has little rigidity. On the other hand, if you make the frame out of two triangles it will stay rigid even in a strong wind.

The geodesic dome's popularity is largely due to R. Buckminster Fuller, who sees this form as the solution to the mass housing of the future. Compared to rectangular frame houses, the dome has a much stronger structure, is more energy efficient due to its smaller surface to volume ratio and unrestricted interior air flow, and uses less building materials for the same area of living space.

In a well-built dome, forces from the weight of the structure, exterior loads and wind pressure pass directly along the curve of its shell to the foundation. In cold climates, domes can support higher snow loads than most conventional roofs. The rounded surface is also less of a barrier to wind. Furthermore, the negative pressure created on the opposite side, where wind flows over and away from the structure, is much less. Some dome manufacturers certify that their homes will survive hurricanes—Geodesic Structures Inc., of Whitehouse Texas states that its domes have hurricane insurance along the Texas coast for winds up to 200 MPH!

Mr. Fuller, who in his eighties still actively promotes his vision of future housing, has an impressive list of structures to his credit. These include radar domes such as the ones on the Arctic's DEW line, the dome at Ford Motor Company's River Rouge plant, the U.S. exhibit dome at Montreal Expo in 1968, and many others.

For industrial or recreational purposes there is no limit, theoretically, to a dome's size. Some city planners foresee whole climate-controlled towns enclosed in covered frame domes of ultra-light materials. The framework of triangles would go up first, and the covering of these "bubbles" then attached with adhesives or fasteners.

One problem with the large number of small triangles required by a geodesic dome is the difficulty of waterproofing the outer surface against leaks.

Manufacturers of dome houses favor panelized modified-geodesic hexagonal construction because this is easier to erect at the site and modify to suit customer's tastes. The larger triangles for the hexagons can be combined with trapezoid or other panels containing standard windows and doors, or other options. Such a package can also be assembled in less time and usually at a lower cost. Buyers may want alcoves for side rooms, dormers, additional entrances, porches, balconies, picture windows or a battery of solar collectors on the outside. Or a buyer may be planning two or three domes connected by an enclosed passageway. The flat trapezoidal sections in a modified-geodesic shell won't undermine its structural strength and are well-suited to such options.

When considering how large a dome house to buy, remember that the structure has an open interior. Unless you plan to put in many partitions and ceilings—which would spoil one of the dome's most attractive features—the air inside will circulate freely. In a dome of moderate size, this means constant convection currents. The air won't form static layers between floor and ceilings, or sink into corner "cold pockets" as it can in a rectangular house. The number of domes erected by the government for exposed shelter in the Arctic are a testimonial to the sphere's energy efficiency.

But the larger the dome, the greater the airspace at the top. More warm air will rise to fill this space and the lower living area will be colder. Some manufacturers avoid this problem by offering "three eighths" and "one half" spheres, and some offer a heat top recovery system.

A dome buyer's life style checklist. When shopping for a dome house try to visit as many such homes as you can, in addition to the manufacturer's display models. This will give you a "feel" for a living space with fewer partition walls.

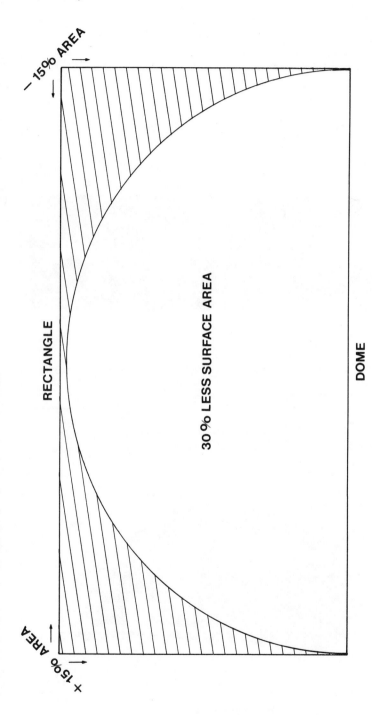

Compared to a rectangle, a dome has less surface area to radiate heat.

Low, medium and high rise domes

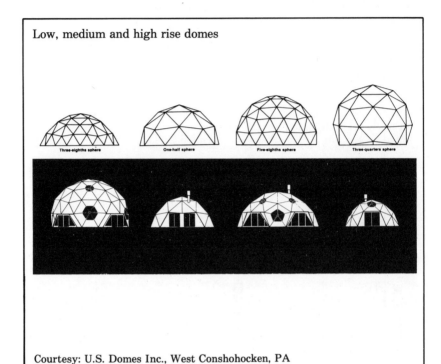

Courtesy: U.S. Domes Inc., West Conshohocken, PA

From the outside: A modified geodesic dome with hexagonal and trapezoidal sections

Courtesy: U.S. Domes Inc., West Conshohocken, PA

Some owners might be willing to talk about any problems they might have had with construction, neighborhood acceptance, long-term mortgage financing and customized options. Most dome owners are innovative and future-oriented.

Before spending time and money on field trips, however, there are some questions you can ask yourself:

- Does the dome shape fit the interior layout you want and the topography of your site? Even a modified geodesic dome is nearly spherical.

- Do any members of your family like to spend time alone? A dome doesn't need interior load bearing walls and its circular floor area is not well adapted to a lot of interior partitions and rooms.

- Noise. If you are a hi-fi buff, you're certain to love the dome's superior acoustics. If you have musical or active children, however, you'll probably want a house with at least one room soundproofed against their decibels. On the other hand, if *external* noise is a problem the shape of a well insulated dome helps shut out this racket. The dome can be a good bet if your land is near a busy street or highway.

- Smells. The superior air flow inside a dome means that odors will also spread quickly. Cooking smells can usually be vented to the outside, using a hood and exhaust fan above the kitchen range. But what about hobbies—for instance, are any of your children model plane builders? If so, will the weather in your area allow them to "dope" the wings and fuselage outside?

If you like the thermal efficiency of the dome's surface but still want interior partitions and private rooms, there are compromise designs available. One such design is the "Vista," in either 30-foot or 35-foot diameters, available from Cathedralite Domes Inc., 820 Bay Avenue, Capitola, California 95010. You get a partitioned floor plan, a ceiling, an attic and a spherical roof.

Buying a dome kit. As with other forms of manufactured housing, the best place to start is with the industry trade organization. This is the National Dome Association, 2506 Gross Point Road, Evanston, Illinois 60201. Their phone number is (312) 475-7530 and they will send you a list of dome manufacturers. The association also publishes a quarterly magazine "Dome Consumer News and Design" and can supply back issues for $1.50 each.

When the manufacturers' literature arrives, you will note differing marketing policies. The following list is far from complete, but here are the replies you can expect from several manufacturers.

Cathedralite Domes Inc. in California sells shells which can be finished either by their distributors or private contractors. They also sell sets of plans and have a building school for owner builders. You will receive a very handsome full-color catalog, along with a price list and a directory of distributors which covers most of the country except the Northeast and Middle Atlantic states.

Monterey Domes of Riverside, California sells kits and will send you a letter and a color brochure. Their 90-page catalog and planning kit costs $6.00 and their assembly manual $5.00. After you have looked these over, their factory personnel can assist you in getting these kits erected locally.

Domes America of Clarendon Hills, Illinois will send you a letter and a sheet which generally describes their marketing policy, design and construction features. They sell only through distributors and not directly to owner-builders. The *minimum* service performed by a Domes America dealer covers the erection of a shell on its foundation and the installation of the roofing (an exacting job on many domes). From this point on, owners may complete the dome by themselves if they want to. A detailed brochure is available for $6.00, postpaid.

U.S. Domes Inc., headquartered in West Conshocken, Pennsylvania is a design and marketing company with representatives throughout the eastern part of the country. Their domes are manufactured by Northern Homes in Hudson Falls, N.Y. and in most areas they can recommend builders familiar with their products. U.S. Domes also market in the Southwest through *Geodesic Domes & Homes,* P.O. Box 176, Whitehouse, Texas. Literature is available upon request. U.S. Domes has 12 different models to choose from, with many custom options.

The Outdoors People, Wyoming, Minnesota (who also belong to the National Association of Housing Manufacturers) will send you a color brochure and a combined specification/price list. This company emphasizes energy efficiency to a great extent (their climate zone has severe winters), and also planning assistance. They conduct weekend "dome schools" featuring on-the-job instruction for owner-builders and will also send supervisory personnel to your site to assist in everything from developing bids to finish carpentry. The motto of this company's owner-builder assistance program is "we travel anywhere." They also have a network of dealers which will erect either a shell or a finished home.

In most cases, a house package of dome panels is more compact than a package for a comparable frame house. Dome manufacturers can market within a fairly wide radius of their factories. To estimate transportation cost as of this writing, figure on roughly $1.50 per loaded mile.

The owner-builder. Those wanting to build their own dome houses will find *Design and Build Your Dome House,* HP Books, a good investment. The author, Gene Hopster, invented the hexadome concept involving only 24 large triangles and 3 trapezoids. These are preassembled and sheathed before being joined together as a dome structure.

This book is a straightforward guide through and around the pitfalls inherent in being one's own prime contractor. The book also describes how to make the components of a dome house and put them together. The sections on recordkeeping, liability, diplomatic handling of neighborhood teenagers, and pouring or laying the foundation should be read carefully. Mr. Hopster's descriptions of a dome's component parts can be particularly helpful to people located far from a factory, but near a shop which can accurately cut the pieces from seasoned, structural grade lumber.

If you do plan to make your own building components as well as assemble them together, it's a good idea to try a smaller dome structure first. More than other owner-builders, those who start a dome should be sure of their skills before trying to cut and join their own panels from lumber and plywood. The reason is the dome shape's low tolerance for dimensional variations in the basic structural components. If the panels don't fit together precisely, the surface may leak and a negative reaction from the building inspector is almost certain. For the same reason, unseasoned or partly seasoned wood should not be used in domes, as it will continue to shrink slightly after being nailed or screwed in place.

Foam Domes

Domes built out of standardized wood-and-plywood panels have tended to give trouble in one area: the skin. Uneven expansion and contraction as the sun's rays move over different areas of the surface can cause creaks and cracks. Most manufacturers of wood domes spend a lot of time and effort making sure that the outer surface is sealed and roofed to high professional standards, otherwise the dome is apt to drip in rainstorms and leak warm air in winter.

There is another approach to a tightly sealed dome: the "foam dome." So far, this approach seems to be limited to builders or to custom manufacturers with their own erection crews. For mass production factories to enter this field, whole new on-site technologies will probably have to be developed. Here are two different types of foam dome construction.

Techmar Construction Inc., Des Moines, Iowa and *Stanbrough Construction Company* of Des Moines have built a dome with 1,844 square feet of living space on two floors. The home was designed by Fredregill Architects of the same city.

In constructing this house, an air form attached to the foundation was first inflated. Next, five inches of polyurethane foam was sprayed against the interior of the air form.

When the foam had cured, a layer of concrete with steel reinforcements was applied to its underside, the thickness ranging from five inches at the base to two inches near the top of the dome. After removing the air form, the openings were finished and sealed. A liquid form of polyurethane was then applied as an elastomeric seal over the entire foam surface. Advantages claimed for this type of dome, in addition to those that are inherent with the shape, are:

- The seamless exterior minimizes infiltration of outside air and leakage of interior air.
- The polyurethane insulation reduces heat loss in winter and heat gain in summer.
- The high heat storage capacity of the concrete inner shell takes full advantage of south facing glass areas for passive solar heating in winter.
- The layer of concrete which separates the interior from the insulation gives the structure an excellent fire rating.

Albert B. Moore Associates Inc., Lakeville, Connecticut has had a long and successful career as a fashion illustrator for *"Esquire"* and some of the leading women's magazines. He also holds strong views about the energy efficiency—or rather the lack of it—in traditional rectangular frame houses.

Like many others, Mr. Moore is concerned about the cost and availability of fossil fuels within another decade or so and does not like what he sees ahead. There is the very strong possibility that many people buying traditional homes today will be unable to pay for the fuel to heat them long before their 25 to 30-year mortgages are paid off.

In his opinion, there are two areas in which private citizens can make significant savings in fuel consumption: use of the automobile and the home. In the case of the automobile, Detroit through federal mandate has made a 180 degree turn and undertaken the massive effort to replace the heavy old gas guzzlers with a whole new generation of fuel-efficient cars.

As far as housing is concerned, however, Moore feels that the approach has been to insulate structures that were not designed to be energy-conserving in the first place. Of the nine elements that make up the building industry: land acquisition, financing, building contractors, building trades unions, industry associations and professional groups, architects and design engineers, materials suppliers, government building code officials, marketing and sales personnel—he believes that all except the second group are opposed to any fundamental change in methods and have always preferred to continue to use traditional designs and techniques.

There is a very basic reason why Mr. Moore singles out the home financing industry as the most receptive to change: economic conditions before the end of the century may involve them in massive foreclosures on unmarketable homes. As mentioned previously, the owners won't be able to afford to both heat their homes and also make the mortgage payments. Presumably, most potential buyers of these homes would be in the same financial predicament. He has convinced a number of banks and thrift institutions in the Northeast that his solutions to the problem have what it takes for future resale despite their often unusual appearance.

Unlike other dome houses, the Albert B. Moore structures allow considerable variation from the spherical form. They can be either a single or a double curving shell made up of a urethane foam/spray-up cement "sandwich" over a triangular net tension frame. He emphasizes that urethane foam, an insulator which won't crush or crack when cured, should not be confused with the formaldehyde foam which has been the subject of health investigations in housing. In 1981 the American Medical Association gave urethane foam a clean bill of health.

The triangular net tension frame used in a Moore home is structurally sound and accepted by most building codes. It's also versatile: a great variety of shapes are possible with only simple variations in frame geometry. As a result, this type of frame will adapt to different foundation plans: square, rectangular or curved. It can be made of wood, steel, or aluminum members used with pre-stretched steel cable and fasteners.

After the design is completed, the foundation is poured and the first step in the construction of a Moore "foam dome" begins. The tension frame is fabricated at the shop and totally assembled in a folding position. It's then transported to the site, unfolded to its tensed pre-determined three-dimensional position and fastened to its support.

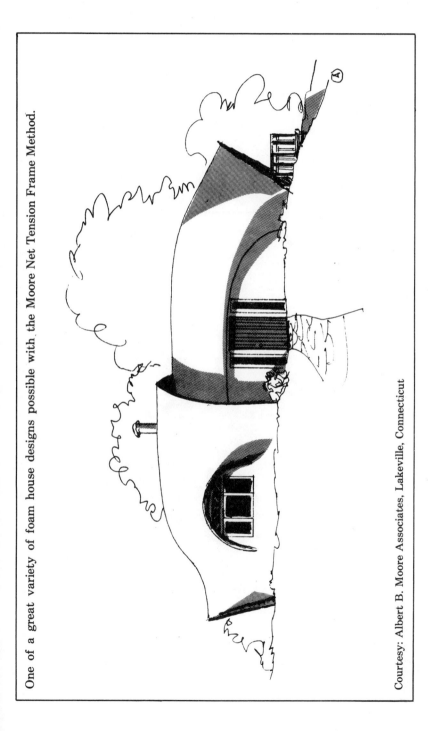

One of a great variety of foam house designs possible with the Moore Net Tension Frame Method.

Courtesy: Albert B. Moore Associates, Lakeville, Connecticut

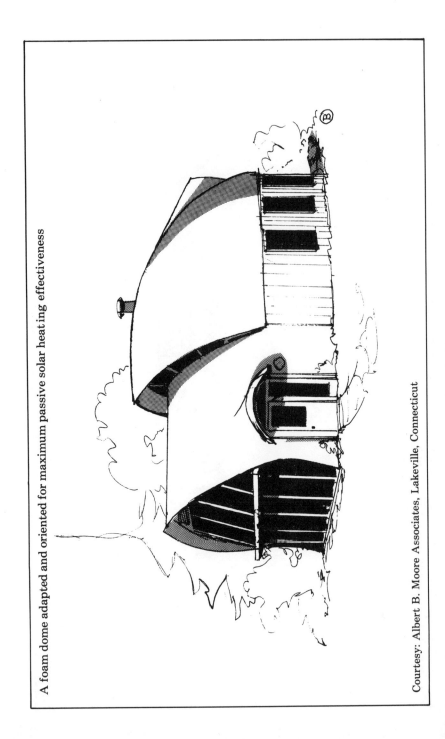

A foam dome adapted and oriented for maximum passive solar heating effectiveness

Courtesy: Albert B. Moore Associates, Lakeville, Connecticut

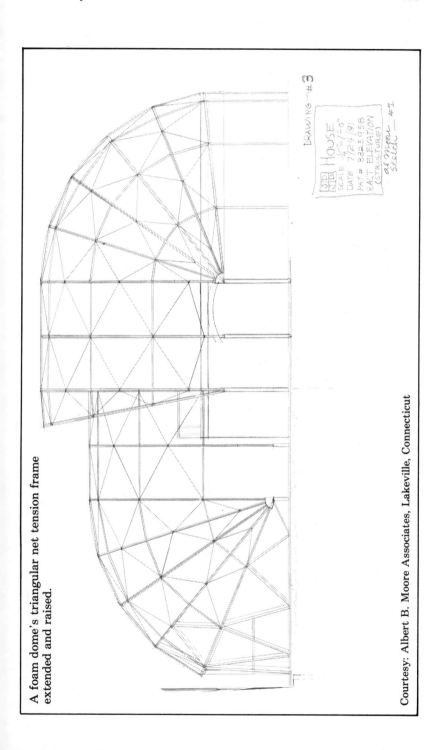

A foam dome's triangular net tension frame extended and raised.

Courtesy: Albert B. Moore Associates, Lakeville, Connecticut

Next, a high-tensile mesh of fiberglass is stretched and fastened over the entire frame. Crews, working from the outside, spray polyurethane foam over the mesh to the desired thickness, usually three to eight inches. When the foam cures, it will have bonded both the frame and mesh into a single homogeneous shell.

After the foam cures, a layer of special fire-retardant cement $5/8$ to 1 inch thick gets sprayed over the interior. At the same time the exterior is sprayed with a special moisture-resistant paint which is also a barrier to ultraviolet rays—other than fire, the sun is urethane foam's only natural enemy. As a last step, doors and windows are molded into the foam/cement sandwich and all joints are sealed against air infiltration. All ventilation is determined by the occupants, either by opening or closing doors or windows, or by special venting provided in the original design.

Depending on the foam's thickness, the completed structure will have an R value between 30 and 50 and can be kept as warm as necessary, if properly sited, by passive solar heating. The cement lining will absorb heat from south-facing windows and massive partitions can be erected behind them to absorb heat during the day and radiate this through most of the night. Or, a swimming pool behind these windows could store enough heat from sunlight to warm the dome after sundown.

Moore Associates' foam domes are not for owner-builders or inexperienced contractors. Special skills and equipment are needed to put up this type of structure, which only factory crews or independent contractors used to this method of construction are likely to have.

Earth Sheltered Homes and Adobe Houses

Both of these approaches appeal to people who like to blend in with their surroundings. "Earth sheltered" means either going underground or else using the earth itself to cover 50 percent or more of a house.

Adobe houses use bricks of local clay, straw and a small amount of emulsified asphalt as a binder. This material has a "natural" look which is popular in the Southwest. Since the bricks are relatively cheap and don't use energy-intensive additives like cement, a larger number can be economically used to build very thick walls. Adobe bricks require no firing and are cured by the sun.

Although stabilized adobe bricks will resist disintegrating in water and can be sealed on the outside against moisture, making them in a rainy climate can be a problem. Unless commercially made bricks are available, adobe construction is probably best suited to areas without heavy rainfall.

Adobe houses are mostly built by their owners, who invest considerable time and effort but get a solid home, at a reasonable cost in building materials. Since this book is intended for people who may only have their weekends free, adobe houses are beyond its scope. Anyone interested in tackling an adobe brick-making and housebuilding project will find these "how to" books helpful:

Making the Adobe Brick Eugene H. Boudreau (Fifth Street Press, 1971) $2.95 paperback

How to Build Adobe Houses Paul Garrison (Tab Books, 1979) $7.95 paperback

The Owner-Built Adobe House Duane Newcomb (Charles Scribners Sons, 1980) $14.95 hardcover

For similar reasons, this book will not attempt to go into earth sheltered housing. Those interested in this type of home presently have two options: (a) invest substantial amounts for architect's services, excavation, massive structures designed to support heavy loads, specialized waterproofing, services of a contractor experienced in this type of construction, filling in, 'berming' or covering the roof and landscaping, or (b) invest considerable time and effort in hiring contractors and building such a home themselves. Two good guides for home-builders are:

Underground Houses Robert L. Roy (Sterling Publishing Co., 1979)

Underground Homes Louis Wampler (Pelican Publishing Company, 1980)

However, earth sheltered housing techniques are being rapidly developed and this may soon be one of the best ways of housing large numbers of people in a limited area with maximum individual privacy. Most of the technology exists, the problem is that builders familiar with it do commercial rather than residential construction.

Two very informative books on the whole subject are also available, both prepared by the Underground Space Center at the University of Minnesota. *Earth Sheltered Housing: Code, Zoning and Financing Issues* (1980), prepared for HUD and available from the U.S. Government Printing Office, should probably be your first purchase since it concentrates more on things that a prospective owner of an earth-covered house would first want to know. The other book *Earth Sheltered Housing Design* (Van Nostrand-Reinhold 1978), is the most detailed, painstakingly researched and complete work available in this field. The technical aspects get a very thorough treatment and the book is available at most larger bookstores.

CHAPTER 9

Low Cost Rural Housing For Moderate Incomes

P eople who plan to buy a house in rural areas generally find conventional financing more difficult to get than homebuyers in suburban communities. A suburban municipality will normally have streets and a full range of services. In this type of setting, a well-built home will usually appreciate in value.

By contrast, a rural home may have to draw its water from a well, generate its own electricity and use a septic tank. Its access road may be dirt or poorly paved. Regardless of how well it's built, there is no guarantee of finding a buyer— unless the house is part of a profitable farm.

To make matters worse, home mortgage money is much harder to come by in rural districts. Many small communities may only have a minor branch office of a commercial bank, and the parent bank may not be interested in financing single-family homes or else the branch office—due to the small volume of such business—won't have anyone qualified to originate a home mortgage.

Many rural houses are bought with a large down payment and a chattel mortgage. A large number of the more isolated homes are paid for entirely in cash.

In short, much of the rural housing scene is simply too sparse and unstructured to interest private lenders. In such a case, rural home buyers in need of financing must turn to the government, either state or federal, for help. The federal agency which provides low-cost financing to rural America is the Farmers Home Administration (FmHA).

Section 502: The FmHA Single-Family Home Loan Program

In 1980 the FmHA completed its 45th year as a supplier of credit to agriculture and rural housing. The agency is part of the U.S. Department of Agriculture, which formally adopted the acronym "FmHA" in 1974 to make a distinction between it and HUD's FHA (Federal Housing Administration). Today, FmHA administers billions of dollars in loan programs.

To qualify, the home buyer must live in a community of fewer than 10,000 which is far enough away from any other large towns to retain its own identity. Communities with populations of between 10,000 and 20,000 may also be included in the Section 502 programs if the Secretaries of USDA and HUD both find that there is a serious lack of mortgage credit.

The borrower's adjusted income must not exceed a specified limit and he or she must be unable to meet the requirements for a conventional mortgage, a loan insured by the FHA or one guaranteed by the VA. Such borrowers may then apply to FMHA for mortgages of up to 33 years at below-market interest rates. Veterans' applications get preference, although they must meet the same requirements as non-veterans.

Unlike the VA guarantees and FHA-insured programs, the FmHA actually originates the mortgage, lends the money and processes or services the payments. As the lender, it reserves the right to periodically review the mortgagor's income, usually every five years or so, to determine whether he or she is still eligible. If the home owner's income has grown enough to handle payments to a private lender, and if private financing is available, the FMHA county supervisor may require that the loan be refinanced.

A modular housing assembly line. A 1,600 square foot house like this, would cost you $33,000 to $41,000.

A double-wide manufactured/mobile home being built.

A double-wide manufactured/mobile home anchored to its foundation, on its own lot. A 1,600 square foot home like this, without land or foundation ($2,000-$3,000), would cost you $28,000 to $36,000.

How a Panelized Home is Erected Courtesy: NAHM

These pictures demonstrate the initial steps in erecting a panelized house. On the first day the floor system is installed.

Later, the interior and exterior wall panels are put in place in a predetermined sequence.

The wall panel sequence insures the efficiency and speed of the work crew.

Roof trusses are then added, followed by the sheathing and waterproof roofing felt.

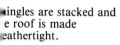

ingles are stacked and e roof is made eathertight.

The final photograph shows the completed home several weeks later.

A completed TECHMAR foam dome. The exterior is coated with a low maintenance elastomeric material which protects the foam from weathering. It is easily cleaned with soap and water. A 1,600 square foot unit would cost approximately $35,000 to $40,000, excluding land.

Courtesy: Better Homes & Gardens Real Estate Service

Spraying steel fiber-reinforced concrete (Shotcrete) over the inside surface of the polyurethane shell. Even in sub-zero weather work proceeds rapidly in a temperature-controlled environment.

Courtesy: Better Homes & Gardens Real Estate Service

FmHA gets most of its funds from fixed-period promissory notes signed by its rural borrowers. When the home buyer receives a check for the loan amount, he or she must also sign a note promising to pay the installments on the dates specified. The agency then sells these notes to *private* investors at the market interest rate, deposits the proceeds with the Rural Housing Insurance Fund, and lends this money out to new borrowers. (FmHA formerly drew funds from the U.S. Treasury to make loans. However, this meant a direct expenditure of federal funds and it was politically expedient to have the private sector supply the money on an insured basis. FmHA can also issue more mortgages this way, without being accountable to anyone except the USDA of which it is a part and the General Accounting Office.)

In any state, the first stage of the pipeline for FmHA's credit and services runs to its state office. Here, the staff is responsible for interpreting policy directions from Washington and supervising and guiding the work of the county offices.

The staffs at the county offices process home loan applications, decide whether applicants are eligible, counsel applicants, appraise existing homes, examine plans and specifications for new homes, inspect construction in progress, and service the mortgages outstanding.

When applying for an FmHA mortgage, the county office may not necessarily be a buyer's first contact. Word may have spread that a builder in the process of putting up a rural development is also assisting buyers to get financing. Builders call this "packaging:" they help applicants to fill out the numerous forms required and then present these to the county office as a completed package. By so doing, they can save an understaffed, overloaded FmHA local office a large amount of processing time.

The next visit for the buyer, however, is always the FmHA county office. When sitting down with the county supervisor, he or she will analyze the buyer's eligibility with respect to family income and assets.

What You Get

Before discussing eligibility, however, you may want to
know what type of shelter FmHA is willing to finance. The
agency provides most of its money for single-family homes
through two programs:

- Section 502 Home Ownership Mortgages to individuals of
  low to moderate income (emergency and special loans come
  under this program).
- Section 504 Home Repair Loans to very low income,
  usually elderly, individuals.

To qualify under either program, a borrower must live in an
area designated on FmHA's state lists and maps as being
rural in character, primarily serving the families who work in
it and in neighboring rural areas.

Making homes available to low and moderate income
families is only a part—though a very large part—of the
agency's Section 502 program. Its general guidelines are to
help borrowers to improve their living standards; to improve
their operations if they are farming or otherwise self-
employed; to obtain safe, decent and sanitary housing; to use
assets, income and credit prudently; to earn enough income
to make the mortgage payments, build equity in their home
and handle day-to-day living expenses; meet their duties and
responsibilities to the community, and move up to conventional or other credit sources in a reasonable period of time.

Section 502 funds may also be used for purposes other than
buying a new or existing homes. According to FmHA: "home
ownership loans may be used to buy, build, improve, repair,
or rehabilitate rural homes and related facilities, and to provide adequate water and waste disposal systems."

The type of home deemed suitable for moderate income
families by FmHA is one that is "modest in size, design and
cost," structurally sound and functionally adequate, with not
more than three bedrooms and a living area not exceeding
1,300 square feet (1,100 square feet is the average). If the
family is a large one, the agency will allow a larger house to
provide more sleeping space.

The FmHA will exempt from the "living area" limitation:
patios, garages, carports, screened or open porches that can-

not be used year-round, unfinished basements, and enclosures for a furnace and hot water heater. These areas, however, must be of reasonable size and not enlarged to get around the space limitation. The site for the home, if not on farmland, should not be larger than one acre.

In addition to the home itself, a Section 502 loan may be used to pay for credit reports charged to the borrower, lawyers' fees, architectural and surveyors' fees, hooking-up utilities, site preparation, plantings around the foundation, lawn seeding, walks, driveways and fences. If other comparable dwellings in the area are normally sold with such appliances, the loan may be used to pay for a kitchen range, refrigerator, washer and dryer. In some cases, the loan may also be applied toward closing costs.

The key phrase governing what you can or cannot use an FmHA mortgage to pay for is "comparable to adequate but modest homes in the area."

For example, if summers are hot but other moderate income houses have no air conditioners, the agency will probably not allow borrowers to buy these appliances with loan money. FmHA will usually veto, or else approve on a case-by-case (large family) basis "desirable but unnecessary" features like an extra bath and bedroom, top-of-the-line bathroom fixtures and kitchen appliances, fireplaces and 2-car garages.

The person who has fairly broad discretion in deciding what you will get for your loan is the FmHA county supervisor. He or she is allowed to advise borrowers on whether the price is right for any given home, and determine whether the price must be lowered. If the seller or builder won't come down, the supervisor can counsel the borrower to look for another house at a lower price. In effect, the county supervisor both sets the maximum amount of the mortgage and also decides the housing options.

The loan may be up to 100 percent of FmHA's appraised value of both site and new home, provided construction inspections are made by FmHA, VA or HUD. A loan may also be 100 percent of the appraised value of a house more than one-year-old, if improvements have been made to it. The maximum repayment period is 33 years.

Who May Qualify?

As currently defined by the Secretary of Agriculture, a family's combined adjusted income must not exceed $15,600 in order to qualify for a moderate income loan. If the family's combined adjusted income is less than $11,200 a year, it may meet the requirements for an interest-credit. These reductions in interest are available for two-year periods and are reevaluated at the end of each period. FmHA also warns that these reductions "will be subject to recapture since (they are) a subsidy that must be repaid."

In addition to meeting the FmHA income requirements, applicants must also:

- Be without decent, safe and sanitary housing.
- Be unable to obtain a loan from private lenders on terms and conditions that they can reasonably be expected to meet.
- Have enough income to pay house payments, insurance premiums, taxes, maintenance costs, other debts and necessary living expenses. Applicants with inadequate repayment ability may obtain cosponsors for the loan.
- Possess the character, ability and experience to meet loan obligations.
- Intend to reside permanently in the house once the loan is issued.

In determining the applicant's earnings, FmHA considers all dependable sources of income including social security, welfare and child-support payments. If adult members of the applicant's family are living with him or her, their income will also be added to the family's total earnings. Excluded from dependable recurring income are things like gifts, bonuses, money earned from jobs which are clearly temporary, payments for foster child care, G.I. Bill payments, scholarships or fellowships which are not paid directly to applicant or spouse, and any one-time sales of machinery, real estate or other property. The income of Section 502 applicants may not be high, but the agency makes sure it's *dependable*.

FmHA will also allow deductions which lower an applicant's annual family income. These are:

- Depreciation expense, as defined by the IRS, stemming from wear, exhaustion and obsolescence of depreciable income-producing property used in the applicant's trade, business or farming operation.
- Business expenses, as defined by the IRS, in excess of the amount actually reimbursed by the employer;
- Expenses paid towards the care of a child or disabled dependent, or an incapacitated spouse, for the purpose of allowing the borrower to continue working at a job. FmHA will not allow a recipient of these payments to be a close relative or dependent of the applicant. There are limits to each type of allowable care expense, and also on total expenses for care.

Interest credits. If applicants whose income does not exceed $11,200 also have a low net worth, they may qualify for interest credits. Elderly couples may usually qualify for these and still retain adequate reserves for medical expenses and hiring others to do maintenance work.

The FmHA adjusts borrowers' income by first lowering total annual income by five percent. Then the total number of minors—members of the immediate family—who live in the homes is multiplied by $300. ("Immediate family" is determined by state law: the term can include children who are the direct issue of the parents, stepchildren, adopted children or those under legal guardianship.) This amount is then subtracted from the lowered annual income.

Mortgagors having interest-credit loans are usually required to make monthly or annual payments equal to at least 20 percent of adjusted income. When these loans are issued, the FmHA county office will usually allow only enough financing for a family's basic needs. The county office will be quite strict in excluding "desirable but unnecessary" features from the house, and will normally limit the living space to 1,060 square feet for an average size family.

An FmHA Closing. The agency states: "the applicant pays for the legal services necessary to guarantee that he has a satisfactory title to the site, for credit reports, and other incidental loan closing costs. These expenses may be included in the loan."

At closing the loan amount will generally be based on the borrower's income at the time the application was approved. If interest credits are involved and 90 days have elapsed between loan approval and the closing, however, the amount of credit will be determined according to the borrower's income at the closing date.

Borrowers earning wages or salary—or who receive other regular monthly income—will repay the loan in equal monthly installments. They enclose their payments with direct payment cards that are mailed to FmHA's financial department. Borrowers who earn income from farming or are similarly self-employed can usually make a single annual payment in the same manner.

As with other closings, the borrower gets a copy of the mortgage or deed of trust. The FmHA also requires that the borrower receive a title insurance owner's policy and a one-year warranty on the house. The agency will also handle any complaints after expiration of the warranty that are justified.

Housing Developments and Section 502

FmHA has this to say about avoiding rural sprawl: "Houses will be located on desirable sites with an assured supply of safe drinking water and suitable arrangements for sewage disposal. In subdivisions, the houses will be sited in an attractive manner to avoid straight line monotony and to accent and preserve the natural advantages of topography, trees and shrubbery. The streets, water and waste disposal systems shall meet FmHA requirements. Funds may be included in the loan to finance lawn seeding and landscaping measures that beautify the home and make it an attractive addition to the community."

The federal government has actually been carrying on a two-pronged community development program. The urban program has been getting most of the publicity and the difficult human problems encountered in cities have generated considerable debate.

The rural program, on the other hand, goes ahead quietly but steadily—except for occasional brushes with environmental groups—building public utilities, water and sewage systems, community recreational facilities, developments for small business and light industry, and single family housing. The Department of Agriculture has estimated that roughly 20 million new housing units will be needed by the year 2,000 to meet rural needs.

Builders who plan rural developments usually prepare a comprehensive proposal for the county supervisor. This proposal will include the plans and specifications for the houses, the mechanical equipment and appliances they will include, their proposed selling price, a map of the site and one showing the subdivisions, street plan, a description of utilities, and an indication of the income categories at which the houses are aimed. It is in the builder's interest to satisfy the comprehensive FmHA regulations covering the planning, location and preparation of building lots.

Applications for these houses will be approved much more quickly, if the county supervisor approves the development and agrees that the builder's houses represent a good value at a fair price. Homes financed by FmHA must meet the same Minimum Property Standards used by HUD-FHA.

Manufactured houses. If a builder is putting up factory-built homes from a nearby manufacturer, FmHA will send its own personnel periodically to inspect these factories.

The agency also requires house manufacturers participating in its program to prepare a statement certifying that the house was constructed in accordance with plans and specifications approved by the FmHA state office. This statement is transmitted to the developer or contractor, who in turn delivers it to the borrower.

PART II:

How to Pay
for It

CHAPTER 10

The Middlemen— How They Can Help You

In any community there will be some owners who sell their homes directly, without listing them with a real estate broker. They usually do this to avoid paying the agent's commission, which can be between five percent and seven percent of the selling price of a house.

Brokers

No real estate agent's commission is paid by you, the buyer, however. Therefore it's to your advantage to consider what good brokers can offer: things like advice about the neighborhood (which they will know thoroughly) and assistance in your house hunting right through to the closing.

So whether you deal directly with homeowners depends very much on your temperament and personal preference. Do you know the neighborhood? Are you tough-minded enough not to overcommit yourself on "just" the house you've been looking for? Can you make "ridiculously" low initial offers to sellers without antagonizing them? Are you perfectly familiar with "creative" financing and able to find institutions to lend you the money you need? In short, are you good at haggling and do you get a kick out of the whole bargaining process? If so, you might do very well in direct dealings with the sellers.

Real Estate Service Agencies

One problem you may face in direct negotiations is that many sellers have very unrealistic notions about the value of their houses. One way to "pre-screen" the owners you talk to—making sure that they have at least been well-counseled—is to contact the Real Estate Service Agencies in the area (for help in locating these write National Association of Real Estate Service Agencies, 6200 Old Keene Mill Court, Springfield, Virginia 22152.)

A Real Estate Service Agency provides all the services of a full-service broker except two important ones: the time-consuming transporting of prospects to and from the houses on sale, with stops for selling and showing; and usually access to a multiple listing service.

By not having to bother with transportation—and the woman or man hours invested in guiding buyers around the neighborhood—these firms can estimate their remaining expenses quite accurately. As a result, they are able to charge sellers a *flat fee* which is usually less than $1,000, even for expensive homes.

For its fee, the service agency will counsel the seller on how to show and price the house. The agency will also advertise the house, supply signs for the front lawn, prepare the sales contract and help with the closing.

But remember that you have no broker or salesperson to mediate if the seller refuses to come down, or to soothe ruffled feelings in the event of a personality clash. If you use service agency listings, getting the house you like at the lowest price will depend entirely on your own talent for dickering.

Using Full-Service Real Estate Brokers

A *good* real estate broker can be the most important single aid to your finding the particular type of house you want at a fair price. This may surprise those who feel that agents will automatically take the seller's side, since the seller pays their commission. Although some do, many are surprisingly impartial.

A broker will usually have a very accurate idea of a home's true current market value. If your initial offer is lower than the seller will accept but within reason, the broker will usually pass it on to the seller to get the negotiating process started.

Don't forget that if the broker can successfully close the sale between you and the seller, it is *you* who will be the new owner of the house. It is to you that future buyers may come for suggestions on where to find a good real estate agent. And brokers are very much aware that, if you should ever have to sell your house, whether or not you become *their* client may depend on whether your buying experience with them was good or bad.

Listings. Houses are listed for sale in three ways. Either way, since the seller pays the commission, the price of the house will not be affected very much.

The *exclusive right to sell* is a widely-used arrangement. Here the broker gets a commission regardless of who sells the house, and consequently will spend the time and money to advertise the house to sell it as quickly as possible.

If an *exclusive agency* is used, the listing broker is entitled to full commission for a period of time specified in the agreement, usually 90 days. If another broker should sell the house during this period, his commission would come out of the selling price after the listing broker received the full agreed percentage.

In an *open listing* only one commission is involved—to the broker who actually closes the sale although all may compete to sell the house. While some real estate agents profess not to like this arrangement, bear in mind that good ones will not waste their time and yours by taking you to houses you don't want. And if they show you a house that you *do* like, the probability of another buyer putting down money on it within 48 hours is not very large—houses at near market prices take time to sell.

One point to remember with open listings: in some cases buyer and seller have tried to close the deal privately, in order to avoid paying the broker's commission. This is against the law in all 50 states—the broker is legally entitled to the agreed commission of the sale. Another thing to keep in mind when bargaining is that sellers have the right to set a minimum price onto which brokers must add their commission. So if the seller won't take a penny less than $50,000, and $50,500 is *your* absolute limit, the $500 difference doesn't leave the agent much incentive to spend further time trying to close the sale. Agents would be spending their time much more profitably in steering you to homes with more flexible sellers or, if you had consistently insisted in offering prices too low for their neighborhoods, on other buyers.

Multiple Listing Service. This is a definite convenience to brokers, sellers and buyers in large metropolitan areas enclosed by a ring of suburbs. An MLS gives each broker an up-to-date computerized list of the houses handled by the other brokers who participate in the service, usually through their local board of realtors. If your agent sells you a home which another participant has listed with MLS, both the listing and participating brokers will split the commission equally. This does not affect the price of the house for the buyer. It is a service increasing your chances of finding a house at a fair price. It also greatly expands the range of choices which your broker can show you. But keep in mind that one of the main reasons for using real estate brokers is their detailed and accurate knowledge of the neighborhood. If you feel that your broker is showing you a house too far from his or her home territory, make sure you can put your questions about schools, commuting, etc., to the listing broker.

Brokers and salespeople. In your dealings with real estate agents you can expect to encounter both brokers, who run their own agencies, and the salespeople who work for them. In all states both brokers and salespeople are classified as professionals and are required to be licensed (states do vary considerably in their educational requirements for licensing, however).

Beyond the licensing requirement, there are those agencies who have joined their local real estate board (which will usually not accept part-timers as members). A smaller portion of the local board members will have joined one of the two national associations. By so doing, these agents have publicly agreed to abide by the ethical standards of their profession and to permit the national association to review their actions if this should be necessary.

Many buyers turn to the most visible group of real estate agents: the heavily advertised nationwide franchises or national real estate companies. These agencies are still staffed by local people, but can draw on the expertise of the franchisor in arranging things like alternate financing between buyer and seller when mortgage money is tight.

To locate a broker, try real estate brokers in your own community for leads on good brokers in the areas where you plan to look. Most real estate brokers have fairly broad information networks, attend trade conventions where they meet their peers and sometimes get feedback from former clients who have moved. You could also try the following sources in your chosen areas:

- The local board of real estate brokers;
- The local chamber of commerce;
- Other homeowners.
- The town clerks in these municipalities (who are usually long-time residents, know the community thoroughly and are involved whenever the town acquires or disposes of real estate.)

Spotting the real professional. When you begin your house hunting, you'll be dealing with people who sell homes for a living not five but seven days a week (most home buyers hold jobs and only have free time on weekends). Many real estate agents might have considerable empathy for the old sailing ditty:

"Six days shalt thou labor, doing all thou art able; The seventh the same, and haul up the cable."

Most agents will be experienced in the art of selling you a house, and some will have had considerable formal training in industry seminars on the subject.

The best agents for *you* are the ones who take a long-term view of their profession. They may have superior persuasive skills of which they're justly proud, but they also know that if they fail to protect your interests as well as the seller's, they've failed to measure up to their profession's code of ethics and have probably lost you as a future customer. In a recent *New York Times* article, "How to Choose a Real Estate Agent," Deborah Rankin said: "Today your best agent may be someone who can skillfully maneuver buyers and sellers through the intricacies of 'creative financing.' There are at least forty different ways of financing a sale, and if an agent can't name at least ten right off the bat, you might want to find someone else."

Here are a few things that a real pro will *not* do:

- Immediately "come on strong" like some door-to-door salesmen. The agent will be relaxed, smile warmly and usually use the soft-sell—although you can expect enthusiasm for the community (if agents did not like the area, they would be working somewhere else).

- Take you on a tour of houses without first going through a detailed interview to find out your likes, dislikes, financial position and seriousness of intent to buy (part of the agent's responsibility to the seller is to screen out "just lookers");

- Take you to a number of houses that you wouldn't want or can't afford (the interview will have given the agent a good idea of what you are looking for and how much you can pay);

- Disagree with you, at least openly. Agents are trained to skip your objections—for the moment—and concentrate on those things about a house that you like. (Side-stepping a customer's initial objections, stressing an item's positive points and then, if the customer shows strong interest, minimizing the negative aspects is a standard technique in most types of selling.)

- Be too concerned at the reduction in commission if your bid of, say, $58,000 is accepted by a seller who was asking $60,000. (A 7 percent commission on $60,000 would have been $4,200. On $58,000 the agent would get $4,060. The difference is $140, and in the case of a 50-50 split would be $70—peanuts!)

*Do, however, avoid agents who try to pressure you into buying *right away* at the asking price. If they're so hungry for a quick profit they may take an equally short term view of a professional broker's other responsibilities to the buyer.

- Offer legal advice or technical advice concerning the construction of a house. They may, however, refer you to local professionals qualified in these fields.

- Deal further with buyers who allow him or her to show them homes they have already seen with another broker (who has the right to sue in such cases);

- Continue to smile warmly and show enthusiasm if a buyer is repeatedly late for appointments, has given the agent incorrect information or otherwise shows a disregard for the value of the agent's time. Real estate agents work on commission, and wasted time can mean lost income.

The interview. As mentioned above, the purpose of the interview is to provide the agents with the information they need in order to do the best job for both buyer and seller. Another reason for the interview is to inform you of the things a home buyer needs to know.

Typically, agents will tell you how an offer to buy is made and what negotations are involved. They will explain about "binders:" these are a written notice of agreement between buyer and seller, which has the effect of withdrawing the house from the market until a regular sales contract can be drawn up. A binder usually involves your paying a few hundred dollars "earnest money."

Agents will also explain what a contract of sale involves and how much deposit you may have to pay. You should make sure you can pay any deposits into an escrow account at the lending bank. Such deposits are protected by state law and you are assured of getting back your money if, through no fault of your own, the deal falls through. The agent will tell you what's involved in getting a mortgage, and what alternative forms of financing may be available. (Be sure to discuss these with the next professional on this list: your real estate lawyer. Sellers participating in alternative financing should also consult *their* lawyers.)

Settlement costs and the closing process will also be explained to you. And the agent will often ask you questions like these:

- "Do you presently own your home?" Then, if the answer is "yes:"
- "How much do you still owe on it?" (If your equity is substantial, you are in a stronger position to buy another. First-time buyers can expect to be asked detailed questions about their other assets.)
- "Do you plan to sell it before you buy another?" (If you have to sell your old home in order to pay for the new one, the broker may have to rule out some sellers who can't wait.)
- If your present home is in the agent's area: "Is your home listed with another broker or do you plan to sell it yourself?" (The answer will tell him if he can acquire another listing.)
- "Do you agree to my calling you any time I find a property that looks right for you? Remember, I'll be working for you seven days a week." (If you reply that you're willing to be called during the evening or on weekends, it's an indication that you really want to buy.)
- "How long have you been house-hunting?" (If it's over six months or a year, the agent may feel that you are more interested in viewing other people's homes than in buying.)
- "Have you had a chance to look at houses with any other brokers?" (Here, the agent hopes to learn about the competition and perhaps pick up a few leads on sales opportunities the other brokers have missed.)
- "What houses did you like best?" (The agent will then know what types of property to show you.)
- "Did you have a reason for not buying any of these?" (If your reasons hinged on something like disagreement between you and your spouse, the agent will at least be prepared if the problem comes up again. If you were actually outbid for the house, you show a motivation to buy.)

Developer's Sales Agents

If you visit new homes offered by developers, the negotiating process is much simpler: the salesperson can describe the houses, answer your specific questions on them and inform you of the price the builder has set. That's it as far as bargaining goes. The builder can and often does help you with your loan financing when mortgage money is scarce and his houses would otherwise remain unsold. If interest rates are very high, the builder can offer a "buy down" in which he will pay the bank an amount of money equal to several percentage points of your interest rate for a specified period of years (see Chapter 14).

You'll Need a Good Real Estate Lawyer

Errors and omissions in housing transactions can be very, very expensive! The seller needs legal advice and so do you, the buyer. Remember that a verbal promise is worthless—if an implied condition is not set forth in the contract for sale, you have no redress later if it is not fulfilled.

The widely varying state laws affecting binders, sales contracts, title searches, title insurance and other necessary documents in real estate transactions mean that you should have legal advice from the start of the negotiations through the closing. And not from just any lawyer, but from one specializing in real estate. For example, most lawyers might be able to handle most of the documentation, but if there should be tenants still living in the property a good real estate lawyer will delay the closing until all leases are cleared up and they are actually off the premises. Removing them after the closing could be very difficult in many areas with tenant protection laws.

When lining up a lawyer, ask at the beginning for an estimate of fees and other legal expenses for the entire transaction. Experienced real estate lawyers should be able to give you a fairly close estimate, and may either agree at this point to a flat fee or else tell you what their hourly charge will be.

It is sometimes easier to locate a lawyer in smaller, more isolated communities. There may only be one or two in

general practice in such areas, who out of necessity are also
involved in real estate.

Locating a good real estate lawyer in heavily populated
built-up areas can be a problem, however. You will usually get
little help from the bar association, since these will not recommend one particular lawyer over another. If the bar association supports a Legal Referral Service, this service may
recommend several lawyers specializing in residential real
estate, which will at least narrow the field for you. Other
people you could contact are:

- The mortgage officers of local savings and loan associations, mutual savings banks and commercial banks who
  deal in home mortgages (preferably banks who will not be
  issuing your loan, if you already have one picked out—he
  may be their own lawyer);
- Homeowners who have recently moved to the area;
- State or local consumer organizations.

Appraisers and House Inspectors

Once you have focused on a house that seems to meet your
requirements, it's a good idea to have its value appraised. If
you are taking out a mortgage, appraisal comes with the loan:
the FHA, VA and most private insurors will not underwrite a
mortgage without an appraisal of the property's market
value.

You will also want to have the house inspected for possible
construction defects: this applies to new homes as well as to
older ones. It is important *not* to use an appraiser for this
work, since not all the things you are checking at this point
affect a home's market value. Many are hidden and difficult
to spot and factor into the appraised price.

One thing to check for is termites. Make sure your contract
requires a termite inspection at the seller's expense. Then if
there is termite damage, the seller will be required to exter-
minate and repair.

For inspecting the rest of the house your best bet is a professional engineer. You can locate them under Building Inspection Service in the Yellow Pages and they usually charge

between \$100 and \$200. For this fee they will go over the house and look at areas such as:

- The foundation (settling, cracks);
- The basement (water seepage, cracks);
- Load-bearing beams (sagging, damp rot);
- Floors (should be solid and level—severely sloping floors can mean structural problems);
- Walls (large cracks which can be caused by settling of the foundation);
- Ceilings (sagging, water seepage);
- Stairs (condition of treads and risers, does whole stair sag to one side—which can be caused by a settling foundation;
- Attic and roof (rafters, roof tiles, quality of insulation);
- Doors and windows (leaks, rot, out-of-square);
- Chimneys (condition of fireproof bricks, flues, dampers, flashing where it joins the roof—which can leak);
- Plumbing and wiring (if outdated or inadequate, these can be expensive to upgrade).

If you buy a home far from the city, check with the county building inspector's office. They may be willing to inspect the house for you. Look at the blank home inspection form from the AA Home Inspection Service, Inc., of Springfield, New Jersey to get an idea of the detailed investigation a good service will give you. It's better to know before you buy, than after, how much restoration needs to be done to your chosen home.

Table VII:
Home Inspection Checklist

Courtesy of:
AA Home Inspection Service, Inc.
P.O. Box 248   Springfield, NJ 07081

Date _____

For _____   Location _____

_____   _____

_____   _____

Phone _____   Inspection Date _____

DESCRIPTION OF HOUSE:

Age _____   Type _____

Rooms: LR _____   DR _____

LR/DR Comb. _____   Kitchen _____

Eat-in Kitchen _____   Rec. Room _____

Bedrooms _____   Bathrooms _____

½ Bathrooms _____   Other _____

_____

Garage: Detached _____   Attached _____

Under _____   No. cars _____

EXTERIOR:

Slope _____   Runoff _____

Foundation Material _____   Cond. _____

Walks: Front _____   Cond. _____

Side _____   Cond. _____

Rear _____   Cond. _____

Veneer _____ Cond. _____

Front Stoop _____ Cond. _____

Rear Porch _____ Cond. _____

Other _____ Cond. _____

Paint _____ Cond. _____

Caulking _____ Cond. _____

Siding _____ Cond. _____

Retaining Walls _____ Cond. _____

Roof/Reroof _____ Cond. _____

Gutters _____ Cond. _____

Leaders _____ Cond. _____

Leaders piped underground to _____

Comments _____

_____

Screens _____ Cond. _____

Storm Sash _____ Cond. _____

Windows _____ Cond. _____

Storm Doors _____ Cond. _____

Weatherstripping: Doors _____ Cond. _____

Windows _____ Cond. _____

Garage Doors & Jambs _____ Cond. _____

Driveway location _____

Width _____ Material _____ Cond. _____

Curbing _____ Cond. _____

Electric Service _____ Conduit _____

Service Cable _____ Outside Equipment _____

Coments _____

_____

_____

GARAGE:

Walls _____   Cond. _____

Floor _____   Cond. _____

Doors _____   Cond. _____

Electric: Y/N _____   RC Units: Y/N _____

Comments _____

_____

BASEMENT:

Full _____   Partial _____   Crawl Space _____

None _____   Finished _____   Part Finished _____

_____

_____

Walls _____   Cond. _____

_____

Floors _____   Cond. _____

_____

Sump pit/pump _____   Cond. _____

_____

Water Penetration _____

_____

Correction Recommended _____

_____

Room _____ Windows _____ Doors _____

Room _____ Windows _____ Doors _____

Room _____ Windows _____ Doors _____

Room _____ Windows _____ Doors _____

Room _____ Windows _____ Doors _____

KITCHEN:

Cabinets _____ Cond. _____

Counter Top _____ Backsplash _____ Edge _____

Cond. _____

Oven _____ Cond. _____

Brand_____

Burners_____ Cond. _____

Brand_____

Vent Fan _____ Cond. _____

Dishwasher: Built-in _____ Portable _____

   Brand_____ Cond. _____

Other equipment _____

Cond. _____

Windows _____ Cond. _____

Doors_____ Cond. _____

Floor _____ Cond. _____

Room _____   Windows _____   Doors _____

Room _____   Windows _____   Doors _____

Room _____   Windows _____   Doors _____

Room _____

Room _____

Room _____

Room _____

Room _____

ATTIC:

Accessability _____   Lighted _____

Insulation _____   Ventilation _____

Floor _____   Rafters _____

Water Penetration _____

_____

FIREPLACES:

Yes _____   No _____   Number _____

_____

_____

PLUMBING:

Water Lines _____ Sewer Lines _____

City Water _____ City Sewer _____

Gas _____ Septic _____

Hot Water _____ Cond. _____

Brand _____ Size _____

Fuel _____ Pressure _____

Comments _____

_____

HEATING:

Forced Air _____ Warm Air _____

Steam _____ Hot Water _____

Other _____

Brand _____ Cond. _____

Zones _____ Output _____

Thermostats _____ Filters _____

Overall Cond. _____

Humidifier _____ Cond. _____

Brand _____ Type _____

Comments _____

_____

_____

AIR CONDITIONING:

Brand _____ Size _____

Condensate Line _____

Location of Compressors _____

Location of Registers _____

Comments _____

_____

_____

ELECTRICAL:

Service _____ Size _____

Breakers _____ Fuses _____

Circuits Used _____ Circuits Available _____

Brand of Panel _____

Comments _____

_____

_____

MISCELLANEOUS EQUIPMENT & INSTALLATIONS:

Water Softener _____ Smoke Detector _____

Burglar Alarm _____ Fire Alarm _____

Patio _____ Outdoor Gas Barbecue _____

Swimming Pool _____ Underground Sprinkler _____

Other _____

Other _____

Other _____

Other _____

Other _____

Other _____

SUMMARY_____

_____

_____

_____

_____

_____

_____

_____

_____

_____

_____

_____

COMMENTS _____

_____

_____

_____

_____

_____

_____

_____

_____

_____

_____

The Insurance Agent's Role

If you already own a house, you'll want to discuss the termination of your present policy with your insurance agent. If you will not be financing the buyer or allowing the buyer to assume your old mortgage, your interest in the house ends with the settlement—then the time to terminate your homeowner's policy is at the closing.

However, if the sale involves arrangements that continue to give you liability for the property, the insurance taken out by the new buyer will also affect you. In such a case, make sure your lawyer and insurance agent tell you what must be included in the new policies to protect your secondary liability. (For example your name and the phrase "as your interest may appear" in the new policies cover you in the event of any property damage which they include.)

And make sure to consult your insurance agent about protection during the move—when your household furnishings are enroute to your new home. Your agent may also be able to help you locate another firm that can write the insurance protection you'll need after you move in.

If you are a first-time buyer planning to take out a mortgage, you'll find that the lender will require you to carry adequate property and fire insurance. You will also have to pay for a title insurance policy which protects the lender in case anything was missed in the title search. If you want title protection as well, you'll have to take out an extra policy.

If you get an FHA-insured loan, you will also be required to take out mortgage insurance, on which there is a ½ of 1 percent service charge that is added to the interest. Private mortgage insurers may also require a mortgage insurance policy. Any insurance companies still in the single-family residential mortgage business will make one of their own life policies a condition for granting the loan.

You will need additional insurance protection when you acquire the deed to your house. Most important is personal liability insurance in case someone is injured on your property—this is normally included in your comprehensive homeowner's policy. Adequate insurance against burglary is also advisable.

If your mortgage is a large one, you may sleep more comfortably if you have mortgage disability insurance. This will guarantee regular monthly payments for a specified period, in case you should be laid up through illness or an accident.

CHAPTER 11

Loan Shopping and Qualifying

When you start looking for the best deal on a home loan, the mortgage officer on the other side of the desk will in turn be looking at your three C's: capacity, credit and character. The first two will be evaluated on the basis of existing facts about your finances, while the third will be largely a subjective opinion.

First put your financial house in order

Capacity means your ability to make the monthly payments. The lender first looks at your present income level and its likelihood of continuing and increasing (in the opinion of your employer).

Credit or creditworthiness is simply your record of having paid off previous loans. The lender will ask you to fill out an application for credit and then have this checked by a firm which specializes in individual credit reports. (If this should happen to be your first application for a loan of any kind, it could be as difficult to prove your creditworthiness as for someone with a record of late or uneven payments.)

Character is what the lender will often evaluate in creditworthy cases where income just barely meets the bank's guidelines for the loan amount at the going interest rate.

Since this judgment will vary from lender to lender, you could well be granted a loan by one bank if rejected by another—provided the credit reports have been favorable. It pays to try them all.

If you've already estimated what you can afford to pay for a house, the next step here is to prepare yourself for your visit to the bank by calculating your net worth. Then there are a number of things that a mortgage loan officer will ask for that can be prepared ahead of time.

Qualifying

If you are working with a real estate broker, he or she will already have outlined some or all of the following things that a lender will want to see.

In fact, if you've found a broker willing to work hard in your interest, it might be a good idea to visit the lender together. Don't worry about revealing private financial matters to a third party—the broker's ability to get you the house you want depends very much on your ability to carry financing. A good agent will already have asked you much the same questions you can expect from the mortgage loan officer.

When you apply for a mortgage the lender will want (and will verify):

- If you are salaried, what you earn each month before taxes, and also your co-borrower's gross monthly income. You will be asked for a copy of the latest W-2 form that accompanied your income tax.
- The name and address of your previous employer, if you've been less than two years with your present one.
- If self-employed, signed copies of your federal income tax returns for the past two years and a financial statement. Should you have an audited profit-and-loss statement, they will also want to look at this.
- Current information on your savings accounts (balances, account numbers, and the names and addresses of the institutions).

- A complete list of your assets (checking accounts, tax refunds, life insurance cash or loan values, pending gifts and bonuses, stocks, bonds, certificates, vacation homes, boats, cars, jewelry, valuable collections, antiques).

- A complete list of your liabilities (name and address of each lender, the amount of the loan still outstanding, the item's current value and the lender's reference number for the loan).

- Your Social Security number and that of any co-signer to the mortgage (such as your spouse or third party).

- Your previous address, if you've not lived at your present one for at least two years.

Also, take along your checkbook. The lender will ask you to pay for the credit check and the appraisal of the house on which the mortgage is being considered.

One of the things the mortgage officer will do with the information you have given him is compute your net worth. Since you've already done this, you have a good idea of what his dollar figure will be. He will then compare this net worth to the amount of borrowing revealed in your debt history.

This comparison will strongly influence his evaluation for the third C, your character. If you've borrowed a lot but have a high net worth, it's an indication that you have used your credit wisely. On the other hand, applicants who have borrowed heavily and have a low net worth to show for it are suspect—unless they can prove that illness or layoffs made the loans necessary to pay for essential living or medical expenses.

And, of course, a high net worth means you have a cushion against inability to make monthly payments. In difficult periods such assets can usually be converted into cash.

For younger buyers who have had less time to accumulate assets, it's also a good idea to bring along any testimonials to their potential for advancement. Favorable letters from employers, good conduct service discharges, even press clippings of solid achievements in business or their community, may serve to mark them in the loan officer's eyes as individuals of promise. After all, mortgage officers *are* human—they will react to positive individual attributes and be much less likely to regard the applicant as a statistic.

Buy your lot ahead of time. You may plan to buy a manufactured home or finish a shell. Your ready cash is probably more than enough for the down payment, but there's a possiblity that your income level may not qualify you at the going interest rate. In this case, try approaching the bank as a landowner—it can add to your stature as well as your net worth *and* will reduce the size of the loan.

The Underwriters—How They Affect Your Mortgage

The need for insuring or guaranteeing a mortgage comes from a small down payment. When the owner's equity in a home is very low the lender runs a greater risk than prudent management of a home loan portfolio normally allows. When a third party steps in and underwrites the mortgage, the risk to both lenders and subsequent investors is transferred to the underwriter.

Insured home mortgages will either be "conventional," insured by a private mortgage insurance company or else government-insured.

Conventional mortgages. There are currently 15 private mortgage insurance companies (13 in the USA and 2 in Canada) who are members of the Mortgage Insurance Companies of America (MICA). These firms are subject to the laws of the states in which they operate, although FNMA and FHLMC—which purchase low down payment conventional loans on the strength of private mortgage insurance—also exercise some supervision of an MIC's financial and underwriting operations.

Up to the present the majority of privately insured mortgages have been originated through savings and loan associations, commercial banks and, increasingly, mortgage companies.

An MIC will insure the "risk portion" of a loan: that part (averaging 22 percent nationwide) which in case of default might not be covered by sale of the house. A local slump in housing prices, neglect of the property by the owner, unpaid interest and principal, and costs of repossession and resale could all contribute to such a shortfall. Typically, the insured risk portion will be the top 20 percent of a 90 percent loan and the top 25 percent of a 95 percent loan. This latter percentage is called the loan-to-value ratio.

While premium plans will vary among the different MIC's, one that is widely used involves a first year charge of ½ of 1 percent on a 90 percent loan and 1 percent on a 95 percent loan. Thereafter, the annual premium is ¼ of 1 percent of the declining balance regardless of the original loan-to-value ratio.

Like the government-insured loan programs, private mortgage insurance enables borrowers to obtain a mortgage with a low down payment. The majority of loans insured by MICs are to moderate income families and in 1980 the average mortgage insured by the industry was slightly under $50,000, the average house purchase price being about $55,000. In the first five months of 1981 the industry insured a total of 139,774 home mortgages.

The industry's figures for 1980 show that 70 percent of the mortgages underwritten were on existing homes and 30 percent on new homes. By neighborhood location 35 percent of MIC-insured homes were in urban areas, 57 percent were in suburbs and the remaining 8 percent in rural or resort areas.

At present the private mortgage insurance companies' total assets are more than $1.7 billion and their contingency reserves at the end of 1980 totaled $834 million (half of every MIC's earned premium dollar goes into a 10-year reserve which cannot be tapped without the approval of the state regulator and then only if losses exceed 35 percent of earned premiums). The companies have a total of 240 regional underwriting offices which function in all 50 states. Thirty states are served by eight or more MICs and no state has less than four. The industry is highly competitive.

A lender wishing to offer conventional insured loans first applies for master policies with several MICs. The insuror's master policy defines the procedures by which a lender will insure the loan, outlines the steps to be followed when borrowers become delinquent on their payments, and explains how to determine the insuror's liability and get reimbursed when a claim is necessary. Overall, the master policy sets forth the terms and conditions that both insurer and lender will follow in doing business.

Both FNMA and FHLMC require MICs to evaluate lenders as to their suitability in originating mortgages for secondary market sale. When an MIC receives a request for a master policy from a lender it will therefore evaluate the lender's:

- Net worth and quality of assets;
- Mortgage servicing ability;
- Methods of handling delinquent loans;
- Appraisal of the underwriting staffs' professional caliber.

Once lenders receive their master policies they can apply for insurance on individual mortgages. First, they will verify the borrower's credit, employment data and appraise the property. After deciding to take on the bulk of the mortgage, they apply to the MIC for underwriting insurance on the risk portion. The MIC will review the lender's loan package of verified information, based on independent underwriting standards, and issue a commitment of insurance.

If a borrower misses a payment, the lender must report this to the MIC who insured the loan. Should delinquent payments continue, the lender must foreclose and acquire a saleable title to the property. On receiving a claim with evidence of title, the MIC will either: (a) pay the lender's entire claim and take title to the property (between 30 and 40 percent of claims are handled this way, or (b) pay either 20 percent or 25 percent of the total claim, depending on the policy's original loan-to-value ratio.

A lender's claim normally includes costs such as accumulated interest, real estate taxes, fire and hazard insurance premiums, attorney's and trustee's fees, court costs, property maintenance fees and unpaid principal balance due on the mortgage.

The lender may cancel the insurance at any point during the term of the mortgage.

MORTGAGE INSURANCE COMPANIES OF AMERICA

MAIN OFFICES

**AMERICAN MORTGAGE
INSURANCE COMPANY**
P.O. Box 27387
Raleigh, NC 27611
5401 Six Forks Road
Raleigh, NC 27609
(919) 782-7810
800-334-9270
800-662-7761 (within NC)

**COMMERCIAL CREDIT MORTGAGE
INSURANCE COMPANY**
300 St. Paul Place
Baltimore, MD 21202
(301) 332-2900

**COMMONWEALTH MORTGAGE
ASSURANCE COMPANY**
1420 Walnut Street, Suite 200
Philadelphia, PA 19102
(215) 545-7200
800-523-1988
800-462-1586 (within PA)

**FOREMOST GUARANTY
CORPORATION**
131 West Wilson Street
Madison, WI 53703
(608) 251-2200
800-356-8159
800-362-8047 (within WI)

**HOME GUARANTY INSURANCE
CORPORATION**
P.O. Box 24718
180 East Belt Boulevard
Richmond, VA 23224
(804) 233-3021
800-446-3874
800-552-3931 (within VA)

**INTEGON MORTGAGE GUARANTY
CORPORATION**
420 N. Spruce Street
Winston-Salem, NC 27102
(919) 725-7261
800-334-8697
800-642-0584 (within NC)

**INVESTORS MORTGAGE
INSURANCE COMPANY**
P.O. Box 570
225 Franklin Street
Boston, MA 02102
(617) 482-0610
800-225-1580
800-882-1686 (within MA)

**MORTGAGE GUARANTY
INSURANCE CORPORATION**
P.O. Box 488
MGIC Plaza
Milwaukee, WI 53201
(414) 347-6442
800-558-9900
800-242-9275 (within WI)

PMI MORTGAGE INSURANCE CO.
601 Montgomery Street
San Francisco, CA 94111
(415) 788-7878
800-227-4666
800-652-1777 (within CA)

**REPUBLIC MORTGAGE
INSURANCE COMPANY**
P.O. Box 2514
Winston-Salem, NC 27102
7820 Silas Creek Parkway Extension
Winston-Salem, NC 27106
(919) 724-1986
800-334-8610 (Eastern US)
800-334-8681 (Western US)
800-642-0833 (within NC)

**TICOR MORTGAGE INSURANCE
COMPANY**
6300 Wilshire Boulevard
Los Angeles, CA 90048
(213) 852-6600
800-421-0791
800-252-0079 (within CA)

UNITED GUARANTY
CORPORATION
P.O. Box 21567
Greensboro, NC 27420
201 North Elm Street, Suite 900
Greensboro, NC 27401
(919) 373-0863
800-334-8966
800-632-0253 (within NC)

VEREX ASSURANCE, INC.
P.O. Box 7066
150 E. Gilman Street
Madison, WI 53707
(608) 257-2527
800-356-8080
800-362-8070 (within WI)

INSMOR MORTGAGE INSURANCE
COMPANY
P.O. Box 56
Royal Trust Tower, Suite 3304
Toronto-Dominion Centre
Toronto, Ontario, Canada M5K 1E7
(416) 868-0880

THE MORTGAGE INSURANCE
COMPANY OF CANADA
Suite 1200
401 Bay Street
Toronto, Ontario, Canada M5H 2Y4
(416) 366-6231

FHA-insured mortgages. The Federal Housing Administration was created by the National Housing Act of 1934 to restructure home mortgage financing and create a stable mortgage market nationwide. FHA's accomplishments are one of the significant federal agency success stories. FHA is now part of HUD.

The agency can point with justifiable pride to an orderly home financing market in which private companies now flourish, and has contributed to forming a strong secondary market for selling packages of home mortgages to investors.

The FHA loan assistance program is a broad one which falls into two broad categories: unsubsidized, where the agency competes with private industry and is allowed to make a profit, and subsidized programs aimed at areas and families where qualifying for a loan would not be possible without government help.

FHA insures 100 percent of a loan, not just the risk portion. The amount of money lent will be based on the FHA-appraised value of a house and its maximum loan limit for the area.

Unsubsidized FHA home loan insurance programs. These currently include the "regular" Section 203(b) home mortgage insurance program, the Section 244 coinsurance program and the Section 270 "245 GPM" graduated payment mortgage program.

Section 203(b). This is the program most prospective home buyers will encounter. It covers one-to-four-family homes and FHA will insure mortgages to finance their construction, purchase or improvement (existing houses) and also to refinance indebtedness on existing houses. The homes must meet HUD Minimum Property Standards which require them to be well built, suitably located and liveable.

The maximum limit on a 203(b) single family home loan is presently $67,500 ($90,000 in certain designated high cost areas). The borrower must pay an annual insurance premium of ½ of 1 percent of the average balance of the year's unpaid principal over the life of the mortgage.

FHA's house appraisal not only determines a "fair value" (which will also be the limit of the loan) but also ensures that it complies with HUD-FHA structural and livability requirements. This certification assures buyers against dilapidated housing and poor construction—beyond this, the house could range from being in reasonably good condition to a superb example of the builder's art.

You compute the down payment on an FHA-insured mortgage by adding 3 percent of the first $25,000 to 5 percent of the balance. On a $67,500 loan this would amount to:

$25,000 $\times$ .03 = $ 750
$42,500 $\times$ .05 = $2,125

$2,875 total down payment

FHA also prohibits the lender from including a prepayment penalty and requires that the mortgages it insures be assumable by subsequent buyers. "Due on Sale" clauses (the right of the lender to call the loan at time of sale) are not allowed.

The maximum allowable interest rate on FHA-insured mortgages is set by the Secretary of HUD. It is usually in line with the interest rate on a VA-guaranteed mortgage. The rate will vary from time to time but is usually several percentage points below the going market rate. This difference is the reason for lenders charging discounts or "points."

Lenders and FHA mortgages. Many lenders follow FHA guidelines in appraising homes for all mortgages, be they government insured, privately insured or non-insured. Mortgage companies, sometimes called mortgage "bankers," have traditionally invested in FHA-insured home loans which followed uniform standards and so could be easily packaged for resale in the secondary market.

The four things that lenders object to in FHA insurance are: (a) prohibition on prepayment penalties; (b) prohibition on a due on sale clause (which means the loan cannot be called in when the house is sold); (c) longer processing time than private insurance (often six weeks vs. a week or two, during which time the house must be off the market); (d) below market interest rate.

Sellers and FHA mortgages. A seller having an FHA mortgage is fortunate if the unpaid principal is high enough. This loan can be assumed by the buyer, who continues to make the lower interest payments. In today's market, an older FHA or VA mortgage is practically the only way a house can be sold outright, without involving seller financing and continued liability for the property.

Sellers who don't have an assumable FHA mortgage view "FHA" buyers differently. The reason is that the agency only allows buyers to pay one of the several discount "points" charged by the lender. The seller must pay the remaining points and many owners either add these to the price of the house or else refuse to deal with buyers who have applied for FHA insurance.

Section 244 coinsurance program. This program provides for loss-sharing between HUD and originating lenders, or with investing mortgagees who subsequently take over the liability of the coinsurance contract. Section 244 has been heavily promoted to those savings and loan associations which have not, in the past, done much FHA business. The 244 property standards and mortgage limits are the same as for Section 203(b).

Section 245 GPM program. This consists of five graduated payment mortgage plans designed to lower the payments in the early years of the plan. If offered through federally chartered banks and thrift institutions, any state laws against usury ("interest on interest") will not apply to their negative amortization.

Subsidized FHA home loan programs. These include Section 221(d)(2), Section 223(e) and Section 237. They are designed for lower income families who are unable to qualify for 203(b) or 245 GPM loans and are backed by HUD's Special Risk Insurance Fund.

Section 221(d)(2). This program is intended to insure low cost housing for families displaced by urban renewal or other governmental action, as well as for other low or moderate income families. The mortgage underwriting standards have been relaxed on income needed to qualify, and the housing tends to be lower priced than with FHA's regular home loan programs.

Section 223(e). Is aimed specifically at housing located in older neighborhoods which are declining and present higher lending risks. HUD requires such areas to be "reasonably viable" and having a need to provide adequate housing "for families of low and moderate income" which makes the risk of insuring property acceptable.

Section 237. Insures lenders against loss on home mortgages they make to people who are marginal credit risks. Between 1968 and 1980 this program insured about 5,200 mortgages of this type.

VA-guaranteed mortgages. For home buyers who are qualified veterans the Veterans Administration will guarantee payment to the lender of $27,500 or 60 percent of the loan, whichever is less, in case of default. This guarantee is greater than the risk portion of the loan and makes a VA mortgage an extremely safe investment.

The actual amount of the mortgage is set by the VA's Certificate of Reasonable Value. This is determined when a VA-authorized appraiser inspects the house for defects and sets a price on it. The VA's interest rates are in line with FHA's, which means they are below market and lenders will charge discount "points." The VA also prohibits prepayment penalties and the "due on sale" clause.

A VA mortgage can also be assumed by a buyer, either a veteran or non-veteran, but make sure first to get a written release from future responsibility from the VA. Without such a release the original mortgagor remains liable if the buyer or any subsequent owner should default.

Unlike an FHA-insured mortgage, one guaranteed by the VA requires no down payment whatsoever. The VA is conservative and prefers a monthly mortgage payment that does not exceed 25 percent of your monthly income.

While the VA takes longer to process loan paperwork than private insurors, it handles this much faster than FHA and is consequently more popular with lenders and sellers. As far as "points" are concerned, however, sellers without an assumable mortgage will treat FHA or VA buyers equally.

The VA can take a lot of the credit for the fast-stabilizing mortgage market in mobile homes, now known as "100 percent manufactured" housing. They were the first to guarantee long-term mortgages on these houses: without such underwriting mobile homes only qualified for medium term chattel mortgages at market interest, same as for a camper. FHA has since followed suit, FNMA has announced it will buy these mortgages if they meet certain conditions, and mobile homes which are solidly anchored to foundations and conform to state building codes are now treated like other houses in many areas.

To find out whether you are eligible, call or write the nearest VA office. They will need your date of birth, social security number, military serial number, date you entered the service, date and place of separation, type of discharge and the name of your unit at time of discharge. If you qualify, the VA will issue you a Certificate of Eligibility.

Points

A point is 1 percent of the loan amount. When applied to mortgages the word means a discount—a reduction in the actual amount of cash you receive when the loan is issued or an upfront payment the buyer pays the seller. Since you must still repay the full amount of the mortgage, this 'up front' charge increases the yield to the lender.

On non-insured or conventional mortgages, a charge of one point may be enough to cover the lender's cost of preparing the loan. This charge is actually a loan origination fee and you can deduct all of it from your income tax.

With FHA/VA mortgages, however, additional points are charged to offset the spread between the market rate and the FHA/VA interest rate ceilings. The number of points is given in specially-prepared tables, and is based on the difference between the two rates.

As a buyer you can still only deduct the single point that FHA/VA allow you to pay from your income on Form 1040. But the seller is in a worse position at income tax time: since the I.R.S. classifies any points he or she pays not as interest, but as a reduction in the selling price of the house, the seller can make no deductions for points. The IRS assumes that the price has been increased to cover the "points" payment. Therefore, the tax situation is yet another reason that sellers dislike points. As a general rule, a seller's wish to avoid dealings with FHA/VA buyers grows directly in relation to the number of points being charged.

When you evaluate the number of points that different lenders may be charging you, keep in mind that this is sometimes an "up front" charge which you pay all at once. At other times it is built into the loan. The lender is required to reveal all points charges. If you were to sell the house within a year or two, paying several points on a large loan could be costly for such a short period. The longer you plan to stay in the house, the more you can spread this one-time expense.

The only way you can *really* compare the different loans offered is to look at them the way the lender does. To determine their yield, lenders combine the interest you pay *plus* other recurring charges, such as real estate taxes, *plus* the applicable portion of the amortized one-time charges (which you pay when the loan is issued). This gives them an amount known as the annual percentage rate, or APR. Ask the lender to show you this rate—he doesn't have to show you during the initial stages, but if you take out a loan the law will require him to show you the APR at time of settlement.

Where to Shop—The Lenders

If you take out a fixed-payment loan, you will probably pay the current market interest rate or close to it. Many lenders will offer you a lower-than-market rate if you agree to tying it to an index, and letting them adjust it as the index rises or falls. Since this could cost you plenty if interest rates drop be sure your contract does not include a prepayment penalty so you can refinance your loan.

The institutions which used to have large, insured deposits on which they paid low interest were the savings and loan associations and the mutual savings banks. These, therefore, had the cheapest money to lend and were the most active in financing private homes.

Today, most savers look for higher rates than the thrift institutions can pay. This drop in deposits has left the thrifts with little cheap money to lend and the necessity for looking for funds in the capital markets. The FHLBB has reacted by permitting lenders to make the rates adjustable (to protect themselves aginst high inflation.)

State-chartered savings and loan associations and mutual savings banks will have to look to their respective state governments for similar help. But until they, too, can raise their rates, the only ones with mortgage money will be those having enough savers who continue to make deposits at low interest. Unfortunately for homebuyers, depositors willing to let their savings be eroded by inflation are becoming scarce.

Banks that *do* have ample money to lend are the commercial banks. Most of these are involved in commercial real estate, but you may find a few in the residential mortgage business. The loans they offer will mostly be conventional and at or near the market rate. You may, however, find a bank that for some reason has been slow to raise its rate—it's worth a try.

Life insurance companies used to be active in single family residential mortgages, but many have now virtually abandoned the field for more profitable multi-family housing. You might still ask your broker if any are issuing residential mortgages.

Remember also that mortgages are not restricted to lending institutions—anyone having the necessary capital can issue one. If you are being transferred, it's worth asking your company or federal agency for a home mortgage.

The following types of banks and thrift institutions offer self-amortizing home loans:

Savings and Loan Associations (called Homestead Associations or Building & Loan Associations in some states) are the long-term home mortgage specialists who usually offer the greatest variety of plans. Federal tax regulations are structured to encourage thrifts to invest at least 80 percent of their assets in residential mortgages.

Although the number of home loans that savings and loan associations write each year varies according to savings inflow, it's usually about 50 percent of all residential mortgages. Home loans are their main business and your application should be quickly and expertly processed.

Savings and loan associations are limited to a 100-mile radius, within the state, of their branches. They tend to acquire a very detailed knowledge of their local home loan market, which allows them to concentrate on more profitable conventional mortgages for their own portfolios. Not needing the federal guarantees, less than 10 percent of their business is in VA or FHA loans.

The type of mortgages you can get from a savings and loan association will depend on whether it is federally or state chartered. If it is regulated by the Federal Home Loan Bank Board, the institution is allowed to offer all federally approved loan plans, including Adjustable Rate Mortgages and Graduated Payment Mortgages. Different savings and loans will have different loan policies, however, so it pays to shop them all.

The savings and loan associations chartered by your state must abide by state laws governing the types of mortgages they can offer. Many states prohibit negative amortization ("interest on interest") or provisions for extending the term of a loan, so most of the plans in chapter 13 may not be available from the state associations. On the other hand, you may be able to get a Standard Fixed Payment Mortgage, or a closely capped Renegotiable Rate Mortgage or Variable Rate Mortgage from a state savings and loan—*if* they have the deposit money to lend.

Mutual Savings Banks. While you'll find these listed with the commercial banks in *Polk's Banking Directory,* they are actually thrift institutions. MSB's were originally established in Pennsylvania and New England to encourage savings by small wage earners who at the time were being ignored by other banks. The idea was that these banks would be operated for the "mutual benefit" of their small depositors.

If you don't live in the Northeast you may not have any MSB's in your area. This concept seldom took hold outside its area of origin—although Delaware, Maryland, Minnesota and the state of Washington have mutual savings banks.

Although residential mortgage lending has always been important to MSB's they, unlike savings and loan associations, are not obliged to invest a specific percentage of their assets in home mortgages. Many do a good business in commercial real estate and consumer loans.

More important to your loan shopping is that, except for five which have switched to federal charters, mutual savings banks are controlled by their respective states. As a result, they will be limited like state savings and loans in the loan plans they are allowed to offer. Within these limits, you can expect their expertise and handling of your application to be of a high standard.

Mortgage companies. There are mortgage brokers, who have no deposit funds of their own. They bring borrowers and lenders together. They *do* have excellent connections with sources of capital throughout the country, and their function is to obtain this money and channel it into packages of mortgages which they originate.

Mortgage bankers are active in both residential and commercial real estate mortgage loans. They are locally oriented with a good feel for their market. They can sell these mortgages in the secondary market and use the proceeds to write new mortgages. They rode the crest of the wave of single-family homes that went up in the 1950's, and originated most of the VA/FHA mortgages on those houses.

Even today, mortgage companies write about 75 percent of all FHA loans insured under section 203. Government-underwritten loans are considered a very safe investment which can be readily sold in the secondary market.

Mortgage companies are not as visible as banks and you may have trouble locating one. Ask your real estate broker—he is almost certain to have worked with several. For the names of mortgage brokers dealing in residential real estate in your area, you could also write or call their trade association: Mortgage Bankers Association of America, 1125 15th Street NW, Washington, D.C. 20005, (202) 861-6500.

Commercial banks. It's hard to characterize commercial banks as a class in regard to their residential mortgage lending activity. As the name implies, the main purpose of a commercial bank is to supply the funds accumulated through time and demand deposits to commerce, agriculture and industry. They are also the leading source of loans for commercial real estate and construction mortgages.

In terms of volume they are second to the savings and loan associations and have almost one third as much as the associations invested in home mortgages. However, there are a *lot* of commercial banks (over 15,000 with almost 30,000 branches) and their ratio of residential mortgages to total assets is slightly under 12 percent (compared to about 75 percent savings and loan associations and about 50 percent for MSB's.)

One might conclude that a commercial bank is not organized to concentrate on home mortgages. Its funds come mainly from short-term checking and savings accounts. It's therefore logical for such a bank to look for short-term loans, where its outflow of funds falls due as its inflow is withdrawn. In fact, when the demand for short-term loans is high, a commercial bank can be expected to gear itself up to meet this demand and put long-term lending on the back burner. There are many exceptions. Some commercial banks are not only very active in residential mortgages but are among the most innovative lenders in designing special loan plans. With the probability of relaxed federal restrictions on the loans they can offer, and the prospect of higher residential yields, activity by the federally-chartered banks should increase.

It will be well worth your time to check all the commercial banks in the area.

Your credit union. If you are one of the 44 million Americans who belong to 22,000 federal and state regulated credit unions, your loan shopping may end right here.

Even if your credit union has so far specialized in short-term consumer loans, try them anyway for a 30-year mortgage. There have been some major changes recently in the regulations affecting long-term lending by credit unions.

Federal credit unions were allowed to write residential mortgages for their members in 1977, and the National Credit Union Administration allowed other credit unions to make long-term home loans in 1978. Some states have allowed credit unions to make these loans for many years.

Credit unions with less than $2 million in assets may now write residential mortgages without getting prior approval from the National Credit Union Administration. Credit unions may also, acting as agents, write mortgages for other lenders and charge origination fees.

In 1979 the Credit Union's National Association established a mortgage corporation in Lafayette, Indiana to package the mortgages originated by the member unions. These will be sold on the secondary market and the money returned to the originator for further lending. Your credit union, through its national association, can now perform some of the functions of a mortgage company.

Table VIII:

1979: Insured 1-Family Home Mortgages by type of originator, as a % of total

Type of Originating Mortgagee	FHA (Section 203b) New Homes	Existing Homes	MICs New & Existing Homes
Mortgage Broker	76.3%	72.7%	20.1%
Savings & Loan Association	6.9	8.6	62.6
National Commercial Bank	4.8	4.4 ⎱	10.3
State Commercial Bank	4.6	2.4 ⎰	
Mutual Savings Bank	.1	2.8	4.4
Insurance Company	.1	.9 ⎱	
Federal Agency	.1	.1	3.3
Private Industry	.1		
Miscellaneous (includes credit unions)	7.0	8.1 ⎰	

Source: FHA 203b supplement S0136, No. 68 and Mortgage Insurance Companies
of America Factbook

CHAPTER 12

Mortgages Explained

Before the first mutual savings and building societies appeared in the early 19th century, most home mortgages were issued by one individual to another.

These secured loans usually ran for 5 or 10 years, their payments covered only interest, and the entire principal fell due when term was up.

Even when the thrift institutions became the major issuers of mortgages, the loans didn't change much—as late as the 1920's your grandparents would have made their regular interest payments to the bank for 5 or 10 years, and then either repaid or refinanced the mortgage.

Sweeping Changes in the 1930's

Faced with a flood of foreclosures, bank failures and general chaos during the depression, the Federal Government deliberately set out to restructure the home financing sector of the economy. Its first moves were aimed at shoring-up bank credit and restoring the confidence of depositors:

1932 • The Reconstruction Finance Corporation (RFC) was created to supply funds to commercial banks.

- The Federal Home Loan Bank (FHLB) was established to perform the same function for S&L's and other home lending institutions.

1933 • Federal Deposit Insurance Corporation (FDIC) created to insure savings deposits in commercial banks.

- Federal charters were made possible for S&L's, and the Government moved to allow families to keep their homes by buying or refinancing mortgages on which they had defaulted.

1934 • The National Housing Act created both the Federal Savings and Loan Insurance Corporation (FSLIC) to insure savers' deposits, and the Federal Housing Administration (FHA) to create a stable national mortgage market with uniform loan documents.

As mentioned earlier, the FHA is chiefly responsible for the availability of self-amortizing long-term mortgages—and the disappearance of 5 or 10 year balloons as senior home loans—at your lending bank.

Joined by the VA after the Servicemen's Readjustment Act of 1944 (which made VA-guaranteed loans possible), the FHA has been carrying out its mandate ever since. By standardizing home mortgage loans and underwriting them, these two agencies have made possible a large and active secondary mortgage market. The existence of this market makes it easier to sell a mortgage once it's written, and facilitates the flow of home mortgage capital to the parts of the country which need it most.

The Secondary Mortgage Market

While most home buyers are familiar with the stock markets and commodities markets, few are aware that lenders who write and issue their mortgages may, if they choose, sell these to investors in other parts of the country.

If your own mortgage is sold, you may never know it, as long as you continue to make your monthly payments. Your dealings will continue in the normal manner, and the lender will usually continue to service your loan for a fee.

When you actually took out your loan, the transaction took place in what is called the "primary" market—where lenders extend credit to borrowers by originating and preparing loans. The secondary market is where these loans are bought and sold by investors after they have been originated. They are usually "packaged" (assembled in groups with similar terms, conditions and interest rates) before being offered to investors. Uniform documentation is required to package "individual" loans into groups to enable them to be resold to large investors who would not be interested in "individual" loans.

We've already seen how MICs and the FHA/VA can lower your down payment by underwriting the mortgage and assuming the risk from the lender. These secured loans are even more attractive to many lenders if they can then sell them to investors. This is especially true of banks and institutions whose savings deposits are low. They can use the money from selling these mortgages to write new ones.

Mortgage Insurance Companies have played an active part in helping institutions to participate in the secondary market. Since they insure loans throughout the country, they know regions and thrift institutions which have a surplus of capital and also those lenders short of capital who need to sell mortgages. As independent third parties, the private insurors bring investor and seller together as a free service to their customers.

This "free" service, however, has large benefits for the private insurers. One result is that capital-short originating lenders can increase their servicing volume—i.e., write more mortgages, most of which will need risk insurance.

Another benefit is that MICs reap considerable goodwill from both the selling originators and the secondary market investors. For example, FNMA and FHLMC have prepared a number of educational and technical support programs for lenders which MICs can easily promote. Furthermore, it has long been the policy of both FNMA and FHLMC to encourage the availability of high loan-to-value mortgages to home buyers.

By the simple means of only buying mortgages insured by "approved" MICs, the private insurers are employed to carry out a large part of this educational work. Not only must they meet requirements for financial solvency and operating standards, the MICs must also see to it that the lenders' mortgages they insure meet FNMA/FHLMC appraisal criteria.

In 1980 FNMA and FHLMC together bought over $6.0 billion of mortgages, over 48 percent of which was MIC insured.

So even if you've never heard of the secondary market in home mortgages, it benefits you directly by:

- Making loan documents uniform, which also makes it easier to compare mortgages from different lenders;
- Making mortgage money available, should you need a mortgage in a part of the country running short of capital to lend.

Flexibility in loan shopping is also definitely affected by the type of mortgage secondary market investors are willing to buy. A good example is adjustable rate mortgages. Until recently lenders issuing these had to keep them in their own portfolios, since the big investors weren't yet ready to buy them.

Now these investors will buy these mortgages because, apart from the federal mandates, they are a safe and relatively high yielding investment over the long term.

FNMA, FHLMC and GNMA together greatly influence the types of loans offered and the availability of money to lend—although making up the shortfall in savings deposits at the lending banks is beyond their resources. They are described below.

Federal National Mortgage Association. FNMA, is the largest owner of residential mortgage debt. A government agency within the Department of Housing and Urban Development since 1950, FNMA was divided into two separate entities in 1968.

GNMA remained within HUD and carried on some of the former FNMA functions. The second entity retained the

FNMA name, but became a private corporation listed on the New York Stock Exchange. It presently has about 60 million shares outstanding.

FNMA is managed by a 15-member board of directors, ten of which are elected by the stockholders and the remaining five appointed by the President of the United States. The Department of Housing and Urban Development still retains some regulatory powers.

Although originally an exclusive investor in the FHA/VA loans which financed most of the moderate income homeowners, FNMA's charter was broadened by the Emergency Home Finance Act of 1970 to buy MIC-insured conventional mortgages. It now buys slightly more conventional mortgages than government-backed loans.

FNMA gets the money to buy its mortgages by selling securities in the private capital markets. The corporation must earn dividends for its stockholders from the difference between its cost of funds and the yield on its mortgage portfolio. If its borrowing cost is higher than its interest income for any length of time, FNMA, like any private business, loses money.

Clearly, FNMA is concerned about the number of her low-interest older FHA/VA mortgages that are being "wrapped" (see Chapter 14): or otherwise assumed through creative financing techniques at these low interest rates. In order to reduce the number of these wraps, the corporation recently came out with plans to refinance its own mortgages.

In addition, there are plans for FNMA to offer a secondary market for second mortgages issued to homeowners who want to tap the equity in their homes for cash. The corporation is also enforcing the "due on sale" clause over as much of its portfolio as it can.

Federal Home Loan Mortgage Corporation. Created also by the Emergency Home Finance Act of 1970, the original purpose of FHLMC was to buy mortgages originated by federally-chartered S&L's. Since 1978 these functions have been widened to include commercial banks and mortgage companies.

The Mortgage Corporation, as FHLMC prefers to call itself, concentrates primarily on conventional loans. This is because S&L's do relatively little FHA/VA business, and most of their loan insurance is handled by MIC's. FHMLC is allowed to buy the government-backed loans, however, in case a mortgage company should offer to sell a package of these.

FHLMC both buys and sells mortgages, using the proceeds of its sales to finance the purchase of new mortgages. It does not borrow in the capital markets as does FNMA.

Government National Mortgage Association. As a part of HUD, Ginny Mae still carries on with the management of FNMA's pre-1968 portfolio of mortgages. It also carries on the "Special Assistance Function," making loans at low interest rates to low-income families who would not otherwise be granted mortgages.

Where GNMA most affects the secondary market is in a newer operation known as the mortgage-backed security program. Its purpose is to attract funds from people who do not normally invest in home mortgages.

What GNMA does is guarantee a certificate, based on a pool of mortgages assembled by an FHA-approved lender, which have been packaged in accordance with GNMA guidelines. These pools may also consist of FHA/VA mobile home mortgages and are not limited to single-family houses.

FNMA and FHLMC work together to assure uniform home mortgage documents in all 50 states. These include the appraisal and loan application forms, the mortgage note and the mortgage or deed of trust.

Privately insured mortgage-backed securities. MICs have also been very active in the packaging of conventional mortgages for investors. They are working with Congress, federal regulatory agencies, FNMA and FHLMC to get the same degree of investor acceptance for securities backed by conventional mortgages now enjoyed by GNMA on those backed by FHA mortgages. Private insurance covering the overall mortgage pool, as well as the individual mortgages in the pool, is proving a key element in winning investor acceptance of the securities it backs.

CHAPTER 13

The New Adjustable Mortgages and Their Predecessors

Today if you can't qualify for a loan at the 18 percent or more market rate, but can qualify at a below market rate, you may have to settle for an Adjustable Rate Mortgage.

Your Adjustable Rate Mortgage Index

The amount you pay monthly with an Adjustable Rate Mortgage depends on the rise or fall of economic indexes, like the "6-Month Treasury Bill Index." Before you sign a loan agreement for an ARM with any bank, make sure the index it is tied to will be beneficial to you. You do this by studying its past performance.

The performance, over the past decade, of the various indexes to which interest rates on ARM plans may be tied is shown in Table IX. It's important to keep in mind that this table only gives an approximate idea of how some of these index rates vary. For the sake of brevity, only the June and December figures are shown. Your bank will be able to give you more detailed information on how these indexes have per-

Table IX

	Cost of funds to FSLIC S&L's	FHLBB Mortgage contract rate	3 Month T–Bill	6 Month T–Bill	1–year T–Security	2–year T–Security	3–year T–Security	5–year T–Security
1970 Mid year	5.24	8.19	6.74	6.91	7.55	N/A	7.84	7.85
Year end	5.36 + .12	8.12 – .07	4.86 – 1.88	4.85 – 2.06	5.00 – 2.55		5.75 – 2.05	5.95 – 1.90
1971 Mid year	5.38	7.38	4.70	4.89	5.64	N/A	6.32	6.53
Year end	5.37 – .01	7.51 + .13	4.02 – .69	4.20 – .69	4.61 – 1.03		5.27 – 1.05	5.69 – .84
1972 Mid year	5.39	7.36	3.87	4.27	4.93	N/A	5.64	5.91
Year end	5.42 + .03	7.45 + .09	5.06 + 1.19	5.29 + 1.02	5.52 + .55		6.01 + .37	6.16 + .25
1973 Mid year	5.46	7.64	7.19	7.23	7.31	N/A	6.83	6.69
Year end	5.72 + .26	8.46 + .82	7.36 + .17	7.44 + .21	7.27 – .04		6.81 – .02	6.80 + .11
1974 Mid Year	6.00	8.66	8.15	8.23	8.67	N/A	8.15	8.10
Year end	6.28 + .28	9.39 + .73	7.18 – .97	7.09 – 1.14	7.31 – 1.36		7.24 – .91	7.31 – .79
1975 Year end	6.31	8.86	5.19	5.46	6.29	N/A	7.17	7.51
Year end	6.34 + .03	9.09 + .23	5.50 + .31	5.93 + .47	6.60 + .31		7.44 + .27	7.76 + .25
1976 Mid year	6.35	8.82	5.44	5.78	6.52	7.06	7.31	7.61
Year end	6.40 + .05	8.90 + .08	4.35 – 1.09	4.51 – 1.27	4.89 – 1.63	5.38 – 1.68	5.68 – 1.63	6.11 – 1.50
1977 Mid year	6.39	8.78	5.00	5.20	5.80	6.13	6.39	6.76
Year end	6.48 + .09	8.93 + .15	6.06 + 1.06	6.38 + 1.16	6.96 + 1.16	7.18 + 1.05	7.30 + .91	7.48 + .72
1978 Mid year	6.54	9.27	6.71	7.20	8.09	8.24	8.30	8.36
Year end	6.79 + .25	9.85 + .58	9.12 + 2.41	9.40 + 2.20	10.30 + 2.21	9.72 + .96	9.33 + 1.03	9.08 + .72
1979 Mid year	7.23	10.46	9.05	9.06	9.57	9.22	8.95	8.85
Year end	7.71 + .48	11.59 + 1.13	12.07 + 3.02	11.85 + 2.75	11.98 + 2.41	11.39 + 2.17	10.71 + 1.76	10.42 + 1.57
1980 Mid year	8.77	12.88	7.00	7.22	8.16	8.73	8.91	9.21
Year end	N/A	13.15 + .23	15.66 + 8.66	14.77 + 7.55	14.88 + 6.72	14.08 + 5.35	13.65 + 4.74	13.25 + 4.09

formed. They have columns of figures which show the variations of an index for each month of the year.

At first glance, the figures in this table are hardly exciting reading, but neither are the stock market reports—unless you happen to own stocks. As more and more families finance their homes with ARMs, the indexes used will probably become a regular feature in the financial section of your daily newspaper.

Many real estate people consider the 3-month and 6-month Treasury Indexes poor bets for home buyers, because of their volatility. Historically, the short-term obligations have had much wider swings than the 3-year and 5-year securities have been more stable.

You may also want to steer clear of the S&L Cost of Funds index. Over the last ten years it has steadily increased even when the other indexes have been dropping.

The New Adjustable Rate Mortgages

In 1981 the Federal Home Loan Mortgage Corporation announced its pilot ARM program of two plans, quickly followed by the Federal National Mortgage Association's announcement of eight ARM plans that they were prepared to buy. These eight plans are compared in tabular form on page 222 (FNMA plans 7 and 8 are identical to FHLMC plans 1 and 2).

Federally chartered Savings and Loan Associations may, if they wish, offer all eight plans. Nationally chartered commercial banks regulated by the Treasury Department's Comptroller of the Currency may, as of this writing, offer plans 5 and 8. Provided other state laws do not restrict their use, state-chartered lenders subject to "interest-on-interest" usury statutes can offer plans five through eight.

Both FHLMC and FNMA are testing the market with these new adjustable rate mortgage programs. Depending on the response from lenders and consumers, the ARM plans that both secondary market investors will purchase could be modified or expanded.

Plan	Index Used	Interest Adjustment Period	Maximum Interest Adjustment	Payment Adjustment Period	Payment Cap for Each Period	Annual Rate	Negative Amortization	How Loan Compares
1	6 Mos. Treasury Bill	Every 6 mos.		Every 6 mos.	7½%	15%	125% of principal	Frequent payment adjustments which cannot increase more than 15% annually or 7½% each period. If inflation pushes the 6 Mos. Treasury Bill rates over your payment limit, excess interest will be added to your loan principal as negative amortization.
2	6 Mos. Treasury Bill	Every 6 mos.		Every 3 years			125% of principal	If you expect interest rates to go down, try this plan. Level payments for 3 years, but with no cap on interest or payment adjustments, expect a sizeable jump at end of 3 years if rates have been going up.
3	1 Year Treasury Bill	Every year		Every year	7½%	7½%	125% of principal	Similar to Plan #1, but adjustments will be less frequent. Annual payment cap of 7½% makes chances of negative amortization even greater than Plan #1 if rates are going up.
4	3 Year Treasury Note	Every 2½ years			18¾%	7½%	125% of principal	Stable payments over a long period of time. 18¾% adjustment still works out as 7½% a year.
5	3 Year Treasury Note	Every 2½ years	5%	Every 2½ years				Conforms to 2% annual limit on changes in commercial bank's interest, so popular loan with banks. Payment periods relatively long, but no negative amortization. Look for sizeable jump when adjustments made while rates are going up.
6	5 Year Treasury Note	Every 5 years		Every 5 years				Offers the greatest potential stability, since 5 Year index is likely to move less than other indexes. Watch out for big payment jump at end of 5 year period if interest rates going up.
7 (FHLMC #1)	FHLBB	Every year		Every year				Because tied to FHLBB rate, expect to pay more for loan initially. No caps and no negative amortization, so you will be charged full cost of funds at each payment period.
8 (FHLMC #2)	FHLBB	Every Year	2%	Every year				Tailored to commercial banking regulations, so popular with banks. Because tied to FHLBB Index, expect to pay more for loan initially.

By its very nature, it's impossible to set forth an exact schedule of an ARM's payments over its term. Borrowers have to make their own estimates of how the economy will affect inflation, interest rates and the plan's index—one approach is illustrated in the following chart for FHLMC #1/FNMA #7. This is strictly a hypothetical projection of possible index performance under "best" and "worst" average inflation rates. You probably have your own views on what sort of inflation the future may hold.

For example, if you feel that the government will soon "get a handle" on inflation and that six percent annually is a reasonable expectation, your monthly payments might resemble the white areas of the chart. By today's standards, these amounts are quite attractive for a $50,000 mortgage and there are also steady reductions in the principal amount outstanding.

If, on the other hand, you take a pessimistic view of what sort of inflation the future holds you may agree on twelve percent average inflation as a possible "worst" case. Under these conditions the monthly payments could be similar to the shaded area of the chart and the loan amortization would also be less. Although the "worst" case average payments are still less than the present rate for a similar fixed-payment mortgage, a borrower with a gloomy view of the future might prefer a capped loan which allows negative amortization (FHLMC #1/FNMA #7 does not, neither does it specify any caps).

Table X: $50,000 Arm; 30-Year Term. Plan: FHLMC #1/FNMA #7. Index: FHLBB Contract Rate, 12 Month Adjustments.

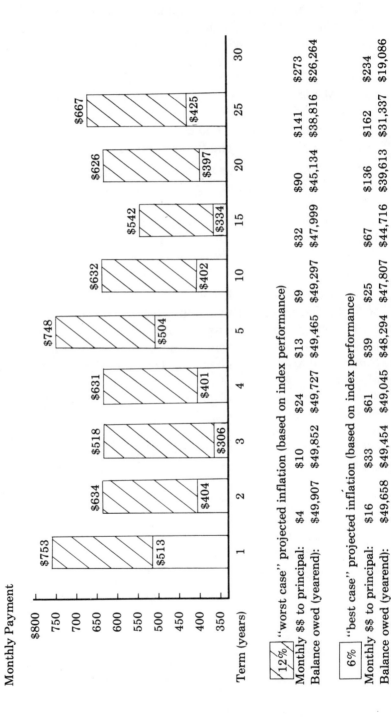

Monthly Payment

Term (years)	1	2	3	4	5	10	15	20	25
12% "worst case" payment	$753	$634	$518	$631	$748	$632	$542	$626	$667
6% "best case" payment	$513	$404	$306	$401	$504	$402	$334	$397	$425

12% "worst case" projected inflation (based on index performance)

	1	2	3	4	5	10	15	20	25
Monthly $$ to principal:	$4	$10	$24	$13	$9	$32	$90	$141	$273
Balance owed (yearend):	$49,907	$49,852	$49,727	$49,465	$49,297	$47,999	$45,134	$38,816	$26,264

6% "best case" projected inflation (based on index performance)

	1	2	3	4	5	10	15	20	25
Monthly $$ to principal:	$16	$33	$61	$39	$25	$67	$136	$162	$234
Balance owed (yearend):	$49,658	$49,454	$49,045	$48,294	$47,807	$44,716	$39,613	$31,337	$19,086

The First Generation of Adjustable Mortgages

The earlier (late 1970's through 1981) mortgage plans, involving adjustable payments or adjustments to outstanding principal, will continue to be used by some state-chartered thrift institutions. These loans can also be offered by many state-chartered commercial banks or national commercial banks regulated by the Treasury Department's Comptroller of the Currency. Unlike some of the newer adjustable rate mortgages, the older plans feature low "caps" or limits on interest rate increases. Borrowers obviously prefer increases in interest to be closely controlled—if they also live in areas where real estate prices are moderate and stable, they are likely to find lenders still doing business in these older mortgage plans.

Here is a brief description of the earlier plans (federally chartered thrift institutions regulated by the FHLBB may no longer offer the VRM or RRM).

Variable Rate Mortgage (VRM). Keyed to the S&L cost of funds index. This was the first adjustable rate home mortgage, with interest rates that could be raised (at the lender's option) or lowered (mandatory). First used by California-chartered S&Ls in 1976, the VRM was authorized for federally-chartered thrifts in 1979. The annual interest rate cap is ± ½ percent and the rate cannot be raised by more than 2½ percent over the life of the loan. Home finance experts predict only a modest activity in future VRM's: although borrowers like their tightly capped increases, lenders can get a better return on mortgages which allow them more latitude in increasing rates.

• When federally-chartered S&Ls were issuing VRMs they were required to offer the borrower a standard fixed-payment mortgage at the same time.

Renegotiable Rate Mortgage (RRM). Keyed to the FHLBB mortgage contract rate. Similar to the Canadian rollover mortgage, RRMs were available in 3- or 5-year periods on an underlying 40-year term mortgage. At each renewal period the lender was required to lower the interest rate if the index has moved downward. With a rising index, the lender was limited to a ½ percent increase for each year of the period (1½ percent for 3 years, 2 percent for 4 years, 2½ percent for 5 years). Upward interest rate over the life of the mortgage was limited to 5 percent.

Still very popular with first-time buyers whose incomes qualify is the *Graduated Payment Mortgage (GPM)*. The purpose of a GPM is to offer lower monthly payments during the early years (incurring negative amortization) and then fully amortize the loan over its 30-year term by increasing the payments in the later years. MICs are quite active in insuring the risk portion of GPMs, which then also makes possible a lower down payment to go along with the initial fixed lower monthly payments. A typical plan would be Mortgage Guaranty Insurance Corporation's SNAP (Simple Negative Amortization program) for which lender applications currently form about 10 percent of the company's business.

Also available is the FHA-insured *245 GPM Program* consisting of three 5-year plans and two 10-year plans. The annual rate increase of the former is limited to 7½ percent, and to 3 percent on the ten year plans. The FHA 245 GPM program was authorized by Congress, which specifically excepted FHA-insured negative amortization loans from state usury ("interest on interest") laws. By the end of 1980 FHA had insured almost $5 billion worth of home mortgages under this program.

Locking in a Low Interest Mortgage for its Full Term: The Wraparound

An alternative approach to applying for an adjustable rate mortgage at a below market rate is to look for an assumable existing mortgage which charges a low interest. If there is a large unpaid balance on such a mortgage you can use considerable leverage by "wrapping" a smaller high interest second mortgage around the older loan—many homeowners are paying less than half today's interest rates. Both mortgages will run for the same term.

The wraparound is easy if the older mortgage has been underwritten by FHA/VA and your lender will be delighted to assist with the details. But most FHA/VA mortgages are sold to secondary market investors and it's unlikely that a lender would have retained one in his own portfolio.

If the older mortgage is non-insured or conventional, with a "due on sale" clause, the process is more complicated—particularly for the seller. Since it cannot be assumed by buyers it must remain in the seller's name. The seller continues to make payments on his or her mortgage, but will personally issue you a new larger mortgage for the full amount needed. This new mortgage will include both the old mortgage and the amount needed to finance the rest of the home mortgage. Sellers still retain a liability for the property.

Someone has to get hurt in this process, and the victims are the large secondary market investors. Their packages of mortgages are normally turned around every 10 years or so, as people sell their homes and the loans are paid up. Wraps keep the old low-yield loans on the books for much longer periods.

The secondary market investor most hurt by wraps is FNMA, which must borrow its funds on the market at current rates. To prevent the slowdown in its loan portfolio's turnover, FNMA is enforcing "due on sale" clauses wherever possible and initiating programs to refinance the FHA and conventional mortgages that it holds. FNMA refinance programs are also available to purchasers of existing homes on which FNMA owns the mortgage. This often means a mortgage to the buyer at well below the market rate.

The Standard Fixed Payment Mortgage

The *Standard Fixed Payment Mortgage (SFPM)*, with its predictable schedule of repayments, is the old standby we met at the beginning of chapter 2. Today, you can expect fixed payments based on current interest rates and lenders would dearly love to see the older low-yield SFPMs called in.

There is no law that prevents any lender, whether federally or state chartered, from offering this type of mortgage and many continue to make SFPMs available to borrowers. The main reason is that the secondary market investors like this type of mortgage and will continue to demand packages of SFPMs.

This traditional self amortizing long-term loan was the only plan available right through the mid-1970's. The large existing portfolios of SFPMs—issued at what then were attractive yields to lenders—are partly responsible for the lack of funds from which much of the home lending industry still suffers.

SAM, Where Lenders Share in Homes' 5 or 10-Year Appreciation

Shared Appreciation Mortgage (SAM). This plan was designed to enable buyers to qualify for a stable below-market interest. With a SAM you would agree to transfer to the lender an agreed upon percentage (usually between 30 percent and 50 percent) of your home's appreciation in value at a specified future date, within either 5 or 10 years.

A SAM can be structured in different ways depending on your needs and the bank's lending policy. For example, if you were short of cash but had the income to carry the monthly payments, the lender could provide all or part of the down payment. Or, if you had the money for the down payment but failed to qualify for a mortgage due to an upward surge in interest rates, the lender could offer you a lower rate on a SAM or else pay part of the monthly charge for an agreed period of time.

In figuring your home's total appreciation, you can deduct your costs in buying and selling it as well as what you paid for improvements made by reputable contractors. (However, the SAM is a poor choice for do-it-yourselfers—it's very difficult to get lenders to accept an owner's estimate of materials and labor costs. The lender will also be suspicious of any bills presented by friends or relatives of the homeowner.)

It pays to be careful about the 5- or 10-year payback provision in SAMs. A borrower who doesn't have the cash to pay the lender's share of appreciation on the date specified will have to refinance the house in order to meet this obligation. This has the effect of adding the lender's share of the appreciation back into the loan balance, and subsequent monthly payments can be much higher.

If you should sell the house before the payment date specified in the SAM, the lender takes his agreed percentage of price appreciation at time of sale.

Other Inflation-Oriented Mortgage Plans

Before FHLMC and FNMA announced their respective adjustable rate mortgage programs, a number of articles in housing trade publications and the financial press discussed several plans designed for continuing high inflation. Most of these have now been dropped in favor of the ARMs described at the beginning of this chapter. Whether they see more activity in future depends on the success of the ARM programs and whether the present and succeeding administrations manage to hold down inflation.

Generally speaking, both lenders and underwriters consider most of these mortgage plans either too risky for middle income borrowers or too complicated to originate and service. It is also more difficult to explain them clearly and fully to applicants when they meet with their mortgage loan officer.

The remainder of this chapter consists of capsule explanations of these inflation-oriented mortgages.

Graduated Payment Adjustable Mortgage (GPAM). Keyed to the FHLBB mortgage contract rate, this plan combines the lower early payments of the GPM with the 3-, 4- and 5-year terms of the RRM. During the early period of the loan the amount you pay monthly cannot rise by more than 15 percent each year. If the rising level of payments and an increase in rates combine to exceed 15 percent, the unpaid portion is added back into the outstanding principal. Since the unpaid balance will increase more during the early years, lenders will usually require a higher down payment than with a regular GPM.

Flexible Loan Insurance Program Mortgage (FLIP). With a FLIP, part of your down payment goes into an interest-bearing escrow account at the lending institution. During the first five years, the lower monthly payments are supplemented by funds withdrawn from the escrow account.

Both the size of the escrow account and the monthly withdrawals can be tailored to your needs. The size of both withdrawals also affects how long the funds in escrow will last—it's usually between two and five years. The lender actually receives constant principal and interest payments over the life of a FLIP, since after the money in escrow is used up the borrower's increased payments cover actual principal and interest charges.

The FHLBB calls this kind of mortgage a Pledged Account Mortgage. Under FHLBB regulations if you need to borrow more than 90 percent of the combined value of the security property and the escrow account, only your employer, yourself and relatives may furnish money for the escrow account.

The Split Rate Mortgage (SRM). The SRM was designed to give borrowers stable monthly payments, while allowing the lender to apply more of the payment against interest should interest rates rise. This allocation is determined by the FHLBB index: if it rises more money goes toward interest and if it falls a greater share goes towards principal. When the 3, 4, or 5 year term expires the new monthly payment is set according to the prevailing rate. This type of loan is also known as a Level Payment Mortgage (LPM).

SRMs use two (i.e. "split") interest rates. One rate remains the same over 3-, 4- or 5-year term and determines the *amount* that you write on your monthly payment check. The second rate changes according to the FHLBB cost of funds index, and determines the *proportion* of your monthly payment that the lender allots to both principal and interest.

Flexible Payment Mortgage (FPM). This plan is best suited to young buyers with secure incomes which are expected to increase rapidly. A number of lenders use this method to issue loans at below market rate. During the first five years you may pay only interest on the loan—nothing is paid against principal and your early payments may be lower. After the 5-year period is up, payments increase enough to amortize the loan over an agreed upon period (not to exceed 35 years).

Due to the 5-year delay in building up equity, a higher down payment is required with an FPM. The interest charges would also be higher than with a normally amortized loan, but higher income buyers would benefit by deducting these on their income tax. The fact that buyers build up no equity in the house during the first five years may not be a disadvantage if they do not plan to live in it for long. Some corporate transferees fall into this category.

Adjustable Principal Mortgage (APM). Although this one is not yet approved for use in the U.S., an Israeli or Brazilian would recognize it immediately: the most complete accommodation to inflation now possible in a mortgage instrument. With an APM the interest that borrowers pay is low and constant—only the outstanding principal is adjusted, either annually or every six months.

The APM is designed to offer borrowers a fixed-rate fixed-term mortgage at an interest rate well below market. At the same time it also protects the lender's investment by securing repayment in *actual,* rather than estimated, real dollars. With rising inflation this can mean the highest negative amortization of any loan plan mentioned so far ($300,000 + owed on a $50,000 mortgage could be possible after a long inflationary period).

CHAPTER 14

Alternative or "Creative" Financing

Alternative financing is what people resort to when they fail to qualify for a large enough loan—or for any loan at all—at a bank or other lender when interest rates are high.

It usually means that the seller puts up the cash or retains his original mortgage after the sale, although sometimes a broker may find a third party willing to invest money in your house.

Many of these financing arrangements have been used for years in the buying and selling of commercial real estate. They were seldom needed in residential real estate transactions because mortgage interest rates for home buyers were so low that most could qualify. Today, with very little cheap mortgage money available anywhere, these arrangements have become common in residential buying and selling.

Unless you get a substantially lower-than-market rate, alternative financing will usually benefit you *only* if there's no way you can get the self-amortizing loan you need. It will certainly increase the fees earned by your real estate lawyer, whose advice should be sought right from the start on these arrangements.

Alternative financing is a product of the very high interest rates imposed to control inflation, coupled with the powerful drive most people have to own their homes. The high interest rates have disqualified entire income categories of people who a generation ago would have routinely been granted a mortgage.

Since it's presently impossible for so many buyers to get the types of mortgages described in Chapter 13, the houses they would otherwise buy remain unsold—unless the sellers themselves put up the money. Most sellers resent their inability to make a clear, final sale and dislike this form of financing. The exceptions are those who can spread their profits over a longer period to minimize their capital gains on the sale.

From most broker's point-of-view, "creative" financing is an unmitigated nuisance which complicates the selling process and which was not included in the qualifying exams for their profession. Exceptions to this are the exceptionally creative agents, whose talent for coming up with new arrangements gives them an edge over the competition.

It is no accident that some of the most original creative financing ideas are coming from the large nationwide real estate franchises. These firms can afford to retain staffs of experts who concentrate on developing new plans for their sales people.

Here are some of the arrangements that the seller or your broker may offer you. Except for the first one, which is pretty straightforward, it cannot be emphasized too strongly that *both* you and the seller should hammer out the details accompanied by your respective lawyers.

Where The Developer or Builder Assists in The Sale

Buy-Down. This is what is happening when you see advertisements for new homes with interest rates several percentage points below the market rate. The builder pays the lending institution a lump sum equal to the reduction for a specified period of years. At the lower rate, there is a much better chance that a buyer will qualify for a mortgage.

Builders do this because otherwise few people would qualify for loans and their houses would remain unsold. Many builders, however, will add the amount of the buy-down back into the price of the house, which could raise the amount— though not the rate—of the mortgage. If the development has been in existence for several years you could check the county records to see the price of similar houses before interest rates shot up. If the difference is substantial, the buy-down may not be a bargain for you.

Land Leasing. Here, by excluding the cost of the lot from the price you pay, the builder is lowering the amount of the loan, the size of the down payment and your monthly mortgage payments. He will lease the land to you separately, for a period which can range from 50 to 99 years, at a fairly low rate—somewhere in the neighborhood of 6 percent of its value. This rent can either increase at an agreed-upon rate, or else be indexed to inflation. The most attractive land lease for you would include an option to buy within five years at a pre-set price, and with your rent payments applicable towards this purchase price.

Home Equity Loan Program (HELP). The way this works is that you buy 80 percent of your house from the builder and rent the other 20 percent from him. This will lower the loan amount enough to qualify. You anticipate that, after several years, your equity in the house will have increased to the point where you can get financing for the builder's share.

Typically, the initial rent you pay the builder will be nominal but will increase as time goes by. Remember that if your house appreciates, the builder's share which you expect to buy will also appreciate.

Where the Seller Assists in the Sale— Installments

Unless you have a lot of cash or can assume an old FHA or VA mortgage, you are likely to need the seller to help you finance your home. Almost all of this financing involves installment payments by you to the seller.

Land contract or Contract for Deed. This can be a very risky way to buy a home, but in times of very high interest rates, or if you cannot qualify for a loan, you might try a land con-tract—*as a temporary measure.*

A land contract is a way of using the seller's low-interest mortgage to help the buyer finance the home. Frequently, these older mortgages carry a "due on sale" clause, which allows the bank to "call in" the mortgage at the time of sale. Ordinarily you, the buyer, cannot buy the property, leaving the old mortgage in place; and the lender gets rid of the low-yield loan he no longer wants to carry.

With a land contract, the seller makes a private agreement with the buyer, and in most cases, does not inform his original lender in order to circumvent the "due on sale" clause. The seller continues to hold title to the property and to make payments on the mortgage. Meanwhile, as you hope for interest rates to drop, you pay the seller in agreed-upon in-stallments. During the contract period you do not have legal title to the property, but you may have "equitable title" the rights and responsibilities of an owner who does not have legal title. And here is where the danger comes in: according to the mortgage lender the seller cannot transfer "equitable title" because of the "due on sale" clause. So legally, the lender can foreclose on the property if he discovers your ar-rangement leaving you with nothing.

Your state law is very important as far as land contracts are concerned. In some states a small mistake in the contract can leave the buyer with no stake in the property and no claim against the seller. In other states these contracts are very dangerous for the seller, who can be tied up in litigation for years if a buyer finds a reason for not making payments and refuses to move out.

If you opt for a land contract, both you and the seller not only need lawyers, you need good ones!

Lease/Buy Agreement. Your advantage in this type of ar-rangement is that the price of the house is "frozen," typically for 12 months, while you try to obtain mortgage financing. It's called a "lease/buy" because the lawyers prepare both a lease and a sales contract at the same time. However, the closing date of the sales contract is post-dated to coincide with the expiration date of the lease.

You pay rent to the seller during the lease period, usually in an amount sufficient to cover the seller's mortgage payments and property taxes. Although you may not deduct these payments from your income, for tax purposes the seller may treat the house as income property for the run of the lease.

Lease with option to buy. No sales contract is involved in this arrangement and it's a good idea to try to fix the price at which the house can be bought.

Most of these leases require the buyer to pay from 10 percent to 20 percent option money and allow a period of one to two years in which to exercise the purchase option. Depending on your negotiations with the seller, all or part of your rent will be credited toward the purchase price if you exercise your option. The seller keeps the tax benefits of ownership until title passes at closing.

If you do *not* exercise your option, both the deposit and rent are kept by the owner.

Purchase Money Mortgage. This is simply a second mortgage issued to you by the seller, which would be junior to the first mortgage in the event of default. Its advantage is that you buy time at a below-market rate until interest rates fall—and meanwhile you are bulding up equity.

Usually, your monthly payments would be set in accordance with a 25- or 30-year amortization period, although the actual term of the loan would be only five or ten years. When the term is up the balance outstanding falls due, much like the "balloon" mortgages common in the 1920's.

Most sellers will insist on "due on sale" clauses so that they can call the loan if you should sell the house.

Second mortgages are not allowed with loans underwritten by the FHA, and are usually prohibited with MIC-insured conventional mortgages. Individual mortgages cannot be sold in the secondary market. Originators must keep them until they are prepaid or until maturity.

Third Party Participation

You may know someone willing to put money into your house. If done in the form of a straight loan, this person could then discount your note to firms that buy these obligations.

Even if you were charged a below-market interest of 12 percent this, plus the discount, could add up to an attractive 20 percent profit for the buyer of the note.

Joint Ventures

But if you lack even enough cash for a down payment, or don't like the houses for which your cash qualifies you, consider a "joint venture." It's a way you can buy a home with an investor, share the down payment and closing costs, monthly mortgage payments, taxes, insurance and the condominium fee, if applicable. And, when the property is sold, the accumulated equity will be shared by both you and the investor, in proportion to what each of you has invested.

Joint ventures have been used in the commercial real estate market for some time, and quite successfully; but only now are being applied to the home real estate market.

You need an agent for this venture: it's complicated. You'll need to carefully work out all the investment details and include them in a "Co-Ownership Agreement" both of you sign. You'll also need to decide upon a "fair market value rent" for your property because in a joint venture you become both owner and tenant, while your investor friend becomes both owner and investor. You receive the same tax deductions for mortgage interest and property taxes on your share of the property that you would receive as a sole title-holder. But you owe your co-owner rent for "leasing" his half of the home.

Here's how one creative real estate professional, Veronica Pickman of The Venture Group in Washington, D.C. describes a joint venture. Ms. Pickman has formed her company expressly to help find investors for homebuyers. In addition, Coldwell Banker and other national real estate firms are using this method to help people buy houses. They call the method "equity sharing" or "equity participation." Here is Ms. Pickman's description:

A joint venture? Some people like to think of this financing vehicle as a team. A prospective home occupant and an investor forming a joint venture team so that both can reap the benefits of one real estate purchase.

Who benefits? Anyone who wants to buy real estate now but finds the down payment or monthly carrying costs too high.

First time buyers especially (but not only) are finding the twin difficulties of high interest rates and down payments are forcing them out of a market they want very much.

Investors also are faced with these same problems *and* the added hurdle of finding very little or absolutely NO investor financing.

But how does this help? By sharing the down payment, monthly carrying costs and tax advantages, both the investor and the home occupant can profit.

The home occupant can buy more house than he thought possible . . . and qualify for the bigger mortgage.

The investor gets the benefits of owner occupant financing, including preferential interest rates and usually LOW LOW LOW PAYMENTS. This adds up to great leverage. The investor also has the added advantage of the other owner living in the property, maintaining it and most probably, improving it. No midnight phone calls from a disgruntled tenant—No worries of months with no rent coming in. This is as close to a trouble free investment as a hands on investor can make.

Could you explain more? Use a real example. The Smiths have looked long and hard for an acceptable house. They found a good bargain but couldn't qualify for the mortgage alone. Investor Jones has also been looking for bargains but was unable to find favorable investor financing.

The house they decided to buy jointly costs $167,000. The down payment and closing costs are $10,000 (which they will split) and the interest is 13½ percent amortized over 30 years. Here is an example:

Table XI: Purchase Analysis

50% OWNERSHIP   monthly—1st year

Sales Price	$167,000
Down Payment	$ 10,000
Mortgage amount	$157,000

	INVESTOR	OCCUPANT
Mortgage amount (P+I)	$ 899	$ 899
Real Estate Taxes	68	68
Condo Fee	18	17
	$ 985	$ 984
Rent from occupant to investor for ½	−300	+300
MONTHLY TOTAL EXPENSE	$ 685	$1284

MONTHLY AFTER TAX BENEFITS

	INVESTOR	OCCUPANT
Interest deduction	$ 884	$ 884
Real Estate Taxes	68	68
Condo Fee	18	
Depreciation on ½ (first year)	729	
Total Monthly Deduction	$1699	$ 952
Rental Income	300	
Net Monthly Shelter	$1399	524
55% tax bracket savings	$ 770	
40% tax bracket savings		$ 380

HOME OCCUPANT AFTER TAX COST TO LIVE IN AND OWN

$1,284		$1,284	
−380		+524	
904	$904	760	$760

INVESTOR PROFIT MONTHLY AFTER TAX

Rental income	$ 300	$85 per month equals a 20% return on
Tax Savings	$ 770	down payment before any appreciation
Monthly In	$1,070	
Monthly Out	$ 985	
Profit	$ 85	

NET APPRECIATION

5% appreciation per year	$ 8,000	monthly	$ 696
10% appreciation per year	$16,700	monthly	$1,391
15% appreciation per year	$25,056	monthly	$2,088

5%	10%	15%
$ 85	$ 85	$ 85
348	696	800
$433×12 mo.=$5196	$781×12 mo.=$9372	$885×12 mo.×$10,620
(103% return)	(187% return)	(212% return)

Again, a warning. "Creative" financing is complicated and if handled incorrectly can be dangerous for you in the future, even if it seems like a great deal now. Be sure you consult a real estate agent and lawyer before getting involved in any of these ventures.

CHAPTER 15

Settlement Costs and the Closing Process

I f you've taken out a loan to buy a house you will be involved in two "closing" procedures.

In the loan closing, you get the cash and the lender executes and delivers all the documents which have been prepared to protect his investment. Your involvement with the loan is just beginning and will continue until it has been repaid or refinanced.

In the real estate closing you sign documents such as the contract for sale, purchase agreement and closing statement. Once title passes to you, that's it and the process ends. It's customary for both closings to be handled in the same meeting.

State Laws Vary

The laws of your state are what most influence the cost of your closing and the number of documents you will have to sign.

You may remember that one reason John and Anne Maxwell chose the state they did was its lower closing costs. Although most of the taxes and fees were on a par with its neighbors, the Maxwells found that in one neighboring state and county title transfer taxes totaled 1½ percent of the selling price while the other neighboring city took 1 percent of the selling price. Their state imposed no transfer tax at all, which meant a saving to the couple of almost $1,000.

The differences between regions of the country can be very great. If you live in the West, the chances are that your state law will only require you to sign the necessary documents and deposit the money with an escrow agent. No formal closing meeting with your banker and real estate agent is necessary.

To set down all the variations nationwide in settlement requirements would make this one chapter as long as the entire book! Your best approach is to begin gathering information on closing right at the start of your house hunting. Some realty companies distribute booklets which include a summary of closing requirements in your area, along with the house advertisements. You can enter these in Table XIII to get an idea of how much the closing will cost.

Real Estate Settlement Procedures Act

The Real Estate Settlement Procedures Act (RESPA), as amended in 1976, is what governs the information you get about your closing costs and when you get it.

The Act as amended requires the lender to provide you a "good faith" estimate of closing charges when you apply for a loan (see Table XIII).

One business day before the closing, the Act requires the lender to give you a detailed breakdown of your settlement costs, and also the Annual Percentage Rate (APR) yield to him on the loan. If these costs should exceed your supply of ready cash, twenty-four hours doesn't leave you much time to borrow money or sell assets. It not only pays to estimate closing costs well ahead of time, but to estimate on the high side.

The Settlement Costs

Settlement costs can be grouped into four main categories. In the order of their appearance in the Housing and Urban Development Settlement Statement form these are:

Loan Charges (801, 805, 901, 902)

Attorneys Fees (1107)

Title Examination and Insurance (1108)

State taxes and fees (1201, 1202, 1203, 1301)

Most of these charges are self-explanatory. Your lawyer, real estate agent or lender can best expand on them as they apply to your state and your particular mortgage. You may find item 901 confusing: this covers the interest on the mortgage between the closing date and the date on which your regular payment period begins. Like the monthly interest, it's tax-deductible.

Item 805 "inspection fee" applies to any inspections, that you or the seller haven't already paid for, which are required by the lender, the government or the local housing code (termites, lead paint, etc).

Title insurance can cost you a few hundred dollars. The *lenders* policy required by the bank only covers the lender. If you want title protection you must take out an *owner's* or *fee* policy. Rather than buy it separately, it's usually much cheaper to purchase them together as a *simultaneous* policy. You might also qualify for an additional discount on a *reissue* rate, if the seller was also carrying title insurance—ask for it. You could also try getting the seller to pay for all or part of the title examination and insurance cost.

Escrow accounts. If you must put money into an escrow account to guarantee certain payments, try to get the lender to pay passbook savings interest rates on it. If the lender won't do this, and if you have a savings account at the same bank, ask if the lender is willing to waive the escrow account and draw the money for these payments from your savings account instead.

From the lawmakers' and lenders' viewpoint, money deposited in escrow assures that service charges will be regularly paid during a homeowner's first few months of occupancy—a period when cash may be short due to the closing and moving expenses. From your point of view, however, this money lies frozen when it could be earning interest for you somewhere else. If you *have* to tie up your money in an escrow account, it's worth shopping around and negotiating so that the lender will make it work for you.

A Typical Closing

A fairly typical closing meeting involves you, the seller, the real estate agent, and in some states a representative from the title insurance company. You will be involved with the lender's agent, and then the real estate broker (acting as agent for the seller) as follows:

The lender's agent:

* Will ask for your paid insurance policy (or binder) on the house;
* Will list what you owe the seller (remainder of the down payment, taxes the seller has prepaid, and so forth):
* Will list what the seller owes you (taxes that have not been paid, etc). These are known as "adjustments."
* Will ask you to sign the mortgage or deed of trust (which allows him to take back your property if the mortgage payments are not made);
* Will ask you to sign the mortgage note (your promise to repay the loan in regular specified monthly payments);
* Will then give you the money to pay the seller for the house.
* Will collect the closing costs from you and give you a *loan disclosure statement* (which lists all the items you've just paid for and which should be kept for tax purposes);
* Will see that both deed and mortgage are recorded in the town or county registry of deeds.

The seller or seller's agent:

* Will ask you to sign the Deed, which transfers title to you (it should be a "General Warranty Deed" which means that title to the property is free and clear, and you can resell it at any time).

The seller or the agent will then give you the keys to the house. You legally own your personal living space and your troubles with landlords are over.

And if you've read this far, you have probably gotten more house for less money than most other buyers in the market. Congratulations!

Table XII: Closing Checklist

BEFORE YOU GO TO THE CLOSING YOU WILL WANT TO ANSWER THE FOLLOWING QUESTIONS:

	Yes	No
1. Are all necessary inspections done? (Bring Inspection reports with you to the closing.)	☐	☐
2. Are all required repairs complete? (Bring certificate of completion to the closing.)	☐	☐
3. Do you have a paid insurance policy or binder in effect the day of the closing?	☐	☐
4. Did you give your old landlord notice?	☐	☐
5. Have you made a final inspection of the house?	☐	☐
6. Have you confirmed with the seller the move-out date?	☐	☐
7. Have you confirmed with your mover the move-in date?	☐	☐
8. Have you confirmed with your mover the time of pick-up and delivery?	☐	☐
9. Have you confirmed with your mover the cost of the move?	☐	☐
10. Do you have enough money for moving?	☐	☐
11. Have you obtained from the lender or escrow agent the exact amount of money you will need for closing? (Ask about prepayable and other costs that didn't appear on your RESPA statement.)	☐	☐
12. Do you have a certified check for that amount?	☐	☐
13. Do you have additional cash "just in case"?	☐	☐
14. Have you confirmed with your lawyer or escrow agent the TIME, DATE, PLACE of the closing?	☐	☐
15. Do you have receipts for those items you have already paid for on the house?	☐	☐

Source: U.S. Department of Housing & Urban Development

Table XIII: Amendment to Application

Lender's Estimate of settlement charges   Date _____

NOTE: You may apply for the loan in your own name or you may wish your spouse (if any) to be a co-applicant. There is no requirement for your spouse (if any) to apply or otherwise become obligated to repay the debt except to the extent that your spouse's income and/or assets are necessary to qualify you for the loan. However, your spouse may be required to execute the security instrument (i.e., Mortgage or Deed of Trust.)

1. Title will be vested in what names?_____
2. How will title be held? (Tenancy)_____
3. Note will be signed by?_____

Good Faith Estimates

This list gives an estimate of most of the charges you will have to pay at the settlement of your loan. The figures shown, as *estimates*, are subject to change. The figures shown are computed based on sales price and proposed mortgage amount as stated on your loan application. The numbers listed on the left correspond with those on the HUD-1 Uniform Settlement Form you will be required to execute at settlement. For further information about these charges, consult your Special Information Booklet.

Estimated Settlement Charges

801	Loan Origination Fee	$ _____
805	Inspection Fee	_____
806	Mortgage Application Fee	_____
901*	Interest	_____
902	Mortgage Insurance Premium	_____
1107	Attorney's Fees	_____
1108	Title Insurance	_____
1201	Recording Fees	_____
1202	City/county tax/stamps	_____
1203	State tax/stamps	_____
1301	Survey	_____

*This interest calculation represents the greatest amount of interest you could be required to pay at settlement. The actual amount will be determined by which day of the month your settlement is conducted. To determine the amount you will have to pay, multiply the number of days remaining in the month in which you settle times the daily interest charge for your loan.

"THIS FORM DOES NOT COVER ALL ITEMS YOU WILL BE REQUIRED TO PAY IN CASH AT SETTLEMENT, FOR EXAMPLE, DEPOSIT IN ESCROW FOR REAL ESTATE TAXES AND INSURANCE. YOU MAY WISH TO INQUIRE AS TO THE AMOUNTS OF SUCH OTHER ITEMS. YOU MAY BE REQUIRED TO PAY OTHER ADDITIONAL AMOUNTS AT SETTLEMENT."

In accordance with the real Estate Settlement Costs Booklet. I/we also acknowledge receipt of the notice required by the Equal Credit Opportunity Act which is located on the inside back cover of the Settlement Cost Booklet. By signing this form, we acknowledge receipt this date of a duplicate copy of this form including the "Good Faith Estimates" of settlement costs, the Settlement Costs Booklet with the notice required by the Equal Credit Opportunity Act.

_____   _____

       Applicant   Co-applicant

_____

Source: U.S. Department of Housing & Urban Development

Table XIV

Form Approved
OMB NO. 63-R-1501

	B. TYPE OF LOAN
U. S. DEPARTMENT OF HOUSING AND URBAN DEVELOPMENT	1. ☐ FHA 2. ☐ FmHA 3. ☐ CONV. UNINS. 4. ☐ VA 5. ☐ CONV. INS.
SETTLEMENT STATEMENT	6. File Number: 7. Loan Number:
	8. Mortgage Insurance Case Number:

C. NOTE: *This form is furnished to give you a statement of actual settlement costs. Amounts paid to and by the settlement agent are shown. Items marked "(p.o.c.)" were paid outside the closing; they are shown here for informational purposes and are not included in the totals.*

D. NAME OF BORROWER:	E. NAME OF SELLER:	F. NAME OF LENDER:

G. PROPERTY LOCATION:	H. SETTLEMENT AGENT:	I. SETTLEMENT DATE:
	PLACE OF SETTLEMENT:	

J. SUMMARY OF BORROWER'S TRANSACTION		K. SUMMARY OF SELLER'S TRANSACTION	
100. GROSS AMOUNT DUE FROM BORROWER:		**400. GROSS AMOUNT DUE TO SELLER:**	
101. Contract sales price		401. Contract sales price	
102. Personal property		402. Personal property	
103. Settlement charges to borrower (line 1400)		403.	
104.		404.	
105.		405.	
Adjustments for items paid by seller in advance		*Adjustments for items paid by seller in advance*	
106. City/town taxes to		406. City/town taxes to	
107. County taxes to		407. County taxes to	
108. Assessments to		408. Assessments to	
109.		409.	
110.		410.	
111.		411.	
112.		412.	
120. GROSS AMOUNT DUE FROM BORROWER		**420. GROSS AMOUNT DUE TO SELLER**	
200. AMOUNTS PAID BY OR IN BEHALF OF BORROWER:		**500. REDUCTIONS IN AMOUNT DUE TO SELLER:**	
201. Deposit or earnest money		501. Excess deposit (see instructions)	
202. Principal amount of new loan(s)		502. Settlement charges to seller (line 1400)	
203. Existing loan(s) taken subject to		503. Existing loan(s) taken subject to	
204.		504. Payoff of first mortgage loan	
205.		505. Payoff of second mortgage loan	
206.		506.	
207.		507.	
208.		508.	
209.		509.	
Adjustments for items unpaid by seller		*Adjustments for items unpaid by seller*	
210. City/town taxes to		510. City/town taxes to	
211. County taxes to		511. County taxes to	
212. Assessments to		512. Assessments to	
213.		513.	
214.		514.	
215.		515.	
216.		516.	
217.		517.	
218.		518.	
219.		519.	
220. TOTAL PAID BY/FOR BORROWER		**520. TOTAL REDUCTION AMOUNT DUE SELLER**	
300. CASH AT SETTLEMENT FROM/TO BORROWER		**600. CASH AT SETTLEMENT TO/FROM SELLER**	
301. Gross amount due from borrower (line 120)		601. Gross amount due to seller (line 420)	
302. Less amounts paid by/for borrower (line 220)	( )	602. Less reductions in amount due seller (line 520)	( )
303. CASH (☐ FROM) (☐ TO) BORROWER		**603. CASH (☐ TO) (☐ FROM) SELLER**	

Previous Edition is Obsolete

HUD-1 (5-76)

Source: U.S. Department of Housing & Development

–2–

L. SETTLEMENT CHARGES	PAID FROM BORROWER'S FUNDS AT SETTLEMENT	PAID FROM SELLER'S FUNDS AT SETTLEMENT
700. TOTAL SALES/BROKER'S COMMISSION based on price $ @ % =		
Division of Commission (line 700) as follows:		
701. $ to		
702. $ to		
703. Commission paid at Settlement		
704.		
800. ITEMS PAYABLE IN CONNECTION WITH LOAN		
801. Loan Origination Fee %		
802. Loan Discount %		
803. Appraisal Fee to		
804. Credit Report to		
805. Lender's Inspection Fee		
806. Mortgage Insurance Application Fee to		
807. Assumption Fee		
808.		
809.		
810.		
811.		
900. ITEMS REQUIRED BY LENDER TO BE PAID IN ADVANCE		
901. Interest from to @ $ /day		
902. Mortgage Insurance Premium for months to		
903. Hazard Insurance Premium for years to		
904. years to		
905.		
1000. RESERVES DEPOSITED WITH LENDER		
1001. Hazard Insurance months @ $ per month		
1002. Mortgage Insurance months @ $ per month		
1003. City property taxes months @ $ per month		
1004. County property taxes months @ $ per month		
1005. Annual assessments months @ $ per month		
1006. months @ $ per month		
1007. months @ $ per month		
1008. months @ $ per month		
1100. TITLE CHARGES		
1101. Settlement or closing fee to		
1102. Abstract or title search to		
1103. Title examination to		
1104. Title insurance binder to		
1105. Document preparation to		
1106. Notary fees to		
1107. Attorney's fees to		
(includes above items numbers;		
1108. Title insurance to		
(includes above items numbers;		
1109. Lender's coverage $		
1110. Owner's coverage $		
1111.		
1112.		
1113.		
1200. GOVERNMENT RECORDING AND TRANSFER CHARGES		
1201. Recording fees: Deed $; Mortgage $; Releases $		
1202. City/county tax/stamps: Deed $; Mortgage $		
1203. State tax/stamps: Deed $; Mortgage $		
1204.		
1205.		
1300. ADDITIONAL SETTLEMENT CHARGES		
1301. Survey to		
1302. Pest inspection to		
1303.		
1304.		
1305.		
1400. TOTAL SETTLEMENT CHARGES (enter on lines 103, Section J and 502, Section K)		

HUD-1 (5–76)

Source: U.S. Department of Housing & Urban Development

TRUTH-IN-LENDING DISCLOSURE STATEMENT

Name(s) _____ Loan Number _____

Mailing Address _____ Type Loan: VA _____ FHA _____ CONV. _____

Settlement Date on which **FINANCE CHARGE** begins to accrue: _____

1. _____ hereinafter called Lender, will lend to the Borrower the amount of $_____ . Borrower will obligate himself to pay said principal amount plus interest at _____% per annum. Payments for principal and **FINANCE CHARGE** , excluding mortgage insurance premium, will consist of _____ monthly payments of $_____ (consisting of principal and interest) beginning on the first day of _____ , 19_____ , and due on the first day of each month thereafter through _____ , 20_____ . In addition, monthly payments will include additional amounts for mortgage insurance premiums, the first of which will be required on _____ 1, 19_____ in the amount of $_____ . Such payments will be made over a total of _____ months and the last monthly payment for mortgage insurance will be due on the first day of _____ , _____ , and will be $_____ . Thereafter, remaining monthly payments will be in the amount of $_____ .

2. While most of the **FINANCE CHARGE** will be spread out over the life of the loan and paid as part of the aforesaid monthly installments, certain **FINANCE CHARGE** will be prepaid at closing and consist of the following:

   a. Origination Fee . . . . $_____
   b. Loan Discount paid by Borrower . . . . $_____
   c. Interest on Loan (_____ _days) . . . . $_____
   d. FHA Mortgage Insurance Premium (2 months) . . . . $_____
   e. Private Mortgage Insurance Premium (Initial and Escrow) . . . . . . $_____
   f. Other _____ $_____

   The TOTAL PREPAID **FINANCE CHARGE:** $_____

3. There will be certain costs to the Borrower which are not part of the **FINANCE CHARGE.** Among these are
   a. Recording Fees:
      Deed of Trust/Mortgage _____ $_____
   b. Other _____ $_____
      _____ $_____

4. The TOTAL **FINANCE CHARGE** to be paid by Borrower consists of the following:
   a. Total Interest. . . . . $_____
   b. Total FHA Mortgage Insurance . . . . $_____
   c. Total Private Mortgage Insurance . . . . $_____

   The TOTAL **FINANCE CHARGE:** $_____

5. The **AMOUNT FINANCED** consists of
   a. Amount of Loan . . . . $_____
   b. Less Prepaid Finance Charges . . . . $_____
   c. Amount Financed . . . . $_____

6. The **FINANCE CHARGE** expressed as an **ANNUAL PERCENTAGE RATE** is . . . . . _____%

7. The total of payments is . . . . $_____

8. In the event of late payment, a late charge equivalent to (FHA-4%/VA-4%) of the amount due must be paid by Borrower to Lender. Further, in the event default be made in the payment of any installment under the Note and if such default is not made good prior to the due date of next installment, the entire principal balance plus accrued interest shall become due and payable without notice at the option of the Note holder.

9. Lender's security interest in this transaction is a first lien on property located at _____

   more particularly described in the recorded security instrument creating said lien. Said security instrument covers all after-acquired property and future advances, the terms for which are described therein.

10. Prepayment Penalty: _____
    _____
    _____
    _____

11. Fire and extended coverage insurance in the amount of $_____ with loss payable clause to Lender is required as a condition of this loan. This insurance may be purchased from any insurance company subject to Lender's rejection for reasonable cause, or through Lender at a cost of $_____ for a _____ year term. Flood Insurance may be required as a condition of this loan.

12. We acknowledge receipt of this completed statement on _____ , 19_____ , prior to the execution of any other documents.

    (Signature of Witness) _____ (Signature of Borrower) _____

    (Signature of Witness) _____ (Signature of Borrower) _____

Source: U.S. Department of Housing & Urban Development

Glossary
&
Appendix

Glossary: House Construction Terminology

acoustical tile—Special sound-absorbing tile for covering walls and ceilings made out of cork, vegetable fibers, wood or expanded minerals.

adobe bricks—Sun-cured bricks made from sandy clay or loam, mixed with water, straw and a small amount of emulsified asphalt stabilizer to resist water erosion when cured.

A-frame—An exterior frame shaped like the letter A where the legs rest directly on the footings. The structure has no vertical exterior side walls and is popular for vacation homes.

aggregate—The sand and gravel which are mixed with Portland cement and water to make concrete.

air-dried lumber—Wood that has been seasoned in yards or sheds instead of a kiln. Its moisture content is usually between 15 and 20 percent.

air ducts—Conduits, usually rectangular in cross-section, which distribute warm/cold air to rooms and carry air back to the furnace or air conditioner.

airway—A space which allows movement of air between roof insulation and the roof boards.

alcove—A recessed area of a room.

alligatoring—A coarse checking pattern in new paint, where the old coating can be seen through the fissures.

American bond—An arrangement in laying brick walls which increases their transverse strength. Some bricks are laid crosswise on every sixth or seventh course. The remaining bricks are laid end-to-end. Also called "common bond".

ampere—A measure of electrical flow through wires. One ampere equals the force of one volt flowing through a resistance of one ohm.

anchor bolts—Bolts which secure a wooden sill plate beam to its concrete or masonry foundation.

annex—A structure attached to a larger building.

apron—A paved area where a driveway joins the street, or the protruding lower flat member of a window's interior trim.

architrave—A molding which surrounds a doorway, window or other square or rectangular opening in a wall. In architecture, the chief horizontal beam which rests directly on a colonnade.

area zoning—Community regulations which establish minimum lot sizes, setback distances, etc.

artist's rendering—A drawing of a building, not necessarily to scale, which is normally used to promote its sale.

asbestos—A mineral silicate of calcium and magnesium, occurring in long threadlike fibers, formerly used to insulate pipes and as a fire retardant in roofs, ceilings and walls. A known cause of lung cancer.

ashlar—Either a square hewn stone used in building, or a thin stone slab used for facing exterior walls.

asphalt—A black tar-like residue from evaporated petroleum, used for sealing driveways and in waterproof roof coverings.

attic—The area above the top story of a house, immediately beneath the roof.

attic ventilator—(1) Screened openings, the inlet ventilators being located in the soffit area under the eaves and the louvered outlet ventilators in the gable walls; (2) A power-driven exhaust fan.

awning—A canvas or aluminum covered frame which extends outward over a window to protect against sun and rain.

backfill—Refilling a trench with excavated earth. Where a foundation has been built, the material is placed against it as a support.

balustrade—A handrail on supporting posts used along the edge of stairs, balconies and porches.

barrel—Forty two gallons of heating oil. A unit of liquid measure which varies in different industries.

baseboard—A molded board placed along the bottom of an interior wall to conceal the gap between finished wall and floor.

baseboard heating—Radiant heaters or panels substituted for the baseboards in order to provide perimeter heating.

base course—In masonry, the lowest course of bricks, blocks or squared stone.

base molding—Strips used to trim the upper edge of baseboard.

base shoe molding—Attaches to baseboard above the floor (sometimes called a "carpet strip").

batt—Blanket insulation sold in roll form and cut to fit snugly between the wall studs. Can be either 16 inches wide for load-bearing walls or 24 inches wide for partitions which do not support loads.

batter boards—Horizontal boards nailed to boards at the corners of an excavation, in order to indicate a desired level.

bay window—A window space curving outwards from the wall of a building, which gives a "bay" or alcove-like effect to the interior.

beam—A principal wood or steel load-bearing structural member. It usually supports joists laid across it at right angles. (See also "false beam")

bearing wall—One which supports vertical loads in addition to its own weight, such as a floor or roof.

bearing value—A measure of the soil's ability to support the weight of a building.

blind nailing—Where nailheads are driven below the surface of a wall and concealed with putty.

board—In lumberyard terminology, a piece of wood more than 4 inches wide and less than 2 inches thick.

board foot—The equivalent of a section of board one foot square and one inch thick. Total board feet for a job is calculated by multiplying the lumber's thickness in inches by its width in inches by the length in feet. Divide by 12

bond—In masonry, the pattern in which individual bricks are laid so that they tie the entire wall into acting as a single unit.

boiled linseed oil—Linseed oil with added lead, manganese or cobalt salts to make it harden more quickly when applied.

bolster—In construction, a short piece of steel or massive wood on top of a column which supports a beam or girder, thus decreasing its unsupported span.

brace—A piece of wood nailed at an angle across vertical studs to form a triangle which stiffens the structure. Might not be employed where thick plywood outer sheathing is used.

braced framing—A light wood frame construction which uses posts and cross braces for greater rigidity.

brick—A rectangular block of kiln-fired clay, often red in color due to the presence of iron. Adding lime or magnesia produces a yellowish color. The dimensions are usually 2½ × 4 × 8 inches.

brick veneer—A non-loadbearing facing of bricks laid against and fastened to the sheathing of a framed wall, forming its outer surface.

bridging—Wooden 2 × 4s nailed diagonally between floor joists. These brace the joists and spread the effect of loads by acting as tension and compression members.

British thermal unit—The amount of heat needed to raise the temperature of one pound of water by one degree Fahrenheit. Used to define the capacity of furnaces and air conditioning units. ("BTU").

broom clean—In contracts, a term meaning that the work area will be free of debris and swept clean after a job is completed.

building code—The laws which control the design, construction methods, materials and electrical and plumbing installation in buildings. They usually also apply to repair and renovation of existing buildings.

building paper—Heavy waterproof paper used in roofs and walls.

butt joint—Where the square-cut ends of two timbers meet.

Bx cable—Electrical cable wrapped in rubber with a flexible steel outer covering. Today its residential use is usually limited to the main exterior wiring which leads into the switchboard.

cantilever—In housing, a beam, block or bracket which projects from a wall and is not supported at the outer end. Cantilevers bear the load of cornices, balconies, breezeway roofs and other extensions from a wall.

casement window—One which is hinged at its vertical sides, allowing it to swing outward.

casing—Moldings of various types used for door and window framing.

cavity wall—A double wall of brick or stone with a hollow area between. Both walls are firmly linked with metal or brick ties and share a common cap at the top and ends.

cellar—That part of the basement which is used for storage.

cement, Keene's—A dense, durable white finish plaster. Used in bathrooms, kitchens and in public buildings where walls are subject to hard wear.

cement, Portland—A mixture of limestone, clay and similar materials used to harden concrete. Large kilns are used in its manufacture and the process is energy-intensive.

cement block—A building block of concrete, usually hollow. (cf. Concrete Block).

cesspool—A pit dug in the earth to hold raw sewage.

checking—(1) Splits or cracks in a board caused by seasoning; (2) Cracks that appear in exterior paint coatings as they age.

check valve—One which prevents the backup of liquids being carried through pipe.

chimney—A flue lined with heat resistant material, which carries the smoke and gases from a fireplace up and out through the roof. (An insulated metal pipe which performs the same function is often called a "smoke pipe").

chimney cap—A device placed over the top of a chimney to keep out rain and snow.

cinder block—A hollow building block of Portland cement and cinders. Lighter and less strong than a concrete block, it is often used in decorative, non-loadbearing garden walls.

circuit breaker—An electrical safety device which, when overloaded, opens or "breaks" automatically. The open switch can then be manually closed or reset, whereas the older safety fuse had to be replaced.

cistern—A tank used to store and catch rainwater in areas where there is no municipal water supply.

clapboard—A long board used in siding. In cross-section clapboards are tapered and wedge-shaped. They are installed with the thicker edge overlapping the thinner edge of the board below.

clear lumber—A high grade of lumber which is "clear" of defects such as splits or knots.

clerestory—That part of a wall which rises above the walls which join it, as in the front of a house. It may contain a line of narrow windows. (cf. "clearstory", the wall of a church at a higher level than the aisles, which contained windows.)

collar beams—Crosspieces which are fastened to opposite roof rafters in order to stiffen them.

column footings—Concrete support bases for load bearing columns.

concrete—A sand, gravel and water mixture which hardens through the action of Portland cement. It will harden under water, and may be reinforced or prestressed.

conduit, electrical—A metal pipe through which wiring is run.

contiguous—Touching, meeting or bordering on.

coping—Tile or concrete used as a cap on a masonry wall, usually sloped to allow the run-off of water.

corbel—A horizontal brick, stone or timber projection from a wall which supports a ledge above it.

corner bead—A strip of wood, two sides of which form a 90° angle, placed in a corner to protect the finished wall edges at the joint. (In wet plastering, a strip of formed sheet metal which reinforces the corner before plaster is applied.)

corner boards—Exterior trim used at the corners of frame houses.

corner braces—Diagonal braces nailed to studs at the corners of wood frame houses in order to stiffen and reinforce the walls.

cornice—(1) A projecting horizontal molding at the top of a wall or building; (2) The overhang of a pitched roof at the eave line.

counter flashing—A waterproof material used over metal chimney flashing at the roofline in order to prevent moisture from entering.

course—A single horizontal row of bricks, concrete blocks or squared stone.

cove molding—A trim with a concave face used for interior corners.

cove lighting—Concealed lights behind a horizontal wall recess which shine upon a reflecting ceiling.

crawl space—A shallow space below the ground floor of a basementless house, usually enclosed by the foundation wall, which allows access to below-floor pipes and ducts.

cripples—Short vertical framing studs used above and below windows.

cross bridging—Diagonal braces between floor joists, usually located near the center of their span, which prevent the joists from twisting under load.

curtain wall—A non-loadbearing outside wall which serves to enclose a patio or area of garden.

dado—A groove, rectangular in cross section, across the width or along the length of a board.

damper—An adjustable metal plate in the flue of a fireplace or furnace, which can be opened or closed to regulate draft.

deck paint—An exterior paint with a high resistance to wear, used on porches and other floor areas with heavy foot traffic.

dimension lumber—Yard lumber in thicknesses ranging from 2 to 5 inches and more than 2 inches wide. Can include joists, rafters, studs and planks.

direct nailing—Nails driven in perpendicular to a surface or where two pieces join.

disposal field—An area lined with porous clay tile and gravel which receives the drainage from a septic tank. The ability of the liquid waste to percolate through the soil determines its size.

door jamb—The case into which a door closes. It consists of two vertical side jambs and a horizontal head jamb.

dormer—An opening in a sloping roof, the framing of which projects outwards and forms vertical walls suitable for a window.

double framing—Double studs or horizontal beams fastened together for extra strength and rigidity.

double glazing—Two panes of glass, with an airspace between, in a window or door.

double hung window—One which moves upwards and downwards, with the lower sash counterbalanced by cords and weights. It usually locks where the upper and lower sashes meet.

dovetail joint—Where the sides of the projecting member and its cavity taper inwards, somewhat like a dove's tail.

dowel—A wood cylinder, inserted through matching holes drilled through two pieces to make a joint.

downspout—A conduit which carries rainwater down from roof gutters and directs it away from the foundation.

dressed lumber—Seasoned wood that has been planed smooth. The widths are slightly less than for equivalent sawn lumber.

drip cap—A projecting molding above a door or window which causes rainwater to drip clear of the sill.

dry rot—A misnomer for "damp rot", where moist wood is attacked by brown rot and other fungi.

drywall—Panels of gypsum board, particleboard or other material which substitute for wet plaster applied over laths. (See Joint Tape).

ducts—Usually rectangular metal conduits which distribute heated or cool air to rooms and return it to a furnace or air conditioner.

eaves—The lower part of the roof which extends beyond the wall of a house.

edge grain—Lumber sawn at an angle of less than 45° to the radius of the annual rings. (cf. "quartersawn lumber").

elevation views—Scale drawings of the vertical surfaces of a building. May be of the front, sides or back.

expansion joint—One which allows the joined members to expand and contract as their temperature changes. In masonry, a bituminous fiber strip used to separate concrete blocks or slabs to prevent their cracking, as higher temperatures expand them against each other.

face bricks—Glossy bricks of uniform appearance, made of selected clays, used on exterior surfaces.

false beam—Long boards joined together to give the impression of a ceiling beam. The interior space is hollow and its purpose is purely decorative.

feathering—Sanding outward gradually to a thin edge, as with drywall joint tape.

fire bricks—Bricks made of heat resistant clay and used to line fireplaces, chimneys and industrial furnaces.

fire clay—Special clay used to make fire bricks. It can withstand very high temperatures without softening, melting or cracking.

fire retardant—A combination of chemicals which retards the spread of flame by making the treated object less flammable.

firestop—In frame housing, a 2 × 4 or 2 × 6 placed horizontally between wall studs to completely block drafts and prevent fire and smoke from spreading between the walls.

fishplate—A piece of wood or plywood placed over two members at a butt joint and fastened to them with nails or bolts. Fishplates are sometimes used where opposite roof rafters join at the ridgeline.

flagstones—Flat stones which split readily into thicknesses of from 1 to 4 inches, used for steps, walks and patios. Available in different grains and colors.

firring—Wooden strips laid across studs or ceiling joists to form an even base on which to fasten tiles or drywall panels (cf. "furring strips").

flashing—Sheet metal or other material used around chimneys at the roofline, around dormers and generally wherever two exterior surfaces meet at an angle. Its purpose is to shed water and prevent moisture from entering the structure.

flat paint—An interior paint that contains a high proportion of pigment and dries to a non-reflective or lusterless finish.

flitch beam—One of metal plates sandwiched between two or more timbers and bolted together to form a compound beam of great strength.

floor joist—One which supports the subfloor and flooring.

floor load—The live load of furniture, fixtures and people which a floor can safely support. Usually stated in pounds per square foot of floor area.

flue—The enclosed passage inside a chimney through which smoke and gases from the fireplace escape. Fireproof lining should extend to its top.

flush—In construction, where two surfaces are at the same level.

footing—A concrete base wider than the foundation wall it supports.

formica—The trade name for a hard, synthetic material often used for kitchen counter tops. Cutting it involves incising the surface with a hard scribing tool and snapping the sections apart.

foundation—That part of a building, extending below the frost line, which supports the superstructure.

framing—The rough structural lumber used in a house such as beams, joists, studs and rafters.

frieze—In construction, a horizontal member which connects the top of the siding with the underside of the cornice.

front footage—The measurement along the front of a lot.

frost line—The depth beyond which the earth no longer freezes, which varies depending on winter climate. Footings must extend below this point to prevent their moving as the soil freezes and thaws.

fuse box—In older houses, the panel with the main electrical wiring and circuits. Circuit breaker panels have replaced fuse boxes in modern houses.

gable—The triangular part of the wall under the inverted "V" of a double-sloped roof, above the eave line.

gambrel roof—One with two slopes on a side, the lower incline being steeper. Its purpose is to provide more headroom around the perimeter of the attic floor.

gazebo—An open structure in a garden, usually containing benches, which affords a view of trees, shrubs and flower beds.

girder—A main beam of wood or steel which supports the joists and flooring. It must be designed to carry anticipated "live" loads of furniture and traffic as well as the "dead" loads of the flooring and partitions. Along with foundations for exterior walls, basement underfloor girders support the entire superstructure of the house.

girt—In post and beam framing, a horizontal member running over supporting posts at ceiling height.

gloss paint—One which contains less pigment and dries to a high sheen or luster (pigment is an opaque substance).

glass block—Blocks of hollow glass used in non-loadbearing walls for decoration and to transmit light.

glazing—The craft of fitting glass into windows and doors (also refers to installed door and window glass).

grade or gradient—The slope of the land, expressed in degrees.

grade line—Where the ground rests against a foundation wall.

grading—Removing soil so that water will drain downwards and away from a foundation.

grain—The direction, appearance, arrangement and size of fibers in a piece of wood.

green lumber—Cut, unseasoned lumber which in drying will shrink across its width and may warp.

grounding—In electrical wiring, "earthing" the circuit to a metal supply pipe or metal rod driven into the earth, in order to prevent lightning damage and possible fire. (In 3-wire grounding, where both outlets and appliances are 3-pronged, the third grounding wire will trip the circuit breaker before the user suffers serious electric shock.)

grounds—Strips of wood, available in different widths, used around door and window frames and along the floorline in plastered walls. They provide a level plaster line for installing skirting, casing and other trim and help the plasterer to strike off a smooth wall.

grout—A thin mortar with enough water added so that it will just flow into the joints and cavities of masonry work and fill them completely.

gusset—A brace or bracket used to strengthen a wood structure, such as a roof truss. May be fastened by nails, screws, bolts or adhesives.

gutter—A channel, running along and below the eaves of a roof, which carries rainwater away to the downspout.

gypsum—Hydrated calcium sulphate, used with sand and water for a wet plaster base coat or in wallboard.

gypsum board—A wallboard of dried gypsum plaster covered on both sides with heavy paper. Also known as "drywall" and "sheetrock". (See Joint Tape).

half timbering—Residential construction which exposes load bearing timbers in exterior walls, the spaces between being filled with bricks and covered with cement or plaster. English Tudor architecture is an example (the "timbers" in modern simulations are boards laid in plaster).

hanger—A vertical tension member which supports a load.

hardboard—Panels made of chopped wood fibers bonded with glue under pressure.

hardwood—The close-grained wood from broad leaved deciduous trees such as oak, maple, birch or hickory. In construction lumber the term does not cover basswood or poplar, which are softer than several "softwoods."

header—(1) A vertical supporting beam nailed to joists to form a frame for openings such as chimneys and stairwells; (2) A horizontal beam over windows and doors which transfers the weight of roof and floors to supporting double studs; (3) The lintel of a fireplace.

hearth—The floor of a fireplace, usually of brick, tile or stone.

heartwood—The harder wood at the center of a tree, under the sapwood, which no longer conducts nutrients.

heel—The lower end of a rafter which rests on a wall plate beam.

hip—The external angle formed where two sloping sides of a roof meet.

hip roof—One that rises on an incline from all four sides of a building. A church steeple is an example of a very sharply inclined hip roof.

humidifier—A device which increases humidity by discharging water vapor. These are available either as room-size units or as part of a central forced-air heating system.

hydraulic cement—A type of cement which resists penetration by moisture.

I-beam—A steel girder with a cross-section like the letter "I". Used for long spans across basements or as a header over wide load-bearing openings such as a double garage door.

imperial gallon—A British measure containing 277 cubic inches of fluid. (A U.S. gallon contains 231 cubic inches.)

insulation, blanket—Rolls of batt, usually fiberglass.

insulation board—Rigid structural building board of pressed wood or vegetable fiber which is available in sheets of different sizes. Many small pockets of trapped air in the panel provide insulation and a variety of flame retardant and water resistant surface treatments are available.

insulation, foamboard—May consist of extruded or expanded polystyrene, polyurethane or polyisocyanurate foam, and is available in solid sheets of different sizes and R values. (Urea formaldehyde continues to give off lingering vapors, has been the subject of health investigations, and its use is declining.)

insulation, foam—Is applied moist under pressure within walls or over a structure, using special agents and nozzles which cause it to foam before curing. Most exterior foam insulation should be sealed and protected from direct sunlight.

insulation, loose fill—Usually blown into wall cavities. May be fiberglass, rock wool or cellulose (made from chopped recycled paper and treated with a fire retardant—which is soluble in water and can wash off.)

insulation, mineral fiber—May be either fiberglass or rock wool made from shale, limestone or steel slag.

jack rafter—A short rafter between the hip of a roof and the wall plate beam. Also, a short rafter extending outwards beyond a wall.

jalousies—Windows with movable horizontal glass slats which can be angled outwards to admit air and keep out rain. The term is also used for exterior wood shutters which are constructed the same way.

jamb—The lining at the sides of a door or window.

joint tape—A perforated paper tape which is placed over the joints of drywall panels. This is covered with two or more coats of joint cement. When dry, these strips are sanded to a feather edge which blends into the panels. The surface is then ready for painting or wallpapering.

joist—One of a series of narrow beams, 2 to 4 inches across, laid on end in parallel. The vertical width is 6 inches or more. Joists are used to support floor and ceiling loads. Floor joists will in turn be supported by beams or girders running underneath at right angles.

kerf—The cut made by a saw.

kiln dried lumber—Lumber dried in a kiln to a lower moisture content. The process is superior to air seasoning and faster.

kilowatt hour—1,000 watt-hours of electricity.

king post—In post and beam framing, a vertical beam which transfers the weight of a roof's ridgeboard to a horizontal beam below it.

knee brace—A corner brace, fastened at an angle between a wall stud and a rafter to stiffen the structure and prevent angular movement.

knot—In boards or lumber, an area in the wood where a branch of the tree met the trunk. Knots lower the strength of structural grade lumber and are considered defects.

lag screws—Strong, large heavy screws used in heavy framing or when attaching ironwork to wood.

lally column—A steel tube, usually filled with concrete, used to support load-bearing beams.

landing—A platform between flights of stairs, or the level surface at the top or bottom of a stair.

lap joint—One in which the lower half of the thickness at the end of the top piece, and a corresponding part of the bottom piece, are removed. Both members are then overlapped and fastened together.

lath—Sheets of gypsum board or wire mesh fastened to framing members as a base for wet plaster. Formerly, wood strips nailed closely together in parallel for the same purpose.

lattice—A framework of criss-crossed wood or metal strips.

leaching field—See Disposal Field.

ledger—In house construction, a strip of lumber nailed along the side of a girder which supports joists.

lintel—A horizontal structural member that supports the load in a wall over an opening, such as a door, window or fireplace.

live load—The variable weight on the floors of a building, such as furniture, appliances and people.

louver—A framed opening, either triangular or rectangular, with angled horizontal slats which allow ventilation but exclude rain and sunlight. Usually made of aluminum and backed with a mesh screen for use in attics.

lumber—A word generally used to describe wood that has passed through a sawmill.

mansard roof—A four-sided roof with each side having two slopes, of which the lower is at a much steeper angle. (The two-sided version is known as a Gambrel Roof).

mantel—(1) A load-bearing lintel above a fireplace; (2) A decorative shelf above the fireplace opening. May be of stone, marble, wood or other suitable material.

masonry—Materials bonded together with mortar by a mason to form a wall, foundation, pier or similar mass. The building materials may be stone, brick, concrete, cinder blocks, concrete blocks, etc.

mastic—A semi-liquid quick drying cement used for setting tile or as an applied waterproof coating.

mechanical room—In a closed-wall panelized house package, the sections for the room that will contain the furnace, air conditioning unit, clothes washer and dryer. A utility room.

millwork—Finished woodwork that has been processed and sometimes completely or partially assembled at a mill. Examples are moldings, other interior trim, railings, panels, door, window and screen frames, and interior or exterior doors. (Exterior siding, wall or ceiling panels, or finish cabinetry done on site by a carpenter are usually not considered millwork.)

miter joint—One where two pieces meet at an angle. An example would be the joint between the side and head casing of a door frame, which meet at an angle of 45°.

moisture barrier—A layer of paint or waterproof material which prevents vapor from passing outward through walls and condensing behind exterior sheathing or siding. Also known as a vapor barrier.

molding—A long strip of milled wood used for finish trim, generally where a wall meets a floor or ceiling. Moldings are available in a variety of cross sectional shapes.

mortar—A mixture of cement, lime, sand and water used to bind bricks, stone and blocks in masonry. (It is a skin irritant and gloves should be worn.)

mullion—The vertical thin piece which separates the panes in a window or the panels in a door. (cf. "Muntin")

newel—The main post which supports the handrail at the top and bottom of a stairway. Also the central post which supports a spiral stair.

nosing—The rounded edge of a stair tread which projects over the vertical riser.

panel—In construction, either a large rectangle of wall or ceiling material or a smaller rectangle of wood or plywood enclosed by a frame.

parapet—A low wall extending above the perimeter of a roof or balcony.

parquet floor—One of inlaid hardwood, cut in geometric sections, to form a pattern of different grains and colors.

parging—A rough coat of mortar applied over a masonry wall as a protection or finish.

particle board—A panel made of compressed wood chips, shavings or sawdust bonded together by resins. It is a hard material which is often used for shelves or behind finished cabinet work.

patio—In modern residential housing, a paved area outside a house which can contain chairs and tables for outdoor meals and entertaining. (Originally, an open inner courtyard common in Spanish and Spanish-American houses.)

patio block—A fairly thin solid block used to floor patios and walkways.

party wall—A common wall on the boundary line between two attached houses that is shared by both owners.

percolation test—Used to determine whether a soil's drainage ability allows enough seepage for a septic tank or cesspool.

perimeter heating—Electric coil or hot water radiant heating installed around a room at baseboard level.

perm—A U.S. measure of the movement of water vapor through a material based on the flow of one grain of water, per square foot of material per hour, for each inch of difference in vapor pressure expressed in inches of mercury. Any moisture barrier material with a perm rating of .05 or less is very suitable.

pier—A pillar of masonry, usually rectangular in cross-section, used in basements to support underfloor main girders.

pigment—An opaque insoluble colored powder used in paints.

pilaster—A decorative column, either load bearing or not, which is partly embedded in a wall.

pitch—In roofing, (1) The ratio of the total rise to the total width of a house (a total rise of 8 feet and a total width of 24 feet means a one-third pitch roof); (2) The incline expressed as inches of rise per foot of run between the ridgepole and the wallplate beam.

pith—The small soft core at the center of a tree around which wood formation takes place.

plan drawing—A detailed two-dimensional outline of a floor in a house as viewed from above. These should be supplied to sub-contractors ahead of time with the desired changes drawn-in and a materials specification attached.

plank—Lumber between 2 and 4 inches thick and more than 8 inches wide. (See Board).

plate—A load-bearing horizontal structural member. (cf. Sill Plate, Sole Plate, top or Wall Plate).

platform frame—Light wood frame construction in which each floor is framed separately, using vertical studs one story (8 feet) high.

plenum—In housing, a chamber which acts as a distribution center for forced air heating and cooling systems. Usually located between floor joists and ceiling panels below.

plumb—Exactly perpendicular. A weighted line (plumb line) determines the exact vertical angle in relation to a level floor, as when building walls or partitions.

plumbing—The pipes and fixtures which distribute fresh water in a house, and which carry sanitary waste along with "grey water" from sinks and baths to the sewage system.

plywood—A panel made of three or more layers (plys) of glued veneer, each layer being laid with its grain at right angles to the grain of the sheets above and below it. Plywood is available in odd-numbered layers, usually 5 to 7, to provide a balanced panel that will not warp. Each outer sheet of a plywood panel is graded from A (best) to D (contains knots and some splits), depending on desired quality of finish and whether one or both sides will be visible. Marine grade plywood uses superior waterproof adhesives and stronger grained sheets throughout.

pointing—Filling masonry joints with mortar to improve their appearance and keep out water.

portico—An open front porch whose roof is supported by columns.

post and beam—Wall construction in which large beams are supported over long spans by heavy posts, as contrasted to platform frame construction where lighter beams are supported at 16 inch intervals by 2 inch thick studs either 4 to 6 inches wide.

primer coat—The first coat of a special paint applied to a surface, providing superior adhesion for the finish coat. A waterproof primer can also be used to seal against moisture.

purlin—A timber parallel to and below the ridgeline, which also helps support the roof rafters.

putty—(1) Wood putty, mixed to a plastic consistency which sets hard, available in different colors to fill cracks and nail holes in wood; (2) Glazier's putty, a soft clay-like mixture of whiting and boiled linseed oil used to seal around door and window glass; (3) White lead putty, used to fill cracks in wood and masonry before painting.

rabbet—(1) A rectangular groove cut longitudinally along a board or plank so that a piece with a matching protrusion can fit into it (as where a stair riser fits into the underside of a tread); (2) Matching rectangular grooves cut along the edges of boards or planks which allow joining them in a flush overlapped joint (as in shiplap lumber).

rafters—Sloping load-bearing planks, laid on end and supported at an angle by the ridgeline and wall plate beam, which bear the load of a roof. Under flat roofs these planks are called joists.

rake—A trim member that slopes parallel to a roof's incline, such as a cornice or the finish between a wall and a gable roof extension.

raw linseed oil—The product as processed from flaxseed with little subsequent treatment (see Boiled Linseed Oil).

receptacle—The electrical wall outlet into which the plug of a light or appliance is inserted.

reflective insulation—Material covered with aluminum foil, which insulates not by R value but by reflecting radiant heat. If the surface gets dull its reflecting efficiency drops sharply.

register—The grille through which heated air from a forced air system enters the room.

reinforced concrete—Concrete which has been poured over steel rods or mesh or form a strengthened slab, beam or column.

resorcinol—A heat resistant glue which is high in wet strength as well as dry strength. Used for wood joints that must withstand severe service.

retaining wall—One which holds back fill or a bank of earth.

ridgeboard—A thick plank, placed on edge at the highest point or "ridgeline" of a roof, to which the tops of the rafters are attached at an angle.

riprap—A wall of rocks loosely thrown together to control erosion, either in a stream bed or on a bank.

riser—The vertical board which encloses the spaces between steps in a stairway, by rising from the back of a tread to the underside at the front of the tread above it.

roll roofing—A roofing material of fiber saturated with asphalt, supplied in 36-inch wide rolls of 108 square feet, which depending on thickness can weigh between 45 and 90 pounds. Roll roofing can be smooth surfaced as an underlayment for roofing shingles, or else mineral surfaced in a limited range of colors for use as a less expensive roof surface on barns, sheds, etc.

roof sheathing—Panels, usually of thick plywood, fastened to the top of rafters or roof trusses which both tie the roof together and support the roofing material.

sapwood—The wood between heartwood and the bark, which in a live tree contains living cells as well as dying and dead cells. It is less resistant to decay than heartwood and is usually lighter in color.

sash—The movable frame in a window, containing one or more panes of glass.

scantling lumber—Lumber with a cross-section ranging from 2 × 4 inches to 4 × 4 inches.

scarf joint—Where two lengths of lumber are overlapped or "spliced" into a long continuous joint. (See rabbet joint)

screed—A horizontal board or plank, moved on edge along the surface of newly poured concrete to smooth it. In plastering, a small strip of wood with the same thickness as the plaster coat, used as a guide.

scribing—Marking two pieces of wood so that when cut they will fit together exactly. Scribing is used both in fitting interior moldings to an irregular surface and in transferring the contours of one log to another so that the cut will match (this allows a close fit in a log house wall).

seepage pit—A sewage disposal system consisting of a septic tank and a connecting cesspool.

septic tank—A settling tank for sewage. Bacteria convert part of the waste into gas and sludge before the remaining material discharges into an underground disposal or leaching bed.

shakes—Edge-grained shingles sawn from a thicker split shingle.

sheathing—The first covering of plywood over a wall or roof structure. On walls, the sheathing is usually covered by foam insulating panels and the siding.

shellac—A transparent coating liquid made by dissolving the secretion of the lac bug (a tropical scale insect) in alcohol. Shellac is vulnerable to liquids and is less resistant to wear than varnish.

shims—Thin tapered wedges, often cut from clapboard siding, driven between stair treads and risers, or between joists and sub-flooring, to eliminate squeaks.

shingles—Pieces of wood, asphalt tile, slate or other material cut to stock sizes, which are used as an overlapping outer covering on roofs and walls.

shiplap lumber—Close fitting boards with overlapped rabbeted eges.

short circuit—A faulty connection between two "hot" electrical wires, or between a hot and a neutral wire, which trips the circuit breaker and stops the flow of electricity in the circuit.

siding—The final outside covering on the walls of a frame house. May be wood clapboards, shingles, aluminum or other weather resistant materials.

sill—The lowest horizontal member in a door or window frame.

sill plate—The lowest beam in the frame of a house, resting directly on the foundation wall (sometimes called a "mud sill").

skirtings—Narrow boards around the margin of a floor (see Baseboards).

slate—A hard fine-grained stone that can be easily split into flat sheets of varying thickness. Used for roofing shingles and also for paving garden walks and patios.

sizing—A coating applied to a surface to prepare it for paint or some other finish.

sleeper—In housing, a wooden beam embeded in or attached to a concrete slab foundation as a support for floor joists.

slope—The angle of grade as measured from a level surface.

smoke chamber—The area directly above the damper in a fireplace, with sides sloping inwards up to the flue. Should be lined with firebrick or refractory mortar.

smoke shelf—A concave horizontal shelf behind the damper, designed to break up cold air downdrafts and make the fireplace "draw" better.

soffit—Usually, the under part of an overhanging cornice or eave.

softwood—Cone bearing evergreen trees which provide most of the lumber used in housing.

soil stack—The principal vertical pipe which receives waste water and sewage. It extends through the roof as a vent.

sole plate—In light platform framing, a horizontal member on which the wall studs rest, usually a 2 × 4.

spackling compound—A cement powder mixed with water for use on gypsum drywall panel joints.

splash block—A masonry or plastic block laid under a downspout to catch the flow of water and lead it away without causing erosion.

split level—A house whose first floor is at two different levels, with less than a full story difference between them.

structural lumber—Clear, strong straight-grained lumber used in framing.

stringer—(1) A supporting board or plank for a stair, notched to receive the treads and risers; (2) A long horizontal timber which supports a floor.

stucco—An exterior finish plaster consisting of Portland cement, lime, sand and water.

stud—A vertical wall framing member 2 inch by 4 inch and eight feet long (except where used above doors and above or below windows).

subfloor—A rough floor of plywood or boards that supports the finished floor.

swale—A wide shallow depression in the ground which acts as a channel for storm water drainage (see Grading).

termite shield—A flat strip of non-corrosive metal placed in or on top of foundation walls, or around pipes, to block the passage of termites. (Termite shields can be bypassed when these insects are swarming.)

terra cotta—A hard, baked clay used in facing and roofing tiles. May be either glazed or unglazed. Literally "baked earth."

terazzo—A flooring in which small chips of marble are set in cement and the whole surface polished smooth.

thermal window—One with two panes of glass and a dead airspace in between. (Due to the short distance between panes, an exterior storm window should still be used in cold climates.)

three way switch—Where two switches in a room, or at the top and bottom of a stairway, control the lighting.

threshold—A strip of beveled wood or metal over which the door swings. The strip extends inwards over the floor and outwards over the door sill.

tie beam—One which ties opposing roof rafters together and prevents them from pushing the wall plate beams out of line (see Collar Beam).

tiles—Thin, square or rectangular pieces used for flooring, exterior wall facing, ceilings, bathroom walls and roofing. May be stone, concrete, glazed or unglazed fired clay. Tiles may also be made of carpeting, plastic, and wood composition for acoustical ceilings.

timbers—Lumber greater than 4 × 6 inches in cross-section, used as support beams in light platform framing and as sills, girts and posts in post and beam framing.

toenailing—Driving nails at an angle through the base of one wood member so that they will also penetrate the piece which it joins.

tongue and groove—Lumber with a groove cut along the center of the edge of one side and having a corresponding center protrusion along the other edge. Boards joined in this manner are used for finish flooring and wall paneling.

trap—In plumbing, a bend in a water pipe that retains water to block gases from escaping out of the pipe and into the house. Traps are used under all sinks and toilet bowls.

tread—The horizontal board in a stairway which forms the step.

trim—Milled wood pieces used in finishing and decorating the exterior and interior of houses. Lumberyards stock a wide variety.

trimmer—A beam or floor joist into which a header is nailed as framing for an opening, such as a stair or chimney.

truss—A rigid frame of structural members designed to support loads over long spans. The framing members are usually arranged as triangular units which eliminate any bending stress, being subjected only to longitudinal stress either in compression or tension (cf. Roof Truss, Floor Truss).

tuck pointing—The repairing of brick or block masonry joints by filling them with fresh mortar.

turpentine—A light, volatile oil distilled from the resins of several species of coniferous trees. Used as a solvent in varnishes and as a thinner for paints (for cleanup the use of mineral spirits is now more common).

underlayment—A layer of material placed under finished floors or roof shingles for cushioning, a more even surface, or waterproofing. Examples would be padded carpet underlay, hardboard sheets under tile floors, and roofing felt or roll roofing under shingles.

underwriters laboratories—An organization which tests components used in electrical wiring and appliances to determine whether they meet minimum safety and quality standards. (The "U/L approved" stamp is accepted nationwide.)

utility room—A room in basementless houses used for laundry, heating and cooling equipment. The term is also used to describe such a room adjoining a finished basement area.

valley—In housing, the depression where two inclined roofs meet at an angle.

vapor barrier—(see moisture barrier).

varnish—A durable transparent finish for wood made by mixing synthetic resins, drying agents and other additives in oil. A polyurethane-based varnish is often favored due to its toughness, long life and resistance to most liquids. The marine-grade varnishes are usually the highest quality.

vehicle—In finishes, the liquid portion consisting of the non-volatile binder and the volatile thinners.

veneer—Thin sheets of wood produced by the rotary cutting of a log. In masonry, a facing of more costly brick or other material over less expensive construction.

verge boards—The boards used as a finish trim on projecting eaves at the gable end of a building. They are often milled or otherwise ornamented.

vermiculite—A mineral similar to mica, which expands when heated to form lightweight material with moderately good insulating properties. It resists high heat and is often used around industrial furnaces.

vestibule—An enclosed entranceway outside the door of a house. Most often used on north side entrances to reduce drafts from cold winds.

vitrified tile—Underground drainage pipe of hard baked clay, glazed when the purpose is to carry away water. Porous unglazed pipe would be used in a sewage disposal field.

volt—A measure of electrical pressure, being the force needed to move one ampere through a conductor having a resistance of one ohm. Household appliances and fixtures usually operate on 110 volt current in the United States, with 220 volt outlets being supplied for heavy appliances such as kitchen ranges and clothes dryers.

voltage drop—The loss in voltage which occurs when current draw exceeds the ability of the wiring to provide it.

wainscoting—Wood paneling which covers the lower half of an interior wall.

wallboard—Rigid sheets of paper-backed gypsum plaster, particleboard, or similar material. These are fastened to the framing studs or joists, taped at the joints, and can then be painted or covered with wallpaper. The term is usually not applied to plywood panels.

wall plate—In light platform frame construction, the horizontal beams above (top plate) and below the studs (bottom plate).

water table—The upper limit of water-saturated soil.

watt—An electrical current of one ampere under one volt of pressure. Produces 1/746 horsepower.

weatherstrip—Thin sections of felt, metal or foam plastic which are installed around doors or windows to keep out drafts and prevent escape of heated air.

weephole—A small drainhole at the bottom of a masonry wall.

wrought iron—Easily formed iron which contains very little carbon, and is tough and crack-resistant. Used for exterior railings, gates, light fixtures and outdoor furniture.

Glossary: Real Estate and Home Financing Terms

abandonment—Where an owner gives up rights in a property by failing to use or maintain it, coupled with intent to abandon. (The term does not apply when the owner is attempting to sell or rent the property).

abstract of title—A written summary of all documents pertaining to the title to a property, following the chronological sequence in which the documents were recorded.

acceleration clause—The clause in a mortgage or deed of trust which states that the entire amount will become due if an unpaid installment is not paid by a certain date, if the ownership of the property changes, or if other events occur which affect the security of the loan.

access right—The right of the owner to enter and leave the property.

accrued interest—Interest, not yet payable, earned since the last interest payment.

acre—A measure of land equal to 4,840 square yards or 43,560 square feet.

action to quiet title—A court action which establishes ownership by removing any other claims to the title of real property.

adverse possession—Where an occupant might acquire title from the owner as result of actual, open, continuous, exclusive occupancy as a result of a valid claim and hostile to the owner. The period of occupancy and the amount of taxes paid will vary from state to state.

affidavit—A written statement which is either notarized or sworn to in the presence of an authorized official.

agent—One who legally represents another (called the principal), from whom the authority may be express or implied.

air rights—The right to use or control the space above a property. Air rights do not include the surface of the property, but may limit the height of buildings on it.

amortization—The gradual repayment of debt along with interest, contrasted to monthly payments which cover only interest.

annual percentage rate (APR)—The rate which includes not only interest but also origination fees and discount points, in relation to the loan amount.

appraisal—When a properly qualified and trained AP-PRAISER sets forth the value of a property in an AP-PRAISAL REPORT.

appurtenance—Anything attached to the land, such as a structure or easement, which passes to the buyer with the title.

assessed value—The value which the tax assessor places on the property for taxation purposes.

assignment—In mortgages, the document that accompanies the transfer of the obligation from one party to another.

assumption—In mortgages, where a buyer takes over primary liability to meet the payments after paying the lender an ASSUMPTION FEE. Unless specifically released by the lender, the original holder of the mortgage continues to retain a secondary liability in case of default.

attachment—The seizing of a defendant's property by court order, as security for any damages that the plaintiff may be awarded.

balloon mortgage—One where the monthly payments are not enough to fully amortize the loan over its term. The unpaid balance then falls due as a lump sum BALLOON PAYMENT.

bankruptcy—When a court relieves an individual or firm of the obligation to pay outstanding debts, after all assets have been turned over to a court-appointed trustee. These are then distributed to the creditors. A bankruptcy may be voluntary (requested by the debtor) or involuntary (requested by creditors).

basis point—A term used by lenders to mean a 1/100 of 1 percent change in the yield on a mortgage.

beneficial interest—One which is equitable rather than legal, as in the case of a land contract.

binder—A written agreement between the buyer and seller or real estate which takes the property off the market until a sales contract can be drawn up. It usually involves a cash deposit by the buyer as evidence of good faith.

bond—In construction, where a lender or homeowner is insured that the builder or contractor completes the work. Usually known as a "performance bond".

blanket mortgage—In cooperative housing, a mortgage which covers the entire building (in contrast to separate mortgages on the individual dwelling units).

call provision—The clause in a mortgage or deed of trust which allows the lender, if certain events take place, to require payment in full by a certain date. An example would be if the homeowner/mortgagor sells the house.

cancellation clause—The clause in a lease which states the conditions under which the agreement may be terminated.

certificate of eligibility—One issued by the Veterans Administration which states that a veteran is eligible for a VA home loan guarantee. The requirements for this certificate are available from the nearest VA office.

certificate of occupancy—A written authorization from the local building department stating that a new home complies with the regulations and is ready to be occupied.

certificate of reasonable value (CRV)—Issued by the Veterans Administration to establish maximum property value and loan amount for a VA-guaranteed mortgage.

certified copy—One which is attested by the holder of the original document to be true.

chattel mortgage—A lien on personal, as opposed to real, property. Examples would be loans for buying a car, camper, boat, furniture, etc.

closing—In real estate, the signing of loan documents and paying of CLOSING COSTS (lawyers fees, title insurance premium, appraisal and inspection fees, survey costs, mortgage origination fees and points) and the delivery of the deed to the buyer.

collateral security—Property which, in addition to the personal obligation of the borrower, secures the repayment of a loan.

common areas—In condominiums and cooperatives, those areas available to all residents and in which each resident owns a proportionate share.

compound interest—That which is paid both on the principal and the accumulated unpaid interest.

condemnation—A court action which allows, by right of eminent domain, the acquisition of private property for public use without the owner's consent. The court also determines the amount paid to the owner as compensation.

conditional sales contract—One where the seller retains title to the property until the buyer has met all the obligations in the contract.

condominium—A structure or development of two or more units, in which the purchaser receives title to a dwelling unit and a proportional interest in the common areas.

consequential damages—Where a property is adversely affected by changes in another property. The amount of compensation and the categories of such damage vary according to state laws.

construction loan—A short term loan, generally at market interest, to finance the work of construction. The lender makes payments to the borrower according to the schedule in the CONSTRUCTION LOAN AGREEMENT.

conventional mortgage—One which is not insured by FHA or guaranteed by VA.

conveyance—A document that transfers ownership of real estate.

cooperative—In housing, a building owned by a corporation in which the residents own shares of stock. A blanket mortgage is available to the corporation, but individual mortgages are not available to the residents since they lack titles to their dwelling units.

cost-plus contract—One where the builder's profit is a specified percentage of the actual cost of materials and labor.

covenants—Binding restrictions written into deeds or mortgages by sellers or lenders. A covenant in a deed is legally enforceable by court action, and failure to observe a covenant in a mortgage can be grounds for default and foreclosure.

credit report—A report to a lender, usually prepared by a firm specializing in this field, on a borrower's history of meeting installment payments.

debt service—The regular payment and collection of interest and principal due on mortgage loans.

deed—A document with a detailed written description of the property, which conveys or transfers title to the buyer at the closing.

deed of trust—An instrument which conveys title in trust to a trustee, as security that a debt on property will be paid. The title is reconveyed upon full payment of the loan. Used in some states instead of a mortgage.

default—The failure to make installment payments on a mortgage, or a breach of its covenants.

defective title—One which lacks all the requirements necessary to transfer full, clear title to a buyer.

defeasance clause—One which gives the mortgagor the right to resume ownership of the property on paying the lender the amount due.

deficiency judgment—In a foreclosure sale, a court order to the debtor to pay the lender the difference between sale receipts and the amount due.

depreciable property—Property for which a useful life can be determined, after which it will have little value due to economic obsolescence or deterioration. For example, the building on a property can depreciate but the land does not.

depreciation allowance—An accounting charge which writes off the original cost of a building by distributing it over the building's useful life, as determined by the I.R.S. At the end of this period, the building is considered economically obsolete regardless of its actual condition.

developer—Either (1) A firm which prepares unimproved land for housing and sells it to builders, (2) A firm which builds houses on the lots; or a firm which does both.

draws—Payments made from a construction loan by the lender as stages of the work are completed according to the schedule of payments.

due on sale clause—One which states that the mortgage or deed of trust is payable in its entirety if the secured property should be transferred to another owner.

earnest money—A deposit by a buyer which accompanies a binder agreement in the purchase of real estate.

easement—A right or interest that individuals or the public may have in the land of others. Examples would be the right to cross a piece of property, or the right of a utility to install electric power lines or a sewer pipe.

eminent domain—A government's right to take private property for public use, paying 'just and fair' compensation. It forms the basis for condemnation proceedings.

encroachment—Construction that illegally intrudes towards or on neighboring property, generally in violation of zoning laws.

encumbrance—Anything that limits or affects a title to property, but does not prevent its transfer. Examples would be liens in the form of mortgages or claims, easements and restrictions.

equal credit opportunity act—As amended in 1977, prohibits a lender from refusing to extend credit on grounds of sex, marital status, age (above legal age), race, color, national origin, or whether part of the borrower's income is derived from public assistance (ECOA).

equitable title—Where a borrower/occupant does not have legal title to the property, as in a land contract.

equity—The homeowner's share of the market value of the property, after mortgage debt or other liens have been subtracted.

escalation clause—In a lease, one which provides for rent increases to cover specified contingencies such as property tax increases, maintenance increases, or a rise in the cost of living index.

escheat—Where the property reverts to the state if the owner dies intestate and without heirs.

escrow account—One administered by the lender for the payment of taxes, insurance premiums or other debts against the property.

exclusive listing—A written contract between a home owner and a licensed real estate agent, giving the agent the exclusive right to sell the property over a specified period and guaranteeing the agent's commission regardless of whether another broker actually makes the sale. Homeowner, however, reserves the right to personally sell the property without paying a commission.

exclusive right to sell—Same as above, except that the agent receives the commission if the homeowner personally sells the property.

execute—In home finance, to sign, notarize and deliver the instrument or document.

face value—The actual value shown on mortgages and notes, without allowing for any discounts.

fair credit reporting act—Title 6 of the Consumer Credit Protection Act as amended in 1971. Prohibits the lender from using the reported information for purposes other than the reason stated. Also prohibits the credit reporting firm from acquiring subjective information, based on interviews, concerning the applicant's lifestyle and character. The lender must tell the borrower which company issued the report and, if refusing credit, must be willing to show the report without charge.

fair market value—The selling price negotiated between a willing seller and a willing buyer, over a reasonable period of time and where neither is under compulsion to buy or sell.

fee simple—Full ownership of real estate, where the right to dispose of the property or bequeath it is unrestricted.

first mortgage—One with a primary lien against the property, having priority over all other mortgages and liens in case of default.

forbearance—Where a lender refrains from foreclosure, usually as a result of an agreement with the mortgagor that installments in arrears will be paid.

foreclosure—An authorized proceeding, stipulated in the mortgage or deed of trust, whereby the lender in the event of default, takes over the property and sells it to recoup the balance outstanding on the loan.

full disclosure—Where a builder or broker must inform the buyer of all known factors (defects, municipal services, highway or airport noise, etc) that might affect a decision to purchase real estate.

grantee—Usually the buyer. The person to whom real property or an interest in it is conveyed.

grantor—Usually the seller. The person who conveys real property or rights in the property.

ground rent—On improved property, that portion of the rent which applies to the land. Otherwise, rent for vacant land.

hazard insurance—A policy where the insuror will compensate the property owner against losses from specified hazards.

holdback—In a construction or improvement loan, that portion of the loan amount which is withheld until the entire job is satisfactorily completed.

home warranty insurance—A policy which insures the home owner against defects, usually in electrical wiring, plumbing, heating and air conditioning systems.

hypothecate—To pledge property as security while keeping possession—i.e. without turning it over to the lender.

improved land—Land which has had improvements or structures erected on it. Legally, the term can apply to land affected by off-site improvements.

installment—The regular payment to the lender of a mortgage.

institutional lender—An organization whose function is to make loans to the public. Examples would be banks and thrift institutions.

instrument—A legal document such as a mortgage, rental lease, or note.

insurable value—The value of that portion of the property subject to damage. Land would not normally be included.

involuntary lien—A judgment or tax lien placed on property without the consent of the owner. (A mortgage lien would be incurred with the owner's consent).

joint tenancy—Where two or more persons have an equal undivided interest in a property, running simultaneously and stated in the same document of conveyance. If one of the owners dies, the interest passes to the surviving joint tenants rather than to heirs.

judgment lien—An involuntary lien decreed by court action on the property of a debtor.

junior mortgage—A mortgage whose claims will be satisfied subsequent to those of the first, or senior, mortgage.

land contract—An installment contract where the seller retains title until paid, usually in full. During the contract period the seller has legal title and the purchaser has equitable title to the property.

landlord—An owner of real estate leased to others.

lease—A document listing the conditions under which an owner of real property (lessor) gives the right of occupancy to another person (lessee) for a specified term and rent.

lease with option to buy—One in which the price and conditions under which the lessee has the right to buy the property are set forth. The option may run for all or part of the lease period.

leverage—Using a small amount of cash and a large amount of borrowed money to increase return on property. To show a profit, the investment's appreciation must be higher than the interest charges combined with the borrowed portion's rate of amortization.

lien—A legal claim against the property of another as security for unpaid debts. Examples are a voluntary mortgage lien, an involuntary judgment lien, or a mechanics lien filed by a contractor to secure payment for materials and labor.

lis pendens—An official notice which is recorded, announcing pending litigation on real estate and advising that any person acquiring an interest in the property after the date of the notice may be affected by the lawsuit.

littoral rights—Those applying to property adjoining an ocean beach or lake front, which normally state how the shore may be used or enjoyed. (See also Riparian Rights).

livability requirements—Minimum standards set by HUD, VA or FmHA for residential housing.

loan-to-value ratio—The amount of the loan in relation to the appraised value or selling price of the property. Unless the loan is insured, the higher the LTV (expressed as a percentage) the higher will be the interest rate.

maintenance fee—In condominiums, the amount assessed each owner to pay for maintaining the common property areas.

market value—The highest price that a willing seller will accept and a willing buyer pay. It may be different from THE MARKET PRICE for which the property is actually sold.

mechanic's lien—In construction, a legally valid claim to secure payment for labor and materials. If not paid, the contractor may in most states file notice of lien, within a specified period, with the county clerk.

mortgage—The written document which pledges the borrower's property as security for the loan. The lender retains a legal claim on the property until principal and interest are paid in full.

mortgage-backed securities—Investments secured by a packaged pool of mortgages, the payments on which are the source of the investors' income (GNMA and private insurors are active in underwriting these securities).

mortgage broker—One who originates a mortgage by bringing together the borrower and lender. Mortgage brokers normally do not continue to service the installment payments.

mortgage company—A private corporation which originates and services mortgage loans, selling these on the secondary market. Sometimes called a mortgage banker, although it operates on the basis of borrowed money, not deposits.

mortgagee—The lender.

mortgage insurance—Insurance written by FHA (100 percent) or a mortgage insurance company (for the risk portion of the loan) which protects the lender against loss in case of default.

mortgage insurance premium—On an insured low down payment mortgage, is paid by the borrower either to FHA or a private mortgage insurance company (MIC).

mortgage life insurance—A term policy taken out by the borrower, covering the declining balance of the loan, in which the lender is the beneficiary. The policy may cover disability as well as death.

mortgage note—The instrument secured by the mortgage. A promise to pay a sum of money over a specified term at a staed interest rate.

mortgage portfolio—May be either the total mortgage loans held by a secondary market investor, or the mortgages serviced by a lender.

mortgagor—The borrower.

multiple listing—An arrangement common between licensed real estate brokers in well populated suburbs, in which each agency pools its listings with the others. A commission is divided between the listing broker and the broker who made the sale.

mutual savings bank—An institution owned by its depositors through certificates of deposit. Along with savings and loan associations, mutual savings banks are active in residential real estate loans.

notice of default—One recorded when the mortgagor is behind on installment payments; or a notice sent to a third party underwriter (FHA, VA, MIC) in the event of default.

option—A continuing agreement in a contract which grants the right to buy, sell or lease property at a specified price within a specified time.

origination fee—A charge by the lender for the work involved in the analyzing, evaluation and preparation of a mortgage loan. Usually one percent of the loan amount.

owner's policy—A title insurance policy in the name of the property owner, not the lender of a mortgage.

plat—A map of a subdivision which shows the boundaries of the individual lots.

point—One percent of the mortgage loan amount. The word is usually used in the context of LOAN DISCOUNT POINTS, a one-time charge levied at the closing to make up the difference between market interest rates and current FHA and VA maximum allowable interest. The spread between the face value of the mortgage and the amount the borrower actually receives make the yields on FHA/VA loans comparable to conventional mortgages. (FHA/VA allow the buyer to pay only one point—the seller must pay the rest). .

prepayment penalty—A clause in a mortgage or deed of trust which specifies an additional fee due the lender if the loan is repaid before it becomes due.

prepayment privilege—A clause in a mortgage or deed of trust which gives the borrower the right to pay all or part of the loan before its maturity.

prime rate—The lowest interest which a commercial bank charges on short term loans (does not apply to mortgages).

purchase money mortgage—One issued by the seller to the buyer as security for the balance of the sale price not paid for in cash at the closing (NOTE: seller-originated mortgages will usually not be insured by MICs and may have to be heavily discounted to interest secondary market investors).

quitclaim deed—One which transfers any title, interest or claim that the grantor (seller) may have when the conveyance on the property is executed. It does not include any warranty (see Warranty Deed).

real estate settlement procedures act—As amended in 1976, requires lenders to provide mortgagors with an advance disclosure of loan settlement costs, other charges and the APR ("RESPA").

raw land—Vacant land in its natural state, unaffected by development.

real property—Land and any structures or natural features on it. Real estate.

realtor—A licensed real estate broker who belongs to a local real estate board which is affiliated with the National Association of Realtors.

receiver—A person appointed by a court to hold and administer property which the owner cannot competently manage, or which is the subject of litigation.

reconveyance—In a deed of trust, the instrument used to transfer title from the trustee to the equitable owner. This takes place when the loan is paid in full.

refinancing—Repaying an existing mortgage from the proceeds of a new loan, usually from the same lender and using the same property as security.

reissue rate—Where the insuror lowers the premium for a title insurance policy on property that he has previously insured.

release of lien—In a mortgage, the instrument which releases the property as security for the loan when this has been paid in full.

restriction—A convenant in a deed which sets forth things that the owner must do or cannot do, on or with the property.

rider—A document added to a mortgage which modifies its meaning, used for example to bring the loan into compliance with VA guaranty regulations.

right of way—An easement upon a property which allows others to pass over it. Also the basis for condemnation proceedings by which a strip across the land can be used for building a public road or highway.

riparian rights—Those applying to property along the banks of a stream or river, which set forth how the land within the natural watershed and the water itself may be used or enjoyed. (See Littoral Rights).

sale-leaseback—An agreement where the seller transfers the property to the buyer for a specified amount, and the buyer then leases the property back to the seller for a specified period. Both agreements form part of the same transaction.

savings and loan association—A stock association which may be chartered either by the FHLBB or the state, and regulated accordingly. Its purpose is to accept and pay interest on insured savings accounts and to make residential mortgage loans.

secondary mortgage market—A term used to describe the buying and selling of mortgages by large investors (FNMA, FHLMC) as well as banks, insurance companies and others. It contrasts with the primary mortgage market, where lenders originate these long term home loans.

second mortgage—See junior mortgage.

servicing—A term used to describe the duties and functions of the mortgagee, such as collecting installment payments, making sure that insurance premiums and property taxes are paid, issuing written notifications and foreclosing in case of default, and preparing a release of lien when the loan is paid in full. A small servicing fee is usually charged.

setback—A requirement in a zoning law which specifies the distance back from the curb or front boundary within which no structure may be built. A common feature in suburban zoning.

settlement statements—Those prepared by the lender and real estate broker for the buyer and the seller, listing the costs involved to each and distributed at the closing.

simple interest—That which accrues on principal alone (see Compound Interest).

subordination agreement—A document which acknowledges that a debt will not be satisfied until other liens on the property have been paid.

tax lien—A claim against property for unpaid taxes.

tax shelter—In residential housing, where interest payments on the property mean a significant reduction in taxable income.

title insurance—A policy which reimburses the lender or property owner a specified amount, in the event of losses due to a defective title.

title defect—Any document or omission which limits or detracts from the full ownership of real property.

title search—A systematic review of all the documents on record for a piece of property. The purpose is to determine whether or not the title is clear of defects.

transfer tax—A documentary tax which many states impose on the transfer of real property. It is usually based on the selling price.

trustee—One who holds property in trust in order to secure payment of an obligation.

unimproved land—Land without structures built on it (see Raw Land).

without recourse—A clause in mortgages or deeds of trust which limits the lender's claim to the secured property in case of default, without additional recourse against the borrower.

warranty deed, general—Where the seller agrees to protect the buyer from any claim against the title (see Quitclaim Deed).

warranty deed, special—Where the seller agrees to protect the buyer from any claims arising from actions by the seller when he or she owned the property.

wraparound mortgage—A junior mortgage that secures both the unpaid balance on an existing mortgage and an additional amount advanced by the current lender. Its face value will cover both outstanding balances, and the current or "wraparound" mortgagee continues to pay the installments on the older senior loan. If the interest rate for the older mortgage is significantly lower than current market rates, the "wrap" can provide the borrower with a lower rate while the current lender still makes a profit on the spread between interest paid and interest received.

yield—The ratio, as a percentage of its original cost, of annual income from an investment.

zoning ordinance—A local law specifying how property in a designated area may be used.

Sources of U.S. Government Publications*

WEST

GPO Bookstore
Federal Office Building
Room 2039,
300 North Los Angeles Street
Los Angeles, CA 90012

GPO Bookstore
Federal Office Building
Room 1023
450 Golden Gate Avenue
San Francisco, CA 94102

GPO Bookstore
Federal Office Building
Room 194,
915 Second Avenue
Seattle, WA 98174

SOUTHWEST

GPO Bookstore
Federal Building
Room 117,
1961 Stout Street
Denver, CO 80294

GPO Bookstore
Majestic Building
720 North Main Street
Pueblo, CO 81003

GPO Bookstore
Federal Building
Room 1050,
1100 Commerce Street
Dallas, TX 75242

GPO Bookstore
45 College Center
9319 Gulf Freeway
Houston, TX 77017

SOUTHEAST

GPO Bookstore
9220 Parkway East-B
Roebuck Shopping City
Birmingham, AL 35206

GPO Bookstore
Federal Building
Room 158,
400 West Bay Street
Jacksonville, FL 32202

GPO Bookstore
Federal Building
Room 100,
275 Peachtree Street, NE
Atlanta, GA 30303

MIDWEST

GPO Bookstore
Everett McKinley Dirksen Building
14th Floor
Room 1463
219 South Dearborn Street
Chicago, IL 60604

GPO Bookstore
Suite 160
McNamara Federal Building,
477 Michigan Avenue
Detroit, MI 48226

GPO Bookstore
Federal Office Building
Room 144,
601 East 12th Street
Kansas City, MO 64106

GPO Bookstore
Federal Office Building
First floor
1240 East 9th Street
Cleveland, OH 44199

GPO Bookstore
Federal Building
Room 207,
200 North High Street
Columbus, OH 43215

GPO Bookstore
Federal Building
Room 190,
517 East Wisconsin Avenue
Milwaukee, WI 53202

GPO Bookstore
Federal Office Building
Room 1214,
600 Arch Street
Philadelphia, PA 19106

NORTHEAST

GPO Bookstore
Kennedy Federal Building
Room G25,
Sudbury Street
Boston, MA 02203

GPO Bookstore
26 Federal Plaza
Room 110,
New York, NY 10278

MIDDLE ATLANTIC

GPO Bookstore and Warehouse
8660 Cherry Lane
Laurel, MD 20810

GPO Bookstore
710 North Capitol Street
Washington, DC 20230·

Other GPO Bookstores in the District of Columbia are located in:

• Department of Commerce Building, Room 1605
• State Department Building, Room 2817
• Department of Health & Human Services, Room 1528
• Pentagon
• U.S. Information Agency

U.S. Government Printing Office Bibliography: The Home, #SB–041, June 1980

*With the exception of the Laurel, Maryland warehouse store, local GPO bookstores
may not stock all titles listed.

Federal Entities Involved in Private Housing

I. Sources of Direct Loans

Farmers Home Administration (FmHA)
U.S. Department of Agriculture
14th Street & Independence Avenue, S.W.
Washington, D.C. 20250
Program: Section 502 rural housing (contact local FmHA county supervisor).

Department of Housing & Urban Development (HUD)
451 Seventh Street, S.W.
Washington, D.C. 20410
Programs: Community Development Block Grants (contact city hall). Section 312 Rehabilitation Loans (contact nearest HUD office).

II. Home Mortgage Underwriting

Federal Housing Administration (FHA)
U.S. Department of Housing & Urban Development
451 Seventh Street, S.W.
Washington, D.C. 20250
Subsidized Insurance Programs: Sections 221(d)(2), 223(e), 237 (contact nearest HUD office).
Unsubsidized Insurance Programs: Sections 203(b), 244, 245 (contact lender).

Veterans Administration
810 Vermont Avenue
Washington, D.C. 20420
Program: Veteran's Home Loan Guaranty (contact lender or VA Regional office).

III. Regulatory Agencies

Federal Home Loan Bank Board (FHLBB)
1700 G Street, N.W.
Washington, D.C. 20552
Regulates: Federally chartered Savings and Loan Associations.

Provides: FSLIC insurance on their savings accounts.

Comptroller of the Currency
U.S. Department of the Treasury
15th Street & Pennsylvania Avenue, N.W.
Washington, D.C. 20220
Regulates: Nationally chartered commercial banks.
*FDIC savings deposit insurance provided by Federal
Deposit Insurance Corporation, a separate agency.

IV. Secondary Mortgage Market Investors

Federal Home Loan Mortgage Corporation (FHLMC—
"Freddy Mac")
1776 G Street, N.W.
Washington, D.C. 20013
(A private corporation created by Congress)
Main function: Buys conventional mortgages not insured
by FHA or guaranteed by VA. Also sells certificates
secured by pools of conventional mortgage loans,
backed by the full faith and credit of the U.S. Government through FHLBB.

Federal National Mortgage Association (FNMA—"Fannie Mae")
3900 Wisconsin Avenue, N.W.
Washington, D.C. 20016
(A private corporation created by Congress)
Main function: Buys and sells FHA-insured or VA-
guaranteed home mortgages, and also conventional
home mortgages.

Government National Mortgage Association (GNMA—
"Ginny Mae")
U.S. Department of Housing & Urban Development
451 Seventh Street, S.W.
Washington, D.C. 20410
Main function: Administers the mortgage-backed se-
curity program designed to bring new investors into
the secondary market.

INDEX